CAR
A Ma

Peter Bills, editor of *Rugby World*
magazine, was highly commended in the
1992 British Sports Journalism Awards for
the 'clarity and authority' of his writing on
the game. He went on to win the 1993
Magazine Sports Writer of the Year award.
His first book was an acclaimed biography
of the former French rugby captain Jean-
Pierre Rives. More recently he collaborated
with Australia's cricket captain, Allan
Border, in *A Peep at the Poms*, and co-
wrote *On a Wing and a Prayer*, the
autobiography of the great Australian
rugby international David Campese.

CARLING

A Man Apart

PETER BILLS

H. F. & G. WITHERBY

LONDON

Contents

Preface

It is the better part of a quarter of a century since I started writing professionally about rugby union. Great game? Of course. Great times, too. Trekking around the world with an assortment of touring teams like the British Lions, the English, the Australians, the French and the Scots: friends, kindness everywhere. Living in Sydney at Chateau Poidevin, overlooking Coogee Bay, and breakfasts on the verandah at Chez Slack in Queensland. I'll never forget, either, those Sunday lunches at Alan Jones's apartment on the rooftops above Sydney, feasting on prawns fresh from the Pacific and chilled wine from the Barossa. Nor riding the train into Johannesburg in 1972 to see England play (and beat) the Springboks, from a suburb close to a township. It was the days of apartheid; I was the only passenger in an entire carriage and the next was so crammed that people were hanging on the running board and standing on the open windows. Because their skin was black. No wonder the place was going up in flames.

France — now there's a tough sporting assignment! Lazy picnic lunches beside the Canal du Midi on a warm May day in Toulouse, the bread, wine and cheese spread out beside copies of *Midi Olympique* and *l'Équipe*. Waiting for a French Championship semi-final to begin and waving happily to the two sets of supporters as they drive through the city, their cars festooned in the scarves and colours of their club, *en route* to the stadium. You haven't lived as a rugby fan until you have experienced that. Everywhere in France, the lavish rugby hospitality: long, late breakfasts with Rives in Paris, an evening on the terrace of Fouroux's splendid home on a hill overlooking Auch; behind, the outline of the Pyrenees sketched as if by water-colour in the fading light. Lunch with Monsieur and Madame Villepreux in Toulouse, the fish so fresh it almost jumps into the pot by itself; a quiet afternoon with Maso in Perpignan and Bertranne in Bagnères. Great men, grand moments. And could they play . . .

Hospitality? *Formidable*. Like standing one night in a private office suite, nine floors above the Champs-Élysées, as a guest of the French rugby coach, gazing upon the floodlit scene below and those monuments of the famous city, the Arc de Triomphe and the Place de la Concorde. And all the while sharing the company of rugbymen from France and Scotland. Or riding the French team bus from the stadium in Toulouse through the cluttered city streets, the loud klaxons on the *gendarmes*' motorbikes drowning out the laughter from a winning rugby squad.

Weekends in Ireland, where the crack is legendary, and the welcome warm, spontaneous and genuine. Quaffing great *cappuccinos* in Milan, where two of the finest players and greatest entertainers the game has ever known, Campese and Ella, have been ensconced in recent years. But don't run away with the notion that splendid people and memorable moments in this game begin at Dover or Heathrow; what about the delight of the annual 'Save and Prosper' dinner at one of the City of London's livery halls each winter? A grand event amid convivial company. There have been countless other occasions and memories, all testifying to the unique spirit of rugby.

It is some game which provides the backdrop to all of this. But then rugby union always has been a special sport. Special, not because it can be the active personification of a Keats poem or a thrill like a Verdi aria, but simply because it is possible to find a warmth, a kindness and a welcome within this game which seems increasingly rare in the world at large. The people within its structure, the kind of folk you meet, make rugby union what it is. When a seventeen-year-old Haileybury schools player, Mark Bowen, was paralysed by a scrummage collapse, rugby rallied round. Players like Brian Moore and Jeff Probyn were there in person at a dinner to raise funds. Will Carling sent one of his England jerseys, which raised £825 at auction to contribute to the fund. Acts like these epitomize the good nature of the game.

Maybe I have just been lucky. I have met only the genuine guys. People like Clem Thomas (the rugby writer), who nearly gave us all a heart attack by almost dying in Paris three years ago, and as he sat gasping for breath ten minutes before kick-off, summoned me to his side and said simply: '900 words on the final whistle. And 500 from the "B" international this morning. Now.' I nearly joined him in the ambulance! He came to stay, quite recently, and thanked me profusely by sitting on a kitchen chair and demolishing it. The sight of this giant of a man of Wales and British Lions fame, sprawled face down on my kitchen floor, the wreckage of the chair all around him, will accompany me for ever! Thanks, Clem – it burned nicely on the log fire!

There are many such folk in the game. During the writing of this book, I received the 'Magazine Sports Writer of the Year' award in the British Sports Journalism Awards. Within days a letter of congratulation arrived from Ian Beer, the president-elect of the Rugby Football Union, a body which has stood many times, silently and tolerantly, in the path of my written attack. Such kindness even to think of taking the trouble.

The writing of this book has emphasized vividly to me, once again, the sort of characters who inhabit the world of rugby football. I was offered limitless time by people with a thousand better things to do than gossip with the likes of myself: Rob Andrew, Bill Beaumont, Eddie Butler, David Campese, Geoff Cooke, Les Cusworth, Jonathan Davies, Peter Dixon, Bob Dwyer, Dusty Hare, Nigel Melville, Andy Mullins, John Reason, Dave Robinson, Kevin Simms, Clem Thomas, Paul Thorburn, Roger Uttley, Mike Weston, Peter Williams, Dudley Wood, Ted Wood; schoolmasters such as Brooke Dowse, Peter Meadows and John Morris, the school archivist at Sedbergh, Mrs Elspet Griffiths and the head of the Aldro school in Surrey, Ian Argyle, to name just a few.

I should like to thank all the above, and also the many others who, although not mentioned individually here, some of them wishing to remain anonymous, gave me generous assistance. Trust, as I outline in the following pages, has to be an implicit part of the relationship between the writer and those interviewed; therefore, I would not dream of divulging to anyone the names of those who assisted me so much on a private basis. However, I would wish them to be aware of my deep gratitude for all their help, which has been considerable.

I wish, also, to state my appreciation for the sage counsel provided by my editor, Richard Wigmore. Thanks also to John Pawsey, my literary agent, for his encouragement, to Giulia Hetherington for the picture research, to Nick May for the design, and to David

Chappell, sports editor of *The Times*, John Goddard and Derek Wyatt, who were among those who meticulously read the manuscript and made many helpful suggestions.

In Durham there was a perfect illustration of the reception I received virtually everywhere during the writing of this book. I invited myself along to Mike Weston's home high above the city, to hear his memories of the subject, and the following was then placed before me: afternoon tea, pre-dinner drinks, a roast dinner with an excellent Chablis, coffee and mints. The master of the house then insisted on turning out to drive me back to my base in the city. Who said hospitality and kindness were nothing special in this sport?

To the subject, I would say simply this. You and your teams helped transform England's international rugby side from a bad joke to a source of pride. We all owe you a debt for that.

The author's individual dedication of a book is traditional, and mine is to be found elsewhere. It is to my wife, Averil. But she will know and understand better than any that I would wish also to dedicate the book to another great love of my life, rugby football, and to all the people in it. It is a sport which gives people so many marvellous friends and wonderful memories. May it remain synonymous with such qualities not just for years to come, but for generations.

> Peter Bills
> Royal Tunbridge Wells
> Kent
> May 1993

1 All Glory Is Fleeting

'Winning isn't everything – it's the only thing.'
Vince Lombardi

It ended in tears. Poetically, perhaps appropriately and most certainly calamitously, all Will Carling's dreams of establishing a record achieved by no other rugby captain England had ever known were broken by the Welsh.

It had been like that for an entire generation. For any follower of the game which, to misquote Oscar Wilde, is all about the physically unbendable in pursuit of a glory that is invisible, the Welsh dragon had been to the English as an ogre is to children. For too long, strong men had returned across the Severn Bridge with tears in their eyes at the unspeakable dejection of defeat in Wales. From 1963 to 1991, England had endured a barren era there. Prior to January 1991, the last time they had won in Wales was when John F. Kennedy was US President, their twenty-eight-year wasteland of failure spanning almost precisely the erection and destruction of the Berlin Wall.

England's gallant but usually defeated rugby team had ended the sequence at the fourteenth attempt, and comfortably too, by 25 points to 6. But if Cardiff on that crisp January day in 1991 signalled a revival of English fortunes, as it was later to appear once England had completed the Grand Slam that season, so, inexorably, it was to beckon the end, too. By the time they returned two years and one month later, in February 1993, the England rugby team were on the trail of immortality.

No side in the history of the Five Nations Championship, that great and glorious sporting occasion which transcends the harsh, grey, monotonous early months of the new year, had traded in such powerful currency. Not even the Irish team of the great Jackie Kyle in 1948–9; nor the physically intimidating squad France put together between 1977 and 1981; nor even the greatest of many fine Welsh teams which strutted the international stage from 1969 through to 1979, an era of such glory and style that none who saw its dominance could begin to contemplate its demise.

True, it had taken the irritating distraction of the First World War to prevent England's rugby team, Grand Slams under their civvy street belts in 1913 and 1914, setting out for sporting glory rather than Gallipoli in 1915. In 1925 it had been the Scots, as opposed to the Turks, who had laid waste all Blighty's best plans. Defeat that year in Edinburgh, by 14–11, and then a 6–6 home draw with Ireland, had denied Wavell Wakefield's side an historic third successive Grand Slam.

So it had never been done. Three Slams in four years? Ah, that didn't count. Wales, Grand Slam winners in 1908, 1909 and 1911, would have had four in four years but for an 11–6 defeat by England at Twickenham in 1910, interestingly enough the first time Wales ever played on Billy Williams's old cabbage patch. England's home matches had been played around the country until then: Leicester, Bristol, Gloucester, and fashionable Blackheath and Richmond.

It was to be sixty-eight years before another captain of a side in the Five Nations Championship set out in pursuit of a third successive Grand Slam. His name was William David Charles Carling, and at the age of twenty-seven he led his team into Cardiff on 6 February 1993. Fifty years earlier, young men of similar cultured background had led their troops into a quite different sort of contest: 1943 was the year when the Germans finally surrendered in North Africa. Nor was the military analogy bizarre; Carling might have found highly instructive the story that behind Roman conquerors returning in triumph from the wars stood a slave carrying a golden crown but whispering a warning that all glory is fleeting . . .

Carling's four-part journey to his personal triumph had begun against France, three weeks earlier. But hints of impending disaster had appeared. France had scored two tries to one, the English score coming after Webb's penalty attempt had struck a post and rebounded, quite fortuitously, into the arms of the on-rushing Hunter for a try beside the posts. Seven points gifted from heaven, the fortune of which was enhanced later when the Frenchman Lafond planted a drop goal attempt firmly against the English crossbar. England, by the close edgy and unconvincing, sneaked home 16–15; it seemed that nothing could go right for the French that day, just as it became apparent three weeks later that a similar fate might be England's at Cardiff.

The unpredictability of a French referee did not help. Jungle warfare was permitted in the line-outs, thought to be an area of certain English ascendancy; consequently, that superiority was rendered mythical. Specific interpretations bewildered the English. The Welsh, intent only on scavenging like a pack of hungry dogs, found circumstances most propitious for such an approach. And where England had found a valuable ally in an upright three weeks earlier at Twickenham, so Wales discovered a similar genie, lurking on the famous turf of the National Stadium. His name was Rory Underwood.

Early in his career, the RAF pilot had been notorious for his spells of public meditation in international rugby matches. The great Australian wing David Campese had berated him for it countless times; he would stand in almost disinterested isolation out on the wing, waiting for the ball to come his way rather than seeking it. Sometimes when it did come, as at Cardiff, he was not ready. In Underwood's grasp, England's hopes of a third successive Grand Slam triumph nestled, a shade uneasily, in the last few crucial seconds before half-time.

A speculative kick out of defence by the Welsh back row player Emyrs Lewis, an angular, heavy Carmarthen police officer who was the Welsh blind-side flank forward in his spare time, rolled past Underwood into space near England's left touchline. The scenario looked predictable – Underwood, with a considerable advantage in time and space, would run back to tap the ball into touch and the referee's whistle would sound for half-time with England leading 9–3. All very much par for the course. But this was the moment when Underwood engaged brain-storm system 1 in his personal lock-on computer. He jogged, not ran, back towards the ball, and promptly compounded the folly by easing up almost totally as he saw his full-back, Webb, coming across. It was Underwood's ball to put away, it had never looked like anyone else's. But Underwood's lethargy and final, blatant blunder allowed the Welsh captain Ieuan Evans not only to make up yards on him but actually to reach the ball first. A hopeful fly-hack by Evans sent the ball rolling over the English line and the race for glory was on. England were not at the races: Evans surged past Webb and scored alone, not an Englishman in sight. Jenkins converted, the half-time whistle blew, and Wales led 10–9.

Forty minutes later, Will Carling led his dazed men away from the scene of their first defeat in the Five Nations Championship since March 1990, almost three years earlier. In the England dressing-room, physically powerful men tried and singularly failed to come to terms with the crushing disappointment of defeat. There it lay, like some downed airliner, in their midst; all they could do was grieve. Carling, the shattered young adjutant, attempted to lift his troops, without conspicuous success. Deep down, England's captain smelt the odour of failure as strongly as his men did. It filled the dressing-room, permeated their every pore; most knew that this was probably their last opportunity to make a unique entry in the record books.

Carling's whole being had been directed towards a unique third Grand Slam. Here was a player in the grand style at his peak as a sportsman. Prior to the opening game of the 1993 tournament, he had played just twelve minutes of rugby in seven weeks, an abstinence which had raised both eyebrows and debate in rugby circles. But Carling had always been a major player, destined for a key role on the grandest stage; all through his career, he had accommodated a step-up in class in an outwardly relaxed and assured style.

Carling had achieved much by one o'clock on the afternoon of Saturday 6 February in Cardiff: the looks, the fame, the reputation, the consummate skills of an outstanding player, the expectation, the background and the future. At five o'clock, his sporting and personal ambitions lay in ruins. To the grim memories of

Edinburgh in March 1990 and Twickenham in November 1991, scenes of England's most notable defeats under Carling's captaincy, was added Cardiff in 1993. The defeat by Ireland at the close of the season in Dublin was, with the greatest of respect to a far superior Irish side on the day, an irrelevance as far as England were concerned. Their great dream had long since evaporated, destroyed in Cardiff: the motivation required to play any international was clearly not present in Dublin. The season was over; by the standards to which England had become accustomed, it would be classified as a complete failure. Thus the mental pain and anguish, which one would anticipate easing with the passage of time, merely intensified. England had only themselves to blame for missing their date with destiny, and their captain knew it.

What no one, or at least very few, really knew was the real Will Carling behind the public image. Perhaps he didn't even know himself. Many of his fellow players, putting him in an 'Army father, public school' pigeon-hole, were equally at a loss to understand him or to get a measure of his true self. Some saw him as arrogant, others insisted that this was to misrepresent him, to mis-understand him totally. His detractors pointed to the occasions when his expression would border on a sneer, an almost snarling look that warned off all comers. He would present an embarrassed silence when what was expected was a few kind words – nothing contentious, just a phrase or two from the great man to send the attendant sycophants home happy. When nothing was forthcoming, hackles were raised. Some people felt aggrieved, others insulted and let down. Behind the criticism lay the most base form of human emotion, jealousy. As Wilde reminds us: 'The public is wonderfully tolerant. It forgives everything except genius.'

There were many contradictions, however. Carling could revel in the publicity, actively seeking it to the point of overkill, then creep away quietly to spend time with old school friends, who had remained close throughout his success. He would present himself at luncheons in regal surroundings before important people and thoroughly look the part, in his immaculate suit with his neatly groomed hair, then tell the most *risqué* jokes imaginable, sometimes in mixed company. The irony would apparently be quite lost on him. He could strike a pose as the supreme leader yet be racked by self-doubt. He epitomized the successful young man but concealed an inner character undermined by the fear of failure. In all he did, in everything he represented, he appeared the suave, confident, swaggering young sporting hero to a generation – yet this was a façade hiding intense insecurity.

Carling could charm and delight, repel and appal. He was capable of deeds of great kindness and words of great hurt; he frequently bewildered and confounded expectation. To outsiders he could seem both gregarious and withdrawn, predictable and unpredictable. Some bemoaned his surliness, yet he would sign autographs, everywhere and for everyone, without demur. His background was ultra-conservative, yet he was in the vanguard of change on the players' behalf, speaking forcefully and to the extreme irritation of senior members of the Rugby Football Union on the theme of financial rewards. Friendships, some of many years' standing, might be hastily broken off; others, after long periods of silence, would suddenly receive as a gift, quite unexpectedly, a cherished personal memento such as an England shirt. Warm words of greeting would accompany it.

Carling delighted some of those who met him and displeased others. Like many modern-day sportsmen of his ilk, he would be quick to criticize the media but would at the same time pocket a lucrative personal contract from a newspaper. Nor, apparently, did he see much contradiction in that. He saw plenty of faults in others, but found it difficult to focus on personal failings. He was as brave as a lion on the field, yet could seem craven off it. He exuded the archetypal English rugby character, yet at the same time somehow contrived to dissociate himself from this image. Personal criticism stung him, overtly so, yet he could hand it out quite oblivious to the feelings of others. As he lapped up great fanfares of publicity, he would carry on working silently, and with genuine pleasure, for charity, happy to have escaped the spotlight.

Carling is the first of a new breed. Back in 1980, when England last won a Grand Slam, the side was captained by the avuncular Bill Beaumont, a warm, friendly man with a reputation commensurate with rugby's image. Beaumont was universally revered; he had a word for everyone and even suffered bores with good grace and a tolerant smile. He has remained that way, his image unimpaired by financial profit from a game he played with distinction. Carling is different. A highly complex individual, he has excited jealousy and admiration simultaneously, resentment and praise. He has also been far and away more successful as a national captain than Beaumont, even though the latter would have become the first man to lead successive British Lions touring teams but for his prematurely enforced retirement through injury.

Yet Carling has never approached Beaumont's popularity off the field, for all his achievements upon it. He

was measured for the job of England captain yet wore
the cloak as loosely as though it were off the peg. He
preferred to distance himself from the throng, whereas
the classic Beaumont image was of a bloke spending
time with his mates at the bar, having a cheery word
even for those total strangers who believe they have
carte blanche to intrude into a sportsman's private time
by foisting themselves upon the company. Beaumont
could handle that; Carling has never learned how.

But then Beaumont, even though he was the captain
who brought England their first Grand Slam for twenty-
three years, was never subjected to the microscopic
intensity endured by Carling. Rugby circa 1980 was a
different beast from rugby in 1991, when England next
won a Grand Slam. The sport has been vastly transformed in popularity. Even as late as the second half of
the 1980s, English cup finals were being played out
before crowds of just 23,000, a figure considered at the
time to be quite acceptable. Tickets for international
matches that England played were usually available, and
if the Varsity match between Oxford and Cambridge
universities attracted anything over 25,000, Twickenham officials wore expressions of smug satisfaction,
albeit with a touch of slight disbelief.

The contrast with today is startling. Cynics suggest,
not altogether mischievously, that if fifteen cardboard
cut-out figures were dressed up in English rugby shirts
and shorts and put out at Twickenham, 15,000 would
turn up to watch. The Varsity match, a fixture which has
fluctuated alarmingly in quality in recent years, is usually
sold out, as is the English cup final. A pair of good seats
together for England's most recent home match in the
Five Nations Championship, against Scotland last
March, were making £800 on the black market.

Hand-in-hand with this explosion of interest has come the mushrooming in the marketing of the game. Commercial companies queue up to associate their firms with rugby, England and Twickenham – three high-quality names with which sponsors are determined to be linked. Millions of pounds are invested – Save and Prosper, chief sponsors of the Rugby Football Union these past years, have enhanced their image and developed their world-wide business interests through their association with the game. Cornhill, incidentally, report a similarly rewarding picture from their sponsorship of England's home series in the world of cricket. The investment might be millions but the value is incalculable.

However, there is a down side, which the game has had to suffer. Even under the circumspect guardianship of men like the secretary of the Rugby Football Union, Dudley Wood, those in authority have had the devil's own task in attempting to keep the lid on the game as the money clouds burst. Not unnaturally, some of those with their arms stretched out to catch any stray notes fluttering down upon the sport have included the players. As a figurehead in such times of fundamental change, the England rugby captain has been subjected to a scrutiny more usually associated with an MI5 target.

To many of those associated with the game in official circles, the England captain must be a character of virgin white. His hands must be spotless, his pursuit of a squeaky-clean image never wavering. He must marshal his troops perfectly, and provide success on the field and immaculate behaviour off it. He must preside over an era of unbroken success for the national team and yet happily ignore the many millions of pounds which are flooding his sport; still less must he ask whether those whom the punters actually come to watch – the players – ought not perhaps to be receiving a cut of the cake. Finally, he must adhere to all of rugby's century-old standards in an age when most others involved with the game are jettisoning them, like impoverished passengers leaving excess baggage at the airline check-in counter.

The game, indeed the world, asks – no, demands – everything from an England rugby captain. He must be a consummate handler of personalities, from the terrace yob to the committee-room bore; he must be a player of sumptuous skills and top fitness. To accommodate the burgeoning media interest in the sport, he must be as suave as the ultimate PR man, able to negotiate the question that goes for the jugular with the smile and subtlety of the master politician. He must be always available, and a ready target for interviewers; he must 'say' enough to satisfy his media detractors, yet 'say' sufficiently little to be acceptable to the diehards of the game, some of whom view media intrusion with barely disguised distaste.

The captain of England's rugby team must cheerfully find the time to promote his sport at official functions, yet must not question whether some monetary advantage may be forthcoming, for that would transgress upon rugby union's sacred laws relating to amateurism. Others can feed greedily at this trough: those administrators and officials who with their wives/sisters/girlfriends/lovers/batmen or whomsoever they choose are flown, expenses paid, to pleasant weekend destinations such as Paris, Edinburgh or Dublin on the coat-tails of the England team; those paid officials who receive an enhanced salary commensurate with the increased profits from the game; and even those in the media who gain financial advantage from the game's increased profile. But not the players.

Convention had to be beaten down simply so that players could profit from activities undertaken at their own expense in their own time. Even then, riders were added: no England player could profit from his association with the game. So if a company wanted Will Carling to stand beside a washing machine in his muddy England kit and promote a specific washing powder, this was considered a heinous crime worthy of lifelong banishment from the sport – no matter what service the England captain had given, no matter the years when he had trained and prepared, at his own financial cost, to become the player he is today.

Experts in the legal field would be hard pressed to comprehend the delicate balance involved in such legislation. For example, a club might approach the star player of a rival team and offer him a job package worth £60,000 a year, together with a £60,000 motor car, to desert his current club and join the other. That would be perfectly legal. But if the club went to the star player and offered him, by comparison, a measly £2,000 in cash just to change clubs, that would be contrary to the laws and render the player liable to expulsion from the game.

Into this minefield of contradictions, this confused world of finance and sport where the traditions of decades were being steadily eroded so that all (except the players) could benefit, was thrust a young man named Will Carling – a player of whom just about everything was expected bar reincarnation. The role he was given, the task he had to perform, was herculean.

2 A Precocious Talent

'Tis God gives skill,
But not without men's hands:
He could not make
Antonio Stradivari's violins
Without Antonio.'
George Eliot

Of course, he had always been groomed for it. Good background, eh? And father was in the military, wasn't he? Well – right sort of chap for the job. The identikit for an English rugby captain fitted rather well. Or so it seemed. The reality, as with all such things, was a little different. He was groomed for leadership all right; that was a natural result of having a father in the Army. But Will Carling, born thirteen days before Christmas 1965 in the picturesque Wiltshire town of Bradford-on-Avon, not far from Bath, was always a lad apart.

The second son of Bill and Pam Carling, the rugby-playing genes were sound. Father William had played the game enthusiastically, as a prop forward, representing among others Cardiff, Cornwall and the Army, and had been stationed at Warminster when Will was born. The boy had an elder brother, Marcus. The family moved around like travellers; father Bill was a Lieutenant-Colonel in the Air Corps, eventually commanding a helicopter squadron. He is remembered at one of Will Carling's schools as the dad who arrived one day by helicopter – clearly a step up from the bog-standard XJ6 sibling-carrying vehicle. A parent to covet.

Given their parents' unpredictable lifestyle, which also took them on service to the Far East, an English public school was the inevitable education for Marcus and William. This was the Douglas Jardine upbringing: the parents, posted overseas, would send their children home to England to boarding school, where the art of making a century at cricket or learning to position oneself properly for the tackle on the rugby field was considered as much a part of the educational process as mastering the intricacies of chemistry, or learning where one could find the source of the Nile.

Will Carling's first school was Montgomery County Infants, in the unlovely Army garrison town of Colchester. He is remembered there as being a bully, a petulant individual who loved success and embraced it willingly enough but had not a clue about handling defeat. This less than flattering trait reached its nadir one day when the youngster was given out at cricket: when he got back to the pavilion he hurled his bat away in disgust. Petulant little Master Carling got what a lot of schoolboys deserved and received in similar circumstances: a box on the ears from his embarrassed mother, who had witnessed the scene.

He spent three years as a young 'Essex man' before changing schools. His parents chose Terra Nova, in Cheshire, a junior boarding school of 100 pupils not far from Jodrell Bank, mainly because their sons' grandparents lived at Alderley Edge, five or six miles from the school. This, it was thought, would provide the close family link which the parents could not offer on a regular basis. But without his parents' day-to-day influence, control and presence, William, aged seven years three months at the start of his first term, leaned heavily on his brother, Marcus, who was nineteen months older and the natural trailblazer for the pair. Perhaps as a further palliative to alleviate the pain of distance from his parents, the youngster threw himself into sport.

Marcus and William, quickly dubbed Carling I and Carling II, became close. The younger lad looked up to the senior boy from an early age; he saw him as more than a family soul-mate – rather, as a role model. Later, William would power past his elder brother in the field of achievement as though he were defeating an opponent with one of those magnificent, classical outside breaks which became his hallmark from his earliest days on the rugby field. Yet he would always praise him. 'Have you heard how well Marcus is doing?' and 'Marcus played ever so well' were two phrases familiar to his contemporaries. A hidden jealousy it palpably was not; the younger brother genuinely derived a pleasure from the elder's albeit modest achievements, and still does to this day, for they have remained extremely close. Shortly before Christmas 1992, when he decided to opt out of English rugby's Divisional Championship, Will Carling flew instead to the Far East to see his brother.

Yet perhaps the need to match and, if possible, improve upon his elder brother's successes sowed the seed for dynamic achievement in the younger Carling. That inner drive for success has without doubt been an integral part of his being throughout his life. There is a strong dynamism, implanted at an early age, that has remained at the core of Will Carling. In adulthood, it translates as almost a craving to achieve, a phenomenon which has been studied extensively at America's Bowling Green University. But that was to become apparent a little later.

What was as clear as the strong winter sunlight which shone in shafts through the trees on to Terra Nova's rugby field was that a boy of most unusual sporting prowess had arrived. His father thought he might make a good rugby player, but he got the position wrong: 'I have a good prop forward for you next September,' Carling senior told Ian Argyle, Terra Nova's master in charge of rugby, when he arrived, by air, for an appointment. Argyle smiled: a father who comes for an appointment by helicopter and a son who plays rugby – how could the school fail to be impressed?

Nor did the reality confound the expectation. Quite the contrary. It was, reflected his headmaster years later, quite remarkable to see a seven-year-old with such quality. Shades of Jardine, although this boy wonder was a genius with a rugby ball in his hand rather than a cricket bat (good though he was to become at the latter sport, too). 'He had such good natural skills and co-ordination,' says Argyle, a quiet, scholarly figure of neat disposition and tidy, orderly mind as befits a schoolmaster. 'I can remember going home one evening and saying I cannot believe there is another seven-year-old in England with his talents, someone who can do with a ball what he can do at such an age. His kicking and handling skills were superb.'

New boys at school are a cross-section of humanity. Some bury their heads at once in schoolbooks, others seek any distraction from lessons. Others still employ the wiliest of tactics to avoid physical exercise, especially a contact sport like rugby. But here was a boy who seemed born for the sport; he took to it with a comfort, a sure touch which belied his tender years. He had the natural skill, but he also possessed the physique to set him apart from others of his age. Even the best paled into insignificance beside him. For he could play, and play magnificently; his was already a precocious, prodigious talent. At his age, at his level, he excelled for what he was — an outstanding young player in the making. His strength, his speed, his intuitive balance and vision; his composure in possession, his cool command of situations; these were qualities which none could have taught. His balance was consummate, his skills exquisite. He could run like the wind and power through tackles like some junior colossus. Those who saw him, this sporting genius in the making, were at once thrilled and captivated; it was as if they realized that they were in at the birth of a master practitioner.

But he was a young sportsman of all-round excellence. He ran, he shot, he batted and bowled, he passed and kicked; the school offered an environment which was made for his talents. Terra Nova required that its participants took their sport seriously, and Carling was more than prepared to oblige. He stood out, initially, through his physical superiority. Ian Argyle remembers his young pupil as being far broader and stronger, especially in the upper body, than opponents of the same age. In matches, Carling's strong legs would enable him to brush aside all but the most determined of tackles. 'He seemed able to create a lot of space for others around him. And he had a rugby brain from the start, no one at the school gave him that. He was a natural player, and perhaps he didn't really learn a lot from anyone there. He just needed the opportunity to bring out his talents.'

Nevertheless, Terra Nova had some worthy coaches to run a shrewd eye over the young hopefuls. Ian Argyle had found a partner with real credentials to assist him on a part-time basis: Jim Roberts had been a good enough wing threequarter in his day to earn three blues for Cambridge University and eighteen caps for England between 1960 and 1964. Clearly this was no reluctant father, unqualified yet pressganged into service to help out. Yet Roberts's summary of the young Carling was to prove flawed. 'We often used to sit and chat, and say we wondered how far young Carling would go,' said Argyle. 'Jim Roberts said that if he got anywhere it would be as a flanker.'

Terra Nova's devotion to sporting excellence was manifest in the amount of time it gave to its brightest prospects. Even at the age of eight, young Carling would spend a minimum of four days a week, very often five, on the training field, working on his skills and developing his awareness of the game. To the ordinary pupil, this would have been tantamount to punishment: to Carling II, the rugby boy, as he became known, it was simply a labour of love.

Ian Argyle believes that at ten he showed more speed than subsequently, certainly more than he did by the age of thirteen, when he was on the point of leaving Terra Nova. This was natural: the young boy's bones and joints were developing into those of a more powerful growing lad. Besides, speed alone is rarely the sole criterion; power is the breaker of tackles.

In Carling's position, the incision is the key; other players, further out, can complete the destruction. At Terra Nova, Carling found just the player to complement his game, a boy named Michael Heathcote. Sometimes the pair might accumulate 100 points between them in a Sevens tournament. Carling scored tries and kicked conversions, while Heathcote's rippling speed was the perfect accompaniment outside him. Together they helped create the finest side Terra Nova had seen in years.

Specific moves with names attractive to young boys were practised assiduously. One of them, 'Spitfire', was especially popular. It involved a dummy scissors between the outside half and inside centre, with the full-back coming in on the outside. Imagine Ian Argyle's surprise, years later, as he sat watching an England international on television at his new school, Aldro, in the gentle Surrey countryside near Godalming, and saw the national team captain and his colleagues perform a set move. Argyle leapt to his feet, astonished, calling out 'Spitfire!' The move was identical to that used first by Carling at Terra Nova.

In 1979, Carling went to Roehampton with his school. The Rosslyn Park National Schools Seven-a-Side tournament has been part of schoolboy rugby folklore for decades; a flip through the old programmes of the four-day event, held each year at the end of the Hilary term, gives a fascinating opportunity for star-spotting. Some notable schoolboy players have appeared at this event: the great Welsh scrum-halves Gareth Edwards for Millfield and Robert Jones for Cwmtawe, plus Chris Oti, also for Millfield, are just three of many. Carling appeared only in the preparatory schools competition.

Roehampton is a social gathering, truly an event; discussion on the first morning is invariably about Ampleforth's brilliant outside half, or the flyer Millfield have unearthed on the wing, or the lovely footballer Rydal have at centre. Much of this is apocryphal: players sure to set Roehampton alight never prosper, while others emerge. The grand leveller, as in all grades of rugby union, is the weather – it is usually foul. Those who study charts of climatic patterns would find the Roehampton week, shortly before Easter, an essential time for that overseas holiday. Lashing rain and cold

winds invariably batter the brave boys; talented foot-
ballers find themselves overpowered by heavier brutes
relishing the appalling conditions. Players step into the
mess underfoot with the enthusiasm of schoolboys given
porridge for breakfast. For years the organizers have
had the ammunition to move the event to early September, when the firm ground would offer every encouragement to the talented player. It might even become
pleasant to watch in warm sunshine. But it has remained
a slave to its tradition, and the appeal, for spectators
and players alike (not to mention for the womenfolk
back home, who are left with the task of scraping the
caked liquid earth of SW15 off their menfolk's ruined
shoes), has often been diminished, which is a pity.

When Carling played for Terra Nova, word had
spread, as on the bush radio, that they were the side
to beat. The 'Seven' had already won tournaments at
Rossall and Stonyhurst; already, too, the exploits of
the young William Carling were known – he had picked
a boy up physically and dumped him over the dead ball
line to prevent him scoring a try in a Sevens match
against Rossall School. Who was this giant from on
high? Could he possibly be as good as some suggested?
The boys of the Welsh prep school Llanarth Court,
Gwent, wouldn't have thought so. The mud was ankle
deep, Terra Nova's forward trio was unable to achieve
supremacy up front, and the team had to rely on Carling
and his colleagues behind the scrum for their salvation.
At 6–10 down with only minutes remaining of the
quarter-final, Carling made the decisive run for the winning score. He brushed aside a challenge or two and
headed for the posts – only to slip over in the mud just
a few yards short and lose the chance. Terra Nova's
hopes slithered away with him; the green and white

hooped jerseys which had scored 100 points in the first round matches disappeared from the tournament. So much for reputations.

So what happened to the great Will Carling? Well, he went back to Cheshire and went on playing superlative rugby in the XV-a-side version. He captained Terra Nova's Under-11s, a team which was totally untroubled by any other school side. By the time he had reached the age of eleven, Carling had won a place in the school's 1st XV; he played two full seasons for the side.

Terra Nova's rugby coaches chose a twenty-strong squad for the 1st XV, working with them in groups and units. 'Sometimes we would go out for twenty minutes during break, and work on a particular discipline,' says Ian Argyle. 'One thing we did was to see how quickly the ball could be moved out to the wing from the scrum-half. We had read somewhere that Blackrock College, the Irish school, had done it in just a few seconds. It had to be done properly; you had to run as you passed and end up with the wing crossing the try-line, from a start position on the 22. I think the best we ever achieved was five to six seconds. But it was a valuable exercise in seeing how quickly the player could move the ball.'

Argyle remembers that Marcus Carling also played for Terra Nova's 1st XV. His coach of the time recalls a fine side-step and a very evasive runner, but adds: 'He was quite a lightweight, fairly fragile compared to Will.' Nevertheless, the younger brother had a target at which to set his sharp sights. The competitive urge was ticking away, pacemaker-like, within, and its intensity would increase with the passing of the years. There was a deep-seated, growing need to match the performances of his elder rival.

The mark of true sporting pedigree among schoolboys

is their prowess at a wide range of games. Carling II was the ultimate 'master proficient' in this respect; a leaf through the pages of the *Terra Novan*, the school chronicle of the period, is a journey of discovery in the pursuit of a rare talent. Carling played for the school's rugby Colts XV in 1975 and they won five of their six matches. The following year, a critique recorded: 'The Colts team were . . . the team who drew the eye towards them. They had a well-disciplined pack . . . and were unusually well captained by William Carling who himself scored 50 points.' By the close of the Lent term, 1977, the younger Carling had represented the 1st XV. Both William and Marcus played in the Sevens team.

And so to June, and that all-too British summer of 1977 when the Queen celebrated the Silver Jubilee of her accession to the throne and the nation, wrapped up in winter coats and scarves, shivered while waiting for the grey days and biting winds at last to relinquish their grip. Will Carling's preoccupations were elsewhere: he was one of six boys to be awarded his cricket colours. His citation read: 'Carling, who still has two more years, has scored nearly 150 runs and taken 25 wickets, a fine achievement in his first season.'

There were some notable individual cricket performances by Carling II: 5–28 against Ryleys School, in the first fixture of the summer, 6–52 against Brocksford Hall, and 35 runs against Pownall Hall. He made 34 out of 86 all out in a losing match against Rydal; took 4–37 and scored an unbeaten 33 against an Old Boys XI, took 4–13 and scored 32 against the Staff and finished with 30 not out against the Fathers. In all, from twelve matches and twelve innings, he made 141 runs with a top score of 35 and an average of 15.6. His bowling figures read: 122 overs, 28 maidens, 349 runs,

26 wickets (the most in the side). In the same season for the 1st XI, Marcus Carling made 100 runs from twelve innings and took four catches, to Will's two.

The pair excelled at shooting, as befits the sons of an Army father. Three shields were competed for each term by preparatory schools all over the country: the St Patrick's (20–25 yards), the St George's (50 yards) and the St Andrew's (100 yards). The hardest to win was the St Patrick's, for more than forty schools usually competed. Terra Nova won this shield in the Michaelmas term of 1976, in the Lent term of 1977 and in the Summer term of the same year. The school also won the other two shields in the Summer term.

Carlings I and II had a profound influence on this success. Marcus scored 94 points from a possible 100 in the Winter term of 1976, and by the following Lent term his younger brother, a chubby-faced, immensely determined, cheery little chap with a thatch of hair as black as the metal on his .22 rifle, had joined the team to considerable effect. In the Lent term St Patrick's Shield competition, Carling senior scored 97 and Carling junior 99 from the possible 100; the scores were reversed in the Summer term. In the Summer term, for the St George's Shield, Carling I scored 87, Carling II, 90. In the St Andrew's Shield, Carling I achieved 88, Carling II, 91. Will was always that crucial bit better than his older brother, although Marcus won the Shooting Cup for the best average, with a boy called Woodcock, in 1977. Both Carlings won their marksman certificate for aggregate scores in excess of 275.

Nor was the family's inherent ability to fire a rifle with deadly accuracy the only other claim to fame of the rugby-playing and cricketing Will Carling. On the athletics track at the 1976 sports day he won the 200 metres for boys of his age group in a new school record time of 30.6 seconds. He finished third in the high jump and threw the cricket ball further than anyone else of his age, 43.05 metres. He was still only ten years old. A year later he set another new school record by running the Under-12 400 metres in 66 seconds dead, and raised his throw with the cricket ball to 50.94 metres.

On 24 June, at last a glorious English high summer day, the critique recorded: 'William Carling had a particularly good day [in the home match with Pownall Hall]. He made appearances in the Under-12 long jump and 200 metres, setting new school records in both [4.39 metres and 29.9 seconds].' At the 1977 sports day, W. D. C. Carling won the Middles 400 metres, the 1,500 metres (in another school record time of 5 minutes, 29.5 seconds), the triple jump (yawn, yawn, another new record, of 9.38 metres!) and the cricket ball throwing competition. He was leading points scorer on the day for the 'Middles', with 28. There were official photographs, too, for posterity (and parents!). There he stands, a wide grin across his chubby little face, the back ramrod straight with pride and the chin up. Look, Mum, look what I've done now . . .

Yet this was no Roger Black in the making. In both 1976 and 1977, Terra Nova competed in the Denstone athletic meeting, for twenty-five prep schools in the area. Triumph at his own school proved insufficient; the best that W. D. C. Carling achieved in 1976 was sixth place in the Under-11 200 metres. It was slightly better the following year: second place in the Under-12 400 metres and fourth in the triple jump. But thoughts of Olympic gold had to be quietly consigned to the dream-time after lights out.

But there was still rugby. 'William Carling,' wrote an

anonymous critic in the following year's chronicle, 'is already dictating the game well from fly-half.' He was in the 1st XV by now, and in the Lent term Terra Nova won six of their seven matches, losing only to Rossall Junior School. He became captain of rugby in the 1978–9 season. Cricket in the summer of 1978 was to be another source of pride in the young breast: Carling junior won the cricket trophy for his fine all-round season and his haul of 36 wickets at an average of just 9.6. He was also the leading run-maker, with 133 from eleven innings.

His shooting was also immaculate during that Summer term: 100 out of 100, which was the top score in the Preparatory Schools Rifle Association competition, earning him the PSRA medal. After that there was only a miserable and humiliating failure in the St George's Shield, a dismal 91 out of 100 (although it was joint top score), followed by a pitiful 90 out of 100 in the St Andrew's Shield! The magic touch had deserted him! By amassing 294 points from a possible 300, dead-eyed Master Will earned a Master Shot certificate from the PSRA. Just about the only activity he wasn't a master at was chess.

At the 1978 school sports day, Carling, now in the seniors, finished second in the high jump and the long jump. At the grandly titled 16th Annual Prep School Meeting at Denstone, he was a member of Terra Nova's 4 × 100 metres relay Under-13 team which won the event in 56 seconds, a record for the meeting in heat and final. He also came second in the long jump. Then, in 1979, his last year at Terra Nova, he was awarded his colours for athletics. Oh, yes, and there *was* time for just a little work when sporting commitments permitted. But Carling, in his own words, was no academic: he won a scholarship from Terra Nova in, of all things, art. (He was in fact to prove an artist of reasonable ability.)

Andrew Keith, Carling's headmaster at Terra Nova, wrote presciently after his first year: 'He has had great success on the rugger field, displaying a nice balance between toughness and skill.' Keith later called his star sports pupil's captaincy 'splendid'. He finished by saying: 'He has dominated much of Terra Nova life for a fair amount of time, and much of our sporting and artistic success is due to him. I hope that William can make the adjustment from being master of all he surveys to being just another lowly new boy with the right degree of humour and humility.'

Did Andrew Keith detect, even at that young age, that the humbling experience undergone by every new boy at school might prove difficult for Carling to handle? Was it an indication that he harboured doubts about his pupil's ability to embrace a life where he would not be, for a while at least, the focal point of attention? Did his last words indicate that already the boy wonder knew just how good he was, and flaunted it – at times, to his detriment?

3 Sedbergh

'How haughtily he cocks his nose,
To tell what every schoolboy knows.'
Jonathan Swift, *The Country Life*

A rocky fell climbs steeply into a clear blue winter sky, its top sprinkled lightly with snow like icing sugar on some vast, strangely contorted cake. Tiny moving white dots are strung out in a line clinging precariously to the steep slope, all heading towards a distant tractor: sheep in search of their morning feed. Below this scene of colour and beauty lies a cluster of incongruously grey, forbidding buildings, lumped together in the lee of the fell. Sedbergh School.

There has been a school on this site since the reign of Henry VIII in 1525. Sedbergh, although gobbled up by the Cumbrian policy of Lebensraum in 1974, has always been a part of the classic Yorkshire Dales and is still within the Dales National Park. It is an area of barren beauty, a remote outpost not un-reminiscent of Dartmoor. The school buildings, austere and imposing, could even, from their grim appearance in winter, be another Dartmoor prison. Like Princetown, the buildings dominate the area: the town has serviced the school through the centuries, its few regular inhabitants running the shops or manning the post office or local inns. Nowadays, when the cold northern winter finally relents, the invasion of tourists provides the only real industry in the region. The views are spectacular, the walks magnificent.

Sedbergh, although mentioned in the Domesday book, has an even older history. Local historians suggest that the name derives from the old Norse word 'Setberg', meaning a flat-topped hill. Certainly, given its location within reach of the Scottish border, it was in an area notorious for raids to the south by the warring Scots. In summer, it can be a blissful delight for visitors and locals; balmy, long, light evenings of solitude and beauty, for strolling beside the rivers Rawthay and Clough, which meet close to the town, and the nearby River Dee. In winter it is a harsh, uncompromising region, not often deluged by snow at the lower levels, perhaps surprisingly, but incessantly wet and made chill by the winds which whistle off the three surrounding fells and sweep through the valley. Given this bleak environment, the young Will Carling, arriving at the school in the autumn of 1979, might have gleaned from Sedbergh an impression of austerity, particularly since flogging and fagging were still practised at the school.

Sedbergh boasted some eminent names down the years of its history. One of these was Hartley Coleridge, the son of the poet, who was headmaster for a time. Another was Brendan Bracken, later to become an associate of Winston Churchill during the Second World War, who arrived unannounced at Sedbergh with an extraordinary story to tell. Bracken, who said he had been born in December 1904 in Australia, recounted how his parents had died in a disastrous New South Wales bush fire and how his father, just before he had expired, had said to him: 'Son, go to England and get yourself an English public school education.' The astonished headmaster, a man who rejoiced in the name of

William Nassau Weech, leaned across his study desk facing the stranger and listened intently to this tale from a young man of sixteen who said he needed one or two more years of education. Weech could not pick up the telephone to Australia and verify the story; he may have suspected a fabrication, but had no means of getting a definitive answer on the matter. So he decided that Bracken could stay, and, when he enquired who might meet the young man's fees, it is said that Bracken heaved an enormous money bag on to the headmaster's study desk and counted out the required sum for the first term's fees as though this were the normal manner of such business.

Sedbergh should be grateful for William Weech's benevolence to Bracken, even though, for unexplained reasons, he was to stay only one term at the school. By the time Bracken died, he had returned to serve the school as Chairman of the Governors and benefactor. He provided money to offer scholarships, in the name of Winston Churchill; these were reserved for boys of Scottish descent, of whom Sedbergh always attracted a sizeable number. He also gave the funds which in 1950 enabled a new school library to be designed, in the eighteenth-century building which had been known as the 'School-house', and which had originally housed the entire school. Today, one still passes solemnly beneath the inscription that Bracken insisted be put above the main door of the building – 'Remember Winston Churchill'. Bracken considered this a suitably inspirational phrase to all boys passing beneath in pursuit of their studies.

It is thought that Sedbergh benefited by around £100,000 from Bracken's generosity. His interest in Sedbergh for the remainder of his life was considerable;

he was a regular visitor. Considering the fact that he had stayed so short a time at the school as a pupil, this may be thought a bit odd, for Sedbergh was hardly an Eton or a Harrow. It was never considered one of England's most important public schools; indeed, a note of derision is apparent in the story of an Harrovian colleague who wrote to Henry Hart in 1879 when he was considering accepting the post of headmaster at Sedbergh. 'Don't, don't,' wrote the friend. 'I have a fair knowledge of geography but I don't even know where Sedbergh is.'

About five miles east of junction 37 off the M6 motorway, actually. But you wouldn't want to be starting from here to get there, as the Irish might tell you! For it can be a lonely, exposed spot. Today, the journey by vehicle from Kendal, some nine miles to the west, is a pleasant interlude of hill climbing and valley trundling. The little stone walls pen the sheep, the views are glorious. It is Postman Pat country; the little red post van comes every day from Kendal, chugging down from the high ground near the motorway, over the bridge which crosses the small, rushing river and along the valley floor into Sedbergh.

The school lads always made it a place with a story to tell. According to a contemporary report, 'One night in February, 1853, some of the "scholar lads" managed to break bounds and carried out some of the wildest freaks, such as tearing off the handsomest of the door knockers in which, at that time, many householders took pride. The same rag-tag-and-bob-tail scholars also took off the ball of the cross. I never heard what became of it and it was never replaced and ere long the whole structure of the Market Cross disappeared, leaving just the open Square.'

Perhaps, too, a so-called 'worthy' scholar found a handsome reward for a piece of larceny in the town one day, as the old school magazine records: 'On the higher side of the street, a few yards back, was an old-time "Tuck" shop kept by "Mother Dilworth" and I do not expect any tuck shop of today could vie with it for home-made cakes. It was a treat to go into the old shop; all was so tempting, from Mrs Dilworth herself, a fine buxom dame with frilled, string-tied cap, to her dainties carefully arranged on the counter and covered with white damask d'oyleys, each edged with crochet. Mrs Dilworth sold gingerbread, jumbles and other cakes, all small and sold in "pennorths" if not "ha'porths", also toffee, which came out of a green ex-tea box.

'With boys in and out constantly there was a little "club-room", I believe, behind the shop. She was much too generous and easily imposed upon to make much profit, but somehow she did get together £200 in the course of many years; this sum she felt could only be safe in her own keeping, so she hid it under the floor. Someone must have known this, for one day it was gone and she never got over the loss and, I believe, went what they call "queer". Sometime in the Sixties, her shop became the Post Office.'

A little over 100 years later, when Will Carling went to Sedbergh, the tradition still lingered of a small club-room where boys could eat and drink out of hours above a restaurant in the town. But sport, and rugby football in particular, was closer to the heart-beat of this school. A questionnaire for Sedbergh sixth-form boys in 1980 asked the following question: 'In one word, for what would you remember Sedbergh after you had left?' The answer, by general consent, was: (1) Rain, (2) Sport, (3) Countryside, (4) Discipline.

Sport was certainly all-pervasive. None other than the immortal Wavell Wakefield, England's rugby captain back in the 1920s, had attended Sedbergh from 1912–16, and plenty of other future rugby internationals, for both England and Scotland, had been this way. More recently, pupils included Scotland's Mike and Alistair Biggar and England's 1971 British Lion, John Spencer, of Spencer and Duckham fame. Alistair Biggar and John Spencer played in the same Sedbergh School 1st XV of 1964; it was a powerful side.

In 1978, the season preceding Will Carling's arrival as a thirteen-year-old, the Sedbergh 1st XV became the first school side since 1966 to emulate the Sedbergh team's record of that year by winning all its regular school fixtures. He might already be a talent apparent, but he was to be educated in a school renowned for its focus on rugby football. As the young man carried his bags up the stairs of Winder House, one of the seven senior houses, he bade farewell once more to his family and began the critical years of his educational career – on the school's rugby fields.

It was a less than auspicious beginning. In a junior game against Stonyhurst, with a lead of 19–8 and fifteen minutes to go, reported a scribe for the Old Sedberghian Club some years later, 'Carling decided to kick diagonally in their 22 and bounced it off their centre who shot through and scored.' Where now the boy wonder who had arrived with the reputation of a saint and had tripped up on his own halo?

Boys less assured, in a playing sense, might have endured miseries for such a crass mistake. Carling, whose elder brother had preceded him to the school, simply atoned in his next match by making a scintillating run which destroyed the opposition defence. Peter

Meadows was there to see it. Meadows, a patrician figure with a round face and ruddy complexion, is now the bursar at the school, but was Carling's housemaster at Winder, throughout his years at Sedbergh. The young man, he says, proved to be academically 'sound', but the more revealing clues to Carling's personality are to be found in Meadows's other remarks. 'Carling had quite a reserve about him. He was difficult to get to know. Pretty single-minded, certainly did not tolerate fools gladly and seemed forceful on the outside. And yet you had the feeling, you never knew quite what he was feeling in his heart of hearts. Boys such as him are in a minority; to be such a private person as a boy is unusual.'

On the games fields, of course, the same style, great assurance and skills he had shown at his prep school were once more in evidence. Naturally: the brilliant young pianist does not lose the art when he plays on a new instrument. So here, we might assume, was a boy confident both on and off the field, one for whom a strange and forbidding public school hundreds of miles away from his parents held no fears. Alas, not so. Carling, a highly sensitive boy, revealed the true inner feelings, the insecurities he normally hid, by the matter of his selection of a house. Marcus was already resident in Winder House, and the school's inclination was to separate the brothers. Young Will had other ideas. 'There was this suggestion about splitting them up but Will said he wanted to be in the same house as his brother,' remembers Meadows. Again, the special relationship was alive and vibrant. What it meant was that Carling junior wanted the close family liaison at hand, not at a distance. Ironically, it was Marcus who suffered most from the decision. 'Will always outshone

Marcus, even though his elder brother was no fool. But Will had the edge in sport and academically, too,' says Meadows.

But even at thirteen Carling showed the quality which was to dog him and damn him in the eyes of so many throughout his young life. The charge of arrogance was an easy one to make; here was the classic case of the boy born with a silver spoon in his mouth. His father flew helicopters, he was outstanding at most sports, playing for rugby sides a year above his age, and he tended to choose his friends from that older group. He was proficient academically and good-looking. The world was laid out before him, like a vast map just waiting for him to explore it. But it was an exclusive chart, open only for Will Carling.

Those most base of human emotions, envy and jealousy, danced dangerously behind Carling's back even from his earliest times at Sedbergh. Many who had heard of his arrival were instantly suspicious and envious. Some who saw him play sport virtually each day, and excel in almost every sphere of the sporting world, were consumed with, one might say, ill-will. Those who clearly lacked his privileged background and, unlike Carling junior, could not arrange their lives so efficiently as to handle their studies as well as playing year-round sport and ending up in the best teams, felt a deep malice. Carling's way did nothing to deflate his critics.

Peter Meadows was, of course, a shrewder, more experienced judge than any boys around at the time. 'You might have thought he was arrogant but I always felt it was more shyness. In his last year, he came out a little more when he was my Head of House. But it was Marcus who was a little more extrovert and consequently more popular. He was easier to get to know. I always felt it was shyness which prevented Will being that way, but it could have been interpreted as arrogance, although I don't think it was.'

Friends, acquaintances, colleagues, fellow team members, media men and countless others would ponder this aspect of Will Carling endlessly in future years. Some, rigid in their beliefs, would insist that he was a conceited, intrinsically aloof individual who never suffered fools gladly and made it plainly obvious to them what he felt, no matter what their feelings or who got hurt. Others, both friends and those who though not especially close to him had observed him over a long period, insisted that he suffered excruciating shyness and was helpless to prevent the image of him which had, erroneously, been formed. It was misleading to accuse him of coldness, they claimed; he had demonstrated time and again that he was far removed from being such a figure.

If his steadily growing physical frame concealed the boy's inner feelings and insecurities, there was no disputing the impression of a champion sportsman in the making. Meadows saw his house, with Carling at the helm, soon win the Junior Juniors final; it was the first of many triumphs to be achieved by sides for which he played during his five years at Sedbergh. This was undeniably the boy with the golden touch. 'He was an outstanding games player, one of the leading lights of the school,' recalls Peter Meadows. 'I can remember watching him play a little inter-house match on the school fields at thirteen, not long after he arrived at Sedbergh, in the autumn of 1979. One knew he was very promising but did not quite know just how far he would go. One sensed, however, it would be a long way.'

Why? 'On the rugby field, he was rather different to others; more mature as a player for a start and surprisingly so for one so young. You always felt he was a little bit older than those around him. He had a measured calm about him, overall. Little disturbed him. He might have got annoyed by things that happened but he never looked rattled or lacking in composure.' Even at thirteen? Definitely different.

These qualities were noticed by other boys, too. Mark Alban, now a sports writer for the *Observer*, played in school sides with Carling through most of his school career. He remembers him as a boy who seemed a lot older than everyone else; and as someone utterly devoted to rugby football. 'The first rugby match of the Upper Sixth season was against St Bees, near Windscale. We went out before the game to walk around the pitch and I remember Will saying, "I have been waiting for this since the season ended last year." He was absolutely incredulous that I preferred cricket. He just loved playing rugby. He wasn't posturing; he just said, "This is what I really love doing."'

Alban's best memories are of playing centre beside Carling in the third year, for the Colts. 'Of course, the school selectors held him back which was quite a shrewd move. With a sport like cricket, you can push people through to a higher level and they adapt. But rugby is different because it is a physical game. He was good enough to play at the higher level but perhaps not physically ready and that gave him time to think about the game. In his last year, he was full-back and I was at fly-half. He was given free rein in that position and made the most of it. The really classy player can do things from there and he did. I can remember him now, stepping through tackles; he just lanced through defences.'

But he detected a sense of frustration in his team-mate. 'I am sure there was that element at school when things were not going well. He felt that no matter how good he might have been, there was a limit to what the side could do in a situation. Rugby is reliant on a team, unlike cricket.'

Sedbergh (fees around £5,000 a year at the time) offered its best sports prospects an expensive but extensive tutelage. Pupils were out most days of the week training and practising, usually in the afternoons, when they would do a two-hour session. Even on busy school-days they would fit in an hour's training. For Will Carling, it was the perfect environment to build his stamina and hone his technique. He did a great deal of weight-training at the school, and five-mile runs were considered the norm. Mercifully, his sports tutors at Sedbergh quickly grasped that a rare jewel had tumbled on to their table and required only intermittent polishing. They could advise and suggest, but somehow, even at thirteen, Carling knew instinctively what to do and where to be on the field.

Such qualities seemed to be part of his make-up. In the words of one of his teachers, he was always pretty organized, meticulously well ordered, as befits a boy from a military family. Each house had around sixty boys, but Carling had a small circle of friends from which he seldom strayed. Holidays took up a third of the year – a month off at Christmas and Easter, two months in the summer – yet the time Carling spent at school helped mould him further into a figure of convention. That was the Sedbergh way.

He was up with everyone else at 7.30 a.m., and, at the end of the day, ready for house prayers at 9.45 p.m. The seniors went to bed later, by 11 p.m. He had earned an art scholarship to the school but was increasingly proficient at the general subjects, English, history and geography. He went on field trips, competed in the school cross-country runs and led a healthy, vigorously active life.

Even the local terrain was in his favour. He had always been a strong boy physically, but Sedbergh boys are renowned for the strength of their legs, from running on the near-by hills and fells. At one time, punishments meant a tortuous run up Winder Fell and back for a cold shower before breakfast, just the thing to induce attention and greater concentration during those indescribably boring maths lessons. Carling was never a great devotee of long-distance running, but the cross-country challenges in which he took part must have helped to strengthen him. As an England international, his capacity to remain on his feet in the tackle, even with two or three opponents driving into him, has been one of his greatest attributes. Such body and leg strength is imperative in the modern game. Carling possessed the quality long before he represented England at senior level.

John Morris was house tutor at Winder House in Carling's time, and was also master in charge of cricket and assistant coach at rugby. He was once a Sedbergh pupil himself, and remembers the school when it really matched the austerity of its appearance. 'It was a far more severe place in the early sixties. All sorts of petty regulations existed with regard to your conduct. No one would speak to people in the year above them, it was that kind of school. In those days, it was a pretty tough existence. But the worst things tended to die out from the middle sixties. The school is now capable of dealing with boys with a wider range of interests. But one aspect still applies – the pride the school takes in its rugby. You are lucky to be here if you are interested in rugby, because it has got a terrific reputation.'

As a junior at thirteen, Carling would have had to accept general duties apart from those of an educational nature. He and the other youngsters were given cleaning tasks, and had to tidy the common rooms, too. Fagging was still practised, and junior boys were employed to run errands for their seniors. Juniors would be told, 'Go and make my tea and clean my shoes,' and would have to take the senior boys' messages to other houses. General tidying-up, vacuuming and cleaning washbasins and corridors also had to be done.

The word fagging is an emotive one in the annals of English public schools. Images arise from *Tom Brown's Schooldays* of small boys held down by brutes of seventeen or eighteen and roasted beside open fires or pushed head first down lavatories. There is no evidence that these practices went on at Sedbergh by the time Carling arrived; and in any case, Carling's sporting prowess would have protected him from any bullying. Those who were the best at sport became close friends in a select group which remained largely impenetrable to outsiders. It may have been regarded with suspicion and resentment by those not privy to membership, but it afforded a kind of protection through strength of numbers – and through reputation.

Carling, though, was regarded with envy and bitterness by those who felt him too good by half at everything with which he became involved. A classic catch-22, no-win situation; and John Morris acknowledges that others had a problem in coming to terms with Carling, still less understanding him.

'He was quite quiet and shy with the people he didn't

know. And he took time to get to know people. It was
easy to get him wrong then, just as it is today. People
might think his aloofness was a pose, but the truth was,
it was quite a struggle for him to handle that. He may
appear to outsiders to be arrogant but he definitely is
not. He is a sensitive sort of person . . . When he was
with people he really trusted and his close friends, he
was marvellous company. He has a terrific sense of
humour and can be very witty. But at school, his biggest
problem was that he was very successful and good at
all games. And people can be so jealous.'

Other pupils in his own year did not know how to
handle this budding sports genius. 'They didn't know
quite what to make of this guy who was almost a year
ahead of them in most things,' says Mark Alban.
Younger boys in the school, like Adrian Scott, saw
Carling's world as quite different from their own.
'Sedbergh was the type of school that if you had won
your 1st XV blazer, people just looked up to you. But
Carling treated people below him poorly. Some boys
who were older you could approach but he wasn't one
of them. He became known as "God". He was regarded
as someone above all else.' Perhaps part of this inner
sense of being apart was induced by others. 'Kerry
Wedd, his 1st XV coach, believed that if a boy was
wearing a brown jersey, he was wonderful. How you
handled that depended on what kind of person you
were,' says Scott.

But Carling was good – very good. Life at Sedbergh
for those wrapped in rugby focused on securing one of
the famous brown jerseys of the 1st XV. To win your
brown jersey gave you a standing, a position automatically above most others. But first you had to work your
way through the ranks. Winder House were never to

win the house rugby cup in Carling's time, but there were to be plenty of other compensations.

In 1980–81, Carling was in the Sedbergh Colts A side which was unbeaten against all other schools. A contemporary report describes him as a fly half who was 'exciting and a controlling influence with quick hands and a maturity rare in one so young'. The Sedbergh 1st XV of the 1981–2 season contained Will Carling for the very first time. But his triumph was laced with disappointment: in the solitary game he played in the team that season, Sedbergh experienced their only defeat of the year, losing to the Scottish school Loretto. Carling had captained an unbeaten Colts A side that season, 'fulfilling', in the words of a later critique, 'and surpassing our wildest expectations. The maturity of his own play in the centre brought out the best in players around him. Few at this stage can produce the awareness of space, angles and timing which singles out the exceptional.'

The 1st XV of that season was captained by Andrew Harle, who remains to this day a close confidant of Carling. Their relationship has survived from school days. Harle, who lives and works in the north of England near Durham, is often visited by the England captain when he is seeking solitude from the immense pressures of his role. One Saturday morning a year or two back, Harle was astonished to receive a telephone call just as he returned home around lunchtime to settle down and watch an England international. The call was from the England captain, anxious to kill time in the team's Surrey hotel and to talk to someone he knew closely and trusted completely.

As one of the favoured inner circle, Harle was regarded as the ideal soulmate on the end of the telephone line, to help Carling counter the building pressure. It was indicative of how he has continued to regard Sedbergh, and the close friends he made there, as an ongoing element of his life. For most young men, the majority of school friends tend to melt away as they embrace life in the outside world. This has not been so for Carling. Until 1993 he shared a London flat with another former Sedbergh boy, Alex Hambly, who captained the school's 1st XV in 1982–3.

This era constituted the golden years for Sedbergh rugby. A succession of outstanding sides carried all before them, and admiration for their skills was widespread. John Willcox, master in charge of rugby at the strong Ampleforth College, and a former England international and British Lion in South Africa in 1962, recalls his initial impressions of the boy destined to be a rugby king. 'He was damned good. Always. In the years he played against us, Sedbergh won all three games. In his last two years he was extremely good and one of the reasons they won each time. In the year he played at full-back, which was his final year, he had a tremendous game. Will could have been anything, he was so good. His attacking running was superb. I can but give a glowing account of him.'

Dick Greenwood, one-time England coach and winner of five caps for England between 1966 and 1969, was another to be struck by Carling's genius, even amid an outstanding Sedbergh side. 'I saw him play a school match at Stonyhurst and although Sedbergh were an immensely good side, he looked class among class. He was a good player right from the start. An ordinary player gets tackled but the good one finds the spaces. Every time there was a space when Sedbergh were playing, Carling was through it.'

Carling possessed the classic attribute of the quality sportsman – he always seemed to have time to spare. Observers recognized it in the play of that wonderful Irish rugbyman, C. M. H. Gibson. It had been apparent, too, during Colin Cowdrey's cricketing days at Oxford, when seemingly languid cover drives zipped effortlessly away to the boundary, turning fieldsmen to stone. Only the best can provide this image of perfect timing. Tom Graveney with a cricket bat, Torvill and Dean on ice skates, the late Bobby Moore with a football. The secret of their skill is timing, that inner sense which separates the great from the good. Carling was always comfortable on the ball, said Greenwood; he was never hurried. True, he was surrounded by good contemporaries, but it was Carling who enjoyed more than others the time and space, because he found them. Others often searched in vain.

Yet the image was abroad even so early in his career. 'There were two schools of thought,' said Greenwood. 'One was that he was an arrogant sod. The second was that any top quality athlete needs cockiness. It is part of his make-up.'

Mere mortals, boys who were useful at rugby football through simply having the physique or the pace to qualify, were bewildered by Carling's craft. By no means all of them were duffers. Brendan Mullin, later to become a player of consummate skills for Ireland and the British Lions, saw at first hand the growing talents of the young Carling when Blackrock College, Mullin's Irish school and traditionally one of the most powerful schools anywhere in Ireland, went to Sedbergh for a fixture. The heavy Irish forwards tested the Sedbergh pack almost to breaking point, and it was always close. What settled the match was one break by Carling, in which he swept upfield on a sixty-yard run. He did not score himself, but a supporting colleague did and Sedbergh squeezed home 13–6. Watching was Brooke Dowse, long-time master at Sedbergh and later to manage a Yorkshire Schools Under-18 tour to Zimbabwe which Carling was to captain. 'I remember it so vividly,' says Dowse. 'He split the whole Blackrock defence wide open before breaking upfield from near half-way. I thought to myself, "Hello, this boy is special."'

That season, with Carling at centre, Sedbergh boasted a fast, skilful threequarter line. There was creativity at centre, a good runner at full-back and two pacy wings. Durham and Bradford Grammar School, traditionally among the North's best rugby schools, were over-whelmed 31–0 and 44–6 respectively. Then, after half-term, St Bees were humiliated, 82–6. Uppingham escaped comparatively lightly with a 35–0 defeat.

Sedbergh School's facilities for rugby would shame many a respectable club. The 1st XV ground, Busk-holme, has a stature to it far beyond the normal par-ameters of a school playing-field. Formerly open land, the boys of the 1930s dug out the entire pitch through their own endeavour. It is one of fourteen rugby pitches boasted by a school which also has a lavish sports hall, an armoury, five courts for Rugby fives and an ideal geographical location for running.

But until the 1970s, when showers were built on to the small pavilion, even boys playing for the 1st XV had to run back to their individual houses for a bath after a match. School supporters attend the major matches in considerable numbers. 'Come on, Brown,' does not refer to some lazy wing shirking the mud and gore of the forward battle, but is the traditional cry of support for the school. To wear the brown shirt and white shorts (the latter only awarded to 1st XV boys), is to ascend into a rugby stratosphere in the annals of Sedbergh School's sporting history.

The honours and the accolades flowed in. 'Sedbergh again chosen as team of the month,' announced *Rugby World* magazine. Michael Stevenson, writing in *The Times*, said: 'The most rewarding thing about covering school rugby . . . is the variety of interesting people with whom one comes in contact. Two of them wrote to me recently, the first castigating me for giving Sedbergh too much prominence, the second taking me to task equally passionately for giving them too little . . . Try again! When Sedbergh defeated Loretto (3–39) recently, they completed a season that clearly established them as one of the best, if not the best, side in the country. Unbeaten, they scored 253 points to 36 conceded, regularly facing appreciably larger schools and, amazingly, only one try was scored against them.'

'Fine achievement by Sedbergh,' headlined the *Daily Telegraph*, when the school finished the 1983 season with a 100 per cent record after ten matches. 'Sedbergh's achievement in winning all their games was particularly notable because they began with only four old colours and were under great pressure following their unbeaten 1982 season. This year's team, if not quite matching their predecessors in attacking flair, had a superior defensive record and a stronger pack.' John Prior, in the schools rugby review of *Country Life* magazine dated January 1983, commented on the outstanding form of Sedbergh and Millfield. 'These two schools stood clearly above all rivals in England. Both played exhilarating rugby of a very high standard.'

In the 1981 season, Carling had played his solitary 1st XV match for the school. By the following year he had established his position at centre, beside boys generally a year or more older. In 1983 he was moved to full-back and again played the entire season. The defeat, rare event as it was, which Carling experienced in his initial outing for the 1st XV at Sedbergh against Loretto (10–13) was to be the last suffered by the senior school side for well over two years against schools opposition. All eleven games were won in 1982–3, all ten the following season. It was an extraordinary testimony to an outstanding collection of players, among whom Carling excelled. But he had emerged extraordinarily quickly by Sedbergh standards. Kerry Wedd, coach to the 1st XV, had put the school's most obvious talent into the side when he was still in the fifth form, dropping a boy who had won his colours the previous season. Both actions were unprecedented at the time.

Privileged? Certainly. Sedbergh's successful rugby sides went off all around the world, like junior Jules Vernes. In 1977 they had gone to Narbonne in the south of France, in 1979 to Portugal. In 1981 there was a short trip to Italy; in 1984 they crossed Canada to visit British Columbia. Shortly after, Carling went to Zimbabwe with Yorkshire Schools.

There is a revealing picture in a Sedbergh School Football Club brochure, documenting the records from that superlative era 1978–83. In pride of place on the front inside facing page, John Spencer, the former Sedberghian, is seen presenting the *Rugby World* award for School Team of the Month, November 1983, to Will Carling, on behalf of the Sedbergh XV. On Spencer's face is a simple expression of open happiness and satisfaction at the success of his old school. Carling, by complete contrast, wears a puzzled, creased expression which could betoken any emotion known to mankind:

delight, disinterest, elation or boredom. As ever, the master player was inscrutably hard to read.

On 12 August 1983, Sedbergh School lost its most famous old boy. Wavell Wakefield, the Rt Hon. The Lord Wakefield of Kendal, Kt, MA, MPS, Sedbergh School 1913–16, captain of Cambridge University, RAF, Harlequins, Leicester and Middlesex, winner of thirty-one caps for England between 1920 and 1927, captain of his country from 1923–7, Governor of the school, President of the Rugby Football Union 1950–51, died. He was eighty-five, and had been a Governor of the school he loved right up to his death. By way of appropriate acknowledgement, the Sedbergh 1st XV of 1983–4, led by James Gray, emulated the achievements of its predecessors by winning all its school matches. It was another outstanding triumph, again marked by Carling's excellence. 'It was Ampleforth [won 10–0] who again tested us to the limits,' records the *Old Sedberghian*. 'In foul weather, two well-matched sides gave us another splendid game – Sedbergh's home advantage and the fine play of W. Carling tipped the balance our way.'

Rossall, usually another strong northern school, were dispatched 28–9, Stonyhurst crushed 28–0 and Durham beaten 13–6. 'At full-back, Carling found room to express himself in delightful and unselfish style which brought the very best out of his colleagues and turned a good side into another all-conquering one,' wrote Peter Meadows.

James Gray, Carling's captain from that season, knew all about him years before they teamed up at Sedbergh. Gray had gone to Terra Nova school for a match with a Sedbergh junior side, and noticed the handily built young lad with the shock of black hair. 'It was apparent even at that early age he was a very talented player. He would have been about twelve at that time,' says Gray, who now works as a marketing manager in Sydney, Australia. 'So when he arrived at Sedbergh not long afterwards, people knew all about him and were aware he was coming. Some people at Sedbergh perceived him as being standoffish. He was good and knew he was good. He had clearly been groomed for success. He is not a very open guy, but if you get to know him he is different. Those like myself who knew him did not think he was arrogant; he never acted the prima donna while I was captain, although he was the most talented player around.'

Gray remembers Carling as physically much stronger than his team-mates of the time, and recalls his excellent co-ordination and natural strength in running. 'Of course, Will thrived in that climate of excellence,' says Gray. 'So much time is given over to sport at Sedbergh, yet it does not present any conflict. Everyone has to play sport all the time. Every boy had to play rugby even if he was completely useless. You exercised every afternoon of the week, one way or another. All this was certainly challenging when you first went there. But it was tough if you couldn't cope with it. There was a lot of emphasis on the physical side of it, for this was a disciplined environment: quite a tough place. Some guys it did present problems to if they weren't particularly into that sort of thing or if they were weak and needed space to be an individual. You don't get that there. Your privacy is non-existent. In the first two years especially, you just don't have any.'

Gray unravels the almost unnaturally close liaison today, a decade later, between Carling and those with whom he shared so many great times at Sedbergh. He explains: 'There is still a strong link between people from the school because there was such a strong sense of belonging there, through the friendships forged among the boys.' This may be explained as much through the school's geographical isolation as anything else. Young boys need a sense of belonging, no matter how exalted their success in a chosen field. With parents living in another country or otherwise rarely seen, the sense of companionship was provided, *in absentia*, by the forging of close friendships among the pupils. These relationships became so close as to seem above fracture when school days finally ended.

'Kerry Wedd was grooming Will for the future, that much was obvious. He singled him out for special attention and was very important in Will's development,' says Gray. 'The backline we had in the 1982–3 season was one of the best ever schoolboy backlines, certainly the best for Sedbergh.'

Today, ten years after all those stirring deeds passed into history, Kerry Wedd lives on the North Devon coast, far from Sedbergh and the rugby fraternity. He concedes: 'I have rather lost my enthusiasm for talk or for writing about my "memories of the young man". He has moved on, and so have I.' What Wedd does claim is that Carling's game was 'on course' long before he had dealings with him at Sedbergh. If there is credit to be awarded, he surmises, then the formative influences of his father and of Ian Argyle, Carling's mentor at Terra Nova, should be examined. 'Since leaving school,' adds Wedd, 'Will has worked hard to put on the bulk and power which are so essential at international level and because of this he can cope at the top. He has also the desire to be the best – and has had that since he was knee high.'

Carling had a long wait to win the captaincy of Sedbergh's 1st XV; too long, in the opinion of many. The only reason he failed earlier was, according to Wedd, that there were other players who were also rated very highly. However, Carling was made captain for the 1984 Lent term, his last rugby-playing term at Sedbergh, and he was Head of Winder House in 1983–4, too.

In 1983 Carling had entered Sedbergh's infamous Wilson run, known as 'The Ten'. This gentle recreational activity for boys over sixteen and a half years involved a ten-mile run up and down the surrounding hills and fells, through mud and bog, wind and rain. It has been run at the school for more than 100 years, having been started by some sadistic Victorian in 1881, much to the chagrin of schoolboys in every decade since. It amounts to a psychological and physical torture spanning the better part of two hours.

Carling, who was never a profound enthusiast for the long run, did it just once. The going was grim: 'Course, very wet and slippery. Weather, cold, fresh westerly wind. Showers.' The motto for the day of the race was as follows:

If all the year were playing Holidays,
To sport would be as tedious as to work.
   (Shakespeare, *Henry IV, Part 1*)

If every day at Sedbergh had been similar to this one, it seems quite possible that Will Carling would have packed up sport completely. He took over 1 hour, 45 minutes to complete a race won by J. P. Holliday in 1 hr, 12 minutes, 51 seconds. The sport was, quite simply, not to Carling's liking.

But though beautifully timed passes flowed from

Carling's hands on the rugby field, as his powerful thighs broke the half-hearted tackles and his scorching pace confounded all but the most secure of defences, this was by no means the zenith of his sporting achievements. He had announced himself as a young cricketer of talent in his first summer at Sedbergh, and subsequent seasons saw him develop his skills promisingly. On a fine, warm summer's day, with Winder Fell providing an imposing backdrop to the cricket ground and St Andrew's church a compass point from the hills for miles around, that essentially English summer game must have made the gods smile in this idyllic setting. Towering trees stood like sentries around the ground; fluffy white clouds floated in skies of Cambridge blue. W. D. C. Carling improved in confidence as the 1982 season wore on, as *The Sedberghian* tells us. 'His final innings against Pocklington was that of a class player. He looked every inch a cricketer and he fielded and bowled his off-spinners with commendable care and attention. He and Alban will be a formidable batting force in the years to come.'

As in winter, amid mud and mire, so in summer, on benign afternoons: Ampleforth fell once more before the Sedbergh sword. Ampleforth 133 all out, Sedbergh 136–2.

Carling averaged 25 with the bat that season but did immensely better the following year, 1983. In a purple patch in high summer, he took 4–27 as Newcastle Royal Grammar School were bowled out for 102, and then made an unbeaten 59 in Sedbergh's 108–1. In the next match, Sedbergh's 256–3 declared contained an unbeaten 100 from Coulthard and 98 from Carling. Coulthard's ton was the first century to be scored by a Sedberghian for fifteen years in a school match, an honour which had been within Carling's grasp when the pair were both on 98 not out simultaneously, having put on 159 in just twenty-two overs. William Hulmes Grammar School, their bewitched, bewildered opponents, were bowled out for 60.

But if the 1983 cricket season further strengthened the reputation of this rugby genius who could also play England's summer game to a commendable level, his absence from Sedbergh's 1984 side was a mystery. Having at last gained the captaincy of the rugby 1st XV, albeit only for the Lent term, it is said that Carling had set his sights on leading the senior cricket team too. When that was denied him – the distinction went to Mark Alban – Carling played no more cricket for Sedbergh. His detractors blame personal pique; his apologists cite pressure of work for end-of-year exams. There was no doubt that he was good enough – perhaps to be captain, as well. His form from 1983 had suggested that he would be a key part of the side. He had, after all, played cricket each summer up to that point. So sudden a rupture in that sequence seemed strange and out of character, given his love for the sport. Other boys who had studying to do still managed to play that term.

It was a suitably enigmatic, puzzling conclusion to Will Carling's five years at Sedbergh. He had dominated the school's sporting life and earned renown far beyond the confines of the school's isolated location. Other schools, other boys, other parents and other masters, who would never know him, had heard of this rugby genius who had lit up Sedbergh's playing-fields. Nor had he played rugby and other sports to the complete abandonment of his studies. By the time he left Sedbergh in the summer of 1984, he had acquired nine O levels, two AO levels and three A levels; the latter an A in geography, a B in English and a C in economics. Yet the mystique somehow endured. As Brooke Dowse says: 'When Will left, I would not have claimed to know him particularly well. There was always a little kept in reserve. In fact, I wondered who did know him.'

4 *The Power and the Glory*

'A Sensitive Plant in a garden grew.'
Percy Bysshe Shelley

If the image presented so far of the young Will Carling has been of a young man possessing solely physical brawn and ball-playing skills, then it is an appropriate time to outline a quite different character. The complexities of this young man continued to baffle most of those with whom he came into contact. The same hands that could haul down stronger opponents on the rugby field or dismiss them with a jolting hand-off possessed the delicate touch of an artist.

'I remember him sitting somewhere near me once during a boring physics lesson at school,' recalls a contemporary at Sedbergh, 'and sketching the back of the cricket pavilion, which we could see from the classroom.' It was good, too. In the written word, Carling could compose a phrase as delicate as the petal of a rose, as evidenced by two of his poems reproduced in the Sedbergh school chronicle. Both poems reveal not simply a sensitivity, but the hand and mind of the loner. And the loner would be, almost invariably, more mature than his contemporaries, making him appear more commanding. 'He got stick because he never was one of the lads. He knew life would be easier if he was one of them, but he could never quite pull it off,' says Mark Alban. 'Winder House was full of talented games players at the time, yet you felt they didn't quite take him aboard.' But did he want it that way? A moment of thought. 'That was never really clear. He blew hot and cold. His natural state was more reserved. He was always quite determined to go off and have time on his own. There is a genuine side of him that really wants to be alone. He tends to drift in and out of friendships; at school, you never quite knew whether you were in favour.'

But these characteristics were part of Carling's basic nature – he either could not or would not alter them. At times he would feel the need to do so, and there would be almost a sense of guilt; at other moments his inner feelings would obviate such sentiments. Such a person is partly inclined towards conciliation while partly attempting to justify an absence of such moves. One facet supersedes the other at irregular intervals. There is rarely a clear pattern.

The enforced ability to stand on his own feet, metaphorically speaking, from an early age, the legacy of a boarding school upbringing, meant that the young Carling knew his own mind. He pursued what he wanted with a vigour most could not comprehend, still less match – 'fiercely ambitious' is a phrase used constantly by his contemporaries. He sought the gold at the end of the rainbow and tracked it with a ruthless dedication. Nor was he to be diverted. Those who threatened to stand in his path received a blunt dismissal.

'When we were in the fourth form at school, I remember someone once handing Will a cigarette,' says Mark Alban. 'But he just let it burn out. He said, "I am not interested." He was neither ashamed of it, nor bound by what his peers would do. He knew what was going on and was well directed. I doubt whether he has been deflected from what he wanted to do since the age of ten. He used to say he wanted to captain England at rugby. So it was no surprise to me when he did that.'

During the 1984 Lent term at Sedbergh, Carling captained the school's 1st XV in a tournament at Durham School. The changes in personnel for the Lent term dictated a transitional period, yet those involved recall an extraordinary achievement by Carling. 'He got this scratch side together and we beat Durham quite comfortably in the final. It was due to the way he managed the side and built it up. I remember thinking his leadership was brilliant. He didn't shout or abuse; he had a natural officer-like quality. He could talk quietly to people. Whether or not you liked him, you wanted to please him,' said Alban.

By now, Kerry Wedd's guidance of his young charge was all-embracing. 'He was a profound influence on Will, there is no doubt of that. He was a very talented rugby coach and had a great eye for the game. He also had a great way of motivating people. He got them to think about the game quite carefully and persuaded people they wanted to do it.'

The night of Sedbergh's triumph in the Durham tournament, the small squad drove home across the North Yorkshire moors, back to the school. 'I remember chatting with Kerry Wedd on the journey. I said I was quite amazed by Will Carling that day, and thought he had a great captaincy gift and could go all the way. Kerry said, "It is a question of whether he will be diverted by the perils of life." We both felt that if he wanted to play for and captain England, it was there and available to him.'

By now, others had seen the fledgling signs of a future leader in Sedbergh School's outstanding player. As early as 1982–3 he had been chosen to represent Yorkshire Schools, and the following year he wore his first ever English jersey, for the England Schools side. This was not so much a case of a boy planting both feet firmly on the ladder, but of an extraordinary talent joining the ladder half-way up. Carling was so good that he never needed to worry about the challenge of others. His playing ability put him light years ahead of most contemporaries. He began to acquire medals like the dictator of a banana republic: Yorkshire Schools Under-18 in 1982, 1983 and 1984; the North school side and England Schools (Under-18) in 1983 and 1984. Sport being a capricious child, prophesying the future is perilous, but 9–4 on Carling making it to the top would have seemed very modest odds.

Yorkshire Schools comprised a powerful unit; it was quite the strongest rugby school county in all of England at the time. 'Sedbergh,' it was reported in *Rothmans Rugby Yearbook* for 1983–4, 'was a team of really exceptional quality.' But Ampleforth ran them desperately close, losing only 18–15. With schools like Ampleforth and Bradford Grammar School, Yorkshire Schools could put together a formidable side. In the 1983–4 season, for example, the county won every match at Schools Under-16 and Under-18 level; a total of eleven matches. Indeed, there was a strong history of Yorkshire-based boys emerging in English rugby, for since the late 1950s such well-known names as Phil Horrocks-Taylor ('The Horrocks went one way, the Taylor went another and I was left holding the ruddy hyphen,' Tony O'Reilly once joked), John Spencer, Les Cusworth, Roger Shackleton, Peter Thompson and David Caplan had all gone on to represent their country at senior level.

In the 1982–3 season, Yorkshire reached the County

Championship final with a team that contained nine former Yorkshire Schools players: Mike Harrison, Nigel Melville, Bryan Barley, David Norton, Simon Tipping, Steve Townend, Peter Buckton, John Ellison and Andrew Mason. All this before Barnard Castle School from nearby County Durham had completed the education of two more likely lads for a rugby side: Rob Andrew and Rory Underwood. There were others, too; the north of England was a gold-mine for emerging young rugby talent in the early 1980s.

Carling captained an unbeaten Yorkshire Schools 18 Group side, its principal win in 1984 being against Lancashire by 24 points to 12. 'Yorkshire gave warning of their pace in the centre,' wrote Graham Tait in the *Daily Telegraph*, 'when Carling used his wing as a foil to score an excellent try out by the corner.' Tait went on: 'In the middle of the half a succession of errors cost Lancashire dearly as Carling, a powerful and accurate kicker, banged over four penalties.' After that, Carling captained the first ever Yorkshire Schools overseas tour, to Zimbabwe.

The power and the glory – both were his from an early age. His stature and presence both inspired colleagues and conspired against opponents, and through his physical strength, which had naturally developed as he approached his twenties, Carling exuded a rare authority on the field.

The England Schools selectors had also quickly spied his talent. On 2 April 1983 he made his début for the Schools side in a 16–0 victory over Ireland at Moseley. Four days later England thrashed France 34–0 at Gosforth, Carling scoring one of the five tries. Just three days after that, England went to Aberdeen and beat Scotland 20–3, Carling again getting a try. Wales, meanwhile, had beaten the Scots 20–0, won 18–3 in France and then crushed Ireland in Cork, 24–10; the first of several Grand Slam matches in which Will Carling would compete was set for Pontypridd on 16 April.

It was always likely to be the closest of encounters and so it proved. England, although they could not manage a try, established an early lead and retained it until three minutes from the end. Then a long-range penalty squeezed Wales from a 10–12 deficit to a 13–12 lead, to which they clung, like the mud to their bodies, until the final whistle. The Welsh try was the only one scored by any side against England that season and the junior Grand Slam could so easily have been theirs. Some familiar names of the future were in that side: Kevin Simms, later the Cambridge University and England centre, who was captain of the England Schools 18 Group that year, Victor Ubogu, of Oxford University, Bath and England, and Andy Mullins, who was to play in the same teams as Carling for Durham University and, later, Harlequins.

The Welsh team included future internationals like scrum half Robert Jones, back row players Rowland Phillips and Alan Carter, and locks Gareth Llewellyn and Huw Richards. Robert Jones and centre Stuart Parfitt also faced the England Schools side captained by Carling the following season. That year, 1984, England again missed out on the Grand Slam even though they started with a comprehensive 18–0 victory over Wales at Cambridge. 'It was not until the 33rd minute that England managed their first try when Hamer ran into the right-hand corner after a half break in the centre by Bill [*sic*] Carling, the captain, had created the gap,' trumpeted the *Daily Telegraph*. 'It took 32 minutes of the . . . second . . . half before Hamer was able to score and again it was an outside break by Carling that created the opportunity.'

Ireland's forwards were too strong for them in a 15–7 win in Belfast, and although England went on to beat France 14–12 in Saint-Nazaire, the season was again flawed. 'All six of England's tries in their three games [of the 1984 season] were scored by the three-quarters,' reported George Abbott, doyen of schools rugby writing, in *Rothmans Rugby Yearbook*. For this, 'the centres W. D. C. Carling (Sedbergh) and J. M. Priestley (Bradford GS) can take considerable credit'.

Stuart Parfitt, formerly at Swansea but now with South Wales Police, recalls his clashes with Carling in 1983 and 1984. 'I remember him being a very correct centre. What he did he always did very well. The talk at that time was all about Kevin Simms and Will Carling, the two England centres. The impression I had was that Carling was like the donkey, he did all the hard work and Simms did the glory stuff. When we kicked our penalty to go 13–12 ahead, Carling got the ball in his own 22 and went for the outside break. I just got to him, with my fingertips, and managed to hold on, but only just. Will had all the skills even then and a rugby brain to go with it. He put in the kicks at the right time and did a lot of hard work, with much tackling. He was the solid man in the defence, hard to get past. Frankly, though, Kevin Simms caused us more trouble individually than Will. Kevin had terrific speed and a nice side-step.'

It was six years before Parfitt and Carling would meet again, at the Hong Kong Sevens with the Barbarians. They later played together, too, at a Sevens tournament in Amsterdam. 'He was still the same type of player, still very correct in what he did. He also seemed a lot quicker than I remembered him.' The arrogance? 'If you are going to be that good, you have to be confident, you need a kind of arrogance,' says Parfitt. 'Will was always a very confident player; you could tell just from the way he stood there and looked. He didn't say anything, but just to look at him you knew. But having said that, I have never found him conceited. He is not the sort of person who is very outgoing but when you get to talk with him and he has relaxed, he is great. He wouldn't be the easiest person to approach, first of all, and perhaps judgements are made from that. In Amsterdam, people were coming up to him all the time and asking for autographs. He signed them but it was obvious he relaxed a lot more when it was just the boys with him. It seemed as though there was a guard up when others were around.'

At Cambridge in 1984, with England set on revenge for their defeat in the junior Grand Slam match with Wales the previous season, English officials warned, 'Watch out for our centres.' Stuart Parfitt says: 'Initially, I thought they were building Will up too much. I thought he was good but not that good. But having watched him since, I think he has done tremendously well.'

Yet Parfitt admits that most people in Wales do not like Carling. 'They have a picture of someone arrogant; a lot of people call him that. Yet many of the great Welsh players were arrogant: Jonathan Davies, even Barry John, had arrogance on the pitch. At that level I think you have got to be a bit that way.' Perhaps he is right. But a critical difference exists between Carling and Davies and John. Whatever the arrogance shown by the Welshmen on the field – and Jonathan Davies even today confirms that this trait has value during an international match – neither of the Welsh fly-halves portrayed such an image in private. You could not have found a less arrogant man than Barry John; he was always, and remains to this day, warm, eminently approachable and friendly, generous with his time and assistance. He has always been a delight to meet, the 'man next door' who might have been teaching at the local school in the valley these past thirty years rather than filling our memories through his exploits on a rugby field. Consequently, he has become renowned for his humility. Jonathan Davies is the same: polite, well-mannered and always with a genuine greeting for those he meets. Like John, he is what he seems, a friendly, open, uncomplicated man, devoid of malice. Not very long ago, Davies drove to Bath from his Cheshire home to keep an interview appointment with Jeremy Guscott and myself. He was stuck in traffic around Birmingham and got back at an ungodly hour. But he had promised and he kept his word, without a suggestion of pain or inconvenience.

The image counts. It is irresistible. Will Carling may very well be a fine player on the field, yet his image off it languishes behind that of Barry John and Jonathan Davies. This may be unfair, unfortunate and inaccurate, and is probably wrong. But that is how it is in the eyes of many people.

Carling was like the Welshmen in one respect: wherever he went and whatever he did with a rugby ball, he possessed that priceless quality enjoyed by so few – he could turn heads. It mattered not a jot at which level he was operating; he seemed able to negotiate with ease hurdles which would be insurmountable to those less gifted. The powerful, thrusting runs in midfield were familiar enough by now, for his reputation had spread far and wide. But he could delight both the novice spectator and the connoisseur alike, both by his more obvious talents as a youngster, such as the rupturing of the defence, achieved through an intimidating combination of speed and strength, and by the subtlety of his evasion. He presented the ball impeccably, like a temptress displaying her best attributes, but this was a lure with which to ensnare rivals, for if his opponent hesitated for a moment he would seize the opportunity and break through.

Another feature of Carling's game was a delightful outside swerve of the entire body, which showed his hips accepting the strain of momentary delay before the whole body spun forward again. In other, less gifted, beings this might have seemed an ugly, fractured manoeuvre. Carling carried it off in a split second, like an especially difficult piece of poetry read at speed. The seed of uncertainty sown by the slight change in the direction of the body was sufficient to confound any defensive alignment. Clever stuff, and not easy to teach – certainly not at the speed involved here.

Carling had always been able to perform at levels beyond his own age group, helped by his innate quality of vision. Vision in sport is an underestimated attribute, yet it was the distinguishing feature of players like the former West German star footballer Franz Beckenbauer, or our own Bobby Moore. Vision can out-pace speed, negating it by carrying its owner to the important part of the field before quicker rivals denied such judgement can react. Without vision, players can resemble automated machines: with it, a player both minimizes his endeavour and maximizes his potential.

Great player, pity about the image. Geoff Sephton, the Cowley school scrum half who captained Lancashire

Schools 18 Group and shared a room with Carling on England Schools duties, agrees. 'He kept himself to himself, he was rather disciplined,' says Sephton. 'One night we had all gone out for a drink but he came in and said, "That's enough." I said to him, "Look, none of us know each other; it's good for team spirit." But you could tell he didn't like it . . . He was a loner, he didn't mix with the other lads. Whether that was because he went to a public school and there were a few of us from grammar schools, I don't know.'

Did Carling strike his colleagues as a player who was set for a glittering career? Hardly, in Sephton's opinion. 'He didn't seem that special. Certainly he was an excellent player, but I always thought Kevin Simms would get to the stage where Will is at now. Will was always strong in attack and defence, and very powerful over ten or fifteen yards. But Simms was a lot quicker.'

The divergence in the careers of two players, Carling and Sephton, from that 1984 England Schools team is astonishing. Today Carling is among the best-known players in the amateur code; Sephton, who turned professional with Widnes before joining Swinton three seasons later, retired at twenty-three. But perhaps the captain had to be different. Jonathan Priestley, his co-centre for Yorkshire and England Schools, believed as much. 'He was an inevitable choice as captain because he was so natural a leader. A bit of the school ethos rubbed off on him. They encourage leadership qualities in the public schools, and Will took to it like a duck to water. I found playing at that level a bit nerve-racking but Will seemed the type who would carry a book with him and casually read it on the bus, on the way to the ground. Very often someone with a leadership quality is like that. You have to have some ability to distance yourself slightly to lead, otherwise no one pays any attention to you.'

Priestley was highly regarded by the selectors of the time. He says: 'Will and I used to knock hell out of each other when we played against one another in school matches. At trials up to the county side we would still play against each other but then they chose us as a pair, and we went right through Northern trials and Divisional trials up to the final trial for England 18 Group. It is always the case with centres that if you can play together, you are stronger than individually. We were encouraged to play as a pair. So we used to get very close before a game for England Schools and go on and on discussing how we would play.'

Priestley felt that Carling always had the nose for a score; and the talent to be a future England international. His physique could become the last resort on days when other strategies had not worked, and power was the final throw. Or the first: 'When we beat Wales at Cambridge that year, my chief memory was of Will and myself hitting the Welsh full-back Bradshaw so hard that he went off after five minutes. The high ball went up and Will hit him on the chest as I hit him lower down. It was hard but perfectly legal . . . As a captain I found him inspirational, because I felt he was such a good player.'

Again there was to be a fascinating divergence of the ways. Priestley himself was highly regarded, as a player of considerable potential, but decided he wanted a career more than he wanted a life in rugby. He therefore rejected the idea of completing his rugby education at Durham, and instead went to University College London to read law. He played a couple of seasons in the Wasps second team, and became frustrated by injuries. He has never had a full rugby season since leaving school but is now a solicitor in Leeds. 'With hindsight, I think I made the right decision. The sporting world is fairly fickle,' he says.

There would be many times in his own career that Will Carling would have ample justification for pondering such a view.

5   *The Veneer Stripped Bare*

'Security is a smile from a headwaiter.'
Russell Baker

They came from far and wide, intrigued and expectant, to see the skills of Durham University's newest rugby recruit. The talent demonstrated by Will Carling, rare in one so young, had brought him quickly to the notice of new selectors at University and Divisional level. Such skills could well have smoothed his passage into Durham, traditionally a sports-minded seat of learning, and the Army, where the ability to excel at sport had never exactly been an impediment.

Carling, who took a three-year psychology degree, had decided to follow his father into the Army and was duly awarded a cadetship at Durham. But the idea of hours of square-bashing while his fellow students lounged against walls or leaned out of windows jeering should be dismissed. There was the occasional weekend exercise, involving overnight tramps on the moors (when rugby permitted), but otherwise military activities were strictly limited. The upside was that Army pay allowed Carling to run a car at Durham; very much a man apart from most of his colleagues.

Durham was the logical destination for a sportsman looking for a career in rugby. The facilities were excellent for rugby, cricket, rowing and a great many other pursuits. From 1982 to 1992, Durham was rivalled by only one other sporting educational establishment, Loughborough. Between them they were to dominate the UAU rugby Championship for British Universities, winning it nine times out of ten in that decade. Durham achieved three titles, Loughborough six.

It was also a wonderful place to be billeted for three years. After all, it had impressed Henry VI, who is reputed to have said after a visit to the city in 1448: 'I have no more noble city in all my realm.' Nor was he alone in such praise. John Ruskin called the city one of the wonders of the world, Nikolaus Pevsner described it as one of the architectural experiences of Europe, and others likened it to Jerusalem. Standing elegantly and magnificently at its heart is Durham cathedral, Norman in origin, on which work began in 1093. Visitors cross the world to see this great building and experience its tranquillity.

We can fairly quickly dismiss study as a serious occupation for Carling at the university. Lectures, he has since confessed, were not high on his priority list, a fact the university tutors soon came to realize. Carling had arrived at Durham in the autumn of 1985, after a year's sabbatical travelling the world, particularly Australia. He had a psychology degree of five levels available to him – Class 1 (highest), Class 2 (Division 1), Class 2 (Division 2), Class 3, or a recommended pass. He was to receive the last category, which gave him a general degree of Bachelor of Science.

Had aptitude upon the rugby field been taken into account, Carling would have achieved the highest honours. Alas, his tutors did not see it that way, even at so sports-minded a university as Durham. 'If Will Carling had not played so much rugby, he would certainly have achieved a better degree,' said Professor

James Barber, Master of Hatfield, rather sternly. 'His mind must have been a great deal on rugby, especially in that last year.' Carling had been assigned to Hatfield College which sits snugly in the lee of Durham Cathedral. The second oldest college in the university, Hatfield has been a very strong sporting centre since the Second World War; before that, the only posts targeted were the higher echelons of the Church, for it was renowned chiefly as a training college for the clergy.

The rugby set were hale and hearty, according to Professor Barber. There were the usual activities: drinking contests, which Carling says he found 'fearsome and revolting'; the pursuit of girls, in which, not surprisingly given his good looks, he earned a reputation for far greater proficiency than in his studies; and the day-to-day life of a typical student – late nights, late mornings, rooms in turmoil, the ubiquitous mugs of coffee. The flat Carling shared, at 28 Young Street, contained all the usual detritus: clothes strewn untidily, the washing-up untouched, papers and books lying in every nook and cranny. It would have been condemned as an abode of ill-repute by any self-respecting cleaning lady. 'It was infamous,' says Andy Mullins, a fellow rugby student at Hatfield. 'It was handed down by people at the University rugby club and a succession of them rented it out year after year. It was very much a bachelors' pad. At the end of every year they threw an all-in party which would end up as a food fight. It was extremely wild and invariably the place had to be redecorated for the next term.'

Once or twice, says Professor Barber, now president of the University's hockey club and vice-president of the rugby club, the rugby set had to be told to toe the line, to rein in the excesses. But Masters at sports-minded colleges like Hatfield should have a perspective beyond the textbook. Thankfully, Barber has. 'If you look for do-ers, you get people that are lively and out-going,' he says. 'Occasionally you have to say, ' You are being a little too lively." Will was one of the group that occasionally required reining in, but you get that sometimes.'

Durham knew of Carling's arrival – his reputation had preceded him. And yet this was no backwater of sporting achievement. The sceptics scoffed at talk of a Sedbergh boy who was a rugby genius, and perhaps with some reason; the list of Durham students who had progressed to represent England at rugby in comparatively recent years was already extensive – Rose, Bailey, Hesford, Hannaford, Clough, Rossborough, Warfield, Dee, Knight, Dixon . . . Tim Curtis, the Worcestershire and England cricketer, also studied there, as did Frank 'Typhoon' Tyson, the legendary fast bowler for England and Northamptonshire.

Peter Dixon, later a tutor in African social anthropology at Durham, had been one of the greatest talents of northern hemisphere rugby during the 1970s. But England were slow to acknowledge his ability. It needed his selection by the 1971 British Lions, shrewdly guided by the late great Carwyn James, and his subsequent appearance in three of the four Test matches the winning Lions played on that memorable tour of New Zealand, to bring his name to the attention of the England selectors. Taking the hint, they finally capped him against the President's Overseas XV later that year, in a match to celebrate the centenary of the Rugby Football Union. Dixon went on to lead England in 1972, and, having won four blues at Oxford, earned a total of twenty-two caps between 1971 and 1978. Unfortunately, England were so disorganized at that time they would not have known had they possessed a Barry John. They won nothing during Dixon's career in the Five Nations Championship. Dixon was a scholar of high repute, a man who studied as hard on the rugby field as off it. He knew the game like few others, and rubbing shoulders with the likes of Carwyn James, perhaps the possessor of the greatest rugby brain in these islands over the past thirty years, had been a learning experience he had wisely and carefully digested.

Durham University was, in a sense, a kind of rugby finishing school for Carling, a place to refine his talents before he exhibited them on the national stage. He possessed the basics, that much was obvious; now he needed to achieve two things. First, he would play at a higher grade, demanding a far sterner physical examination than any before. His body would need to adapt to the stronger tackles, the harder blows that grown men would inflict. Second, he would encounter a higher level of coaching – from Peter Dixon and Ted Wood, both of whom were well regarded – and would need to prove his ability to take on board the word of those who had played at the summit of the world game, or coached at a consistently higher level than was the norm in schools. The process was often to prove painful, more so mentally than through any physical challenge.

Peter Dixon remembers Carling as a player with pedigree, one who quickly excited interest and approval. It wasn't so much his ability to move swiftly through the gears; most players had that. Rather, it was the turbo effect that once engaged gave such effortless, purring acceleration. The body charged with that ultimate impetus was a great sight to see. 'Carling had that extra bit of pace that he could inject very rapidly. He wasn't afraid to try for the break, he had good vision and a good long kick.'

Another clue – he was very good under the high ball, and shrewd at choosing the line to get through in attack. The solution? Durham played him at full-back, just where he had been positioned in his final year as a schoolboy. But it was only a short-term option to assist the balance of the side; he played at that position for a spell in his first year, but moved to centre after that. In his last two years, he played only at centre.

Meanwhile, on the wing, Durham had a player with a reputation almost as grand as Carling's. Chris Oti had been the star of a highly successful Millfield School side, and had the kind of blistering pace which is enjoyed by so few. The pair of them offered Durham a potency in attack which destroyed all but the securest of defences. 'Carling had such speed, and he could check and then take off again and totally confound the defender,' says Peter Dixon. 'He was also played at full-back to create space on the outside for Oti.' It was a dynamic combination. They cut defences to ribbons like a pair of modern-day d'Artagnans, doing so with an elegance and verve that thrilled the onlookers. The breach in the defence was frequently established by Carling, the execution performed by Oti, who could prove as elusive a runner as a fox evading the hounds.

They were great days. Even in adversity there was the justified hope at every stage of a match that the pair might conjure the critical break-out, turning desperate defence into compelling attack. Dixon remembers: 'There was always the feeling, the belief that if we could win the ball and get it out to Carling, he could well create the space to release Oti. And Chris was capable of scoring from ninety yards range. He would get scores from nowhere – just give him the ball and he would do something decisive.'

Ted Wood, who had first seen Carling as a schoolboy, was responsible for his coaching in the first year and was joined by Peter Dixon for the next two seasons. When they first saw Carling's skills for themselves, both men knew the youngster would one day be an England centre. The possibility of either or both players going on later to Oxbridge was raised. Dixon's links with Oxford remained strong, and many rugby followers envisaged a Dark Blues side at Twickenham one December with Carling and Oti included – like Pavarotti and Carreras on the same bill at the Royal Albert Hall. In the event, neither of them went there.

Sportsmen applying for Oxford in the 1970s and early 1980s were admitted only if they possessed exceptional academic qualifications, although this policy was to be relaxed. Even so, Carling's academic record would have barred him, and Oti did not apply, preferring Cambridge. Oxford rugby was the poorer for their absence, and Cambridge were to prove the happy beneficiaries, Oti making a considerable impact. He pursued the time-honoured Light Blue path of a Land Economy degree, and even managed to do some work associated with that subject as well as playing rugby and establishing the reputation which was to bring him England honours.

Carling, too, had the chance to go to Cambridge, but did not follow it up. He admitted later: 'I was probably going through a self-righteous period and I didn't think I would get in on intellectual merit. That would always have been at the back of my mind. It was a matter of honour.' Why this should have bothered him is hard to say. It certainly didn't trouble a whole generation of rugby players who, while not exactly being dim-wits, might have struggled to make a team for *University Challenge*. But they got their blues at rugby and contributed immensely to the university's profile, so there were benefits both ways.

At Durham, Peter Dixon was as hugely impressed with Carling's defence as with his offence. 'He was strong enough to take a wing seven or eight yards from play into touch. In a number of games we might see an opposition wing running free but Carling would get across and tackle him into touch. It was effective tackling, too – not the old British style, bottom of the legs stuff, but straight through him. His power was always evident in attack when he had the ball but it was just as clear in defence.'

Dixon had been introduced to the English rugby writer John Reason during his days at Oxford in the late sixties, and they toured with the Lions in New Zealand in 1971, after which they kept in contact. Shortly after Dixon became involved with the coaching of Durham University's 1st XV, he called Reason at his home in the south of England. 'I have seen two players here at university who ought to be playing for England,' Dixon told him. 'Who are they?' inquired Reason, a reporter who was well able to sniff a story and who greatly respected Dixon's judgement. 'Their names are Will Carling and Chris Oti,' Dixon told him. Reason, now rugby correspondent of the *Sunday Telegraph*, wrote the story, and immediately a wider audience came to hear the names of Carling and Oti and follow their increasingly rapid progress.

But there were aspects which brought fewer smiles to Carling's coaches. 'He was good and he knew it,' says Dixon. 'He wanted to have an input into what the team was trying to do. Ted (who coached him for all three years) and myself had some difficulty in trying to control him, to persuade him he should be trying to play within a team format and not do just what he wanted to do which was run a lot of ball. It took a couple of years working on him to achieve that. The trouble is, at school you have a hell of a lot of running. Will eventually came to realize he was running ball that he should have kicked and he was getting knocked down and putting the rest of the team in danger.'

The relationship between star player and coaching staff was often difficult. 'Will felt we had the players to play a more expansive game and run the ball a lot more than we did. We knew that Carling would make breaks and that Oti would score from anywhere, yet it was not always possible to do that. We could not always get good ball. There had to be a balance.'

Working with Carling, discussing rugby and life with him so closely over a long period of time, offered Peter Dixon a revealing insight into the character he regards as the real Will Carling. Not the glossy magazine version, the author of a sanitized newspaper column and after-match interviews, or the man who retreats behind a mask when out and about in public. 'The arrogance is because he has always been slightly unsure of himself. That filters back to his rugby. He is a *Boy's Own* hero and you can get carried away with the image. You think all will go well but when it doesn't, it is a shock to the system. I remember seeing him in London once, after he had left Durham, and he was already worrying about his place in the England team. He was unsure of his position, concerned that Guscott and Halliday would be paired at centre.

'The arrogance thing is, he is unsure of himself in the

social world. At the heart of the man is that doubt, that inborn insecurity, yet he has no reason to doubt. He doesn't like criticism and reacts against it. He would go off if people confronted him. But if you kept on and on, he would listen to people he considered to be on his own level. Others, he sees as not being worthy and he doesn't have to suffer. He has no time for them. It all comes down to this thing about being unsure. But God knows why ... He is a shy and sensitive man yet up here [Durham], he was in this situation where he was in the Army. He is not totally one of the boys; he is standoffish. But then perhaps that is part of leadership.'

Whatever the reason, Dixon had seen Carling's old uncertainties re-emerging. This deep-rooted self-doubt, this constant fear of failure which induced an air of insecurity, had been with Carling since his school days. It was a two-edged sword: it nagged away at him in his quieter moments, but proved a catalyst to achievement at other times. It made him difficult to analyse and even harder to predict.

This was a view with which Ted Wood concurred. Wood speaks of a theory put forward in a paper concerning achievement by Brian Sutton-Smith, of America's Bowling Green University, in Ohio. Basically, it proposes a view that early socialization as part of one's upbringing creates in some people a tremendous need to achieve. It suggests that those taught or reminded all the time of the importance of being success-ful become worried, concerned and insecure. 'It clearly applies to Will because there was always this restlessness within him, this need to succeed. The paper also talked of the need of the person to behave impeccably and this, too, was a very strong part of Will's make-up. Will is obviously a worrier, a very serious guy deep down, and he is insecure,' says Wood.

On the other hand, the opposite also applies, for Carling can be a great humorist and wit, at times seeming the perfect extrovert. His mood dictates which emotion is in place at any particular moment, and attempting to prophesy which will apply at any given time is a hopeless task. Wood thought him a loner, and had a deep concern for the young man. The two developed a close friendship, and when Ted Wood had a breakdown during his time at Durham, Carling could not have been kinder. 'He was very concerned and kind to me. He came up to see me. Before that, when he had left Durham, he took my wife Pam and myself out for dinner one night to say "thank you" for what I had done. He also presented me with an England shirt. I appreciated both gestures enormously. He is a very thoughtful, sensitive boy. A lot of people in the north were very rude to him after he joined Harlequins. They didn't like him, for northerners don't understand people wanting to play for anyone else. At the time I thought he was very sensitive to people who were uncivil to him.'

The kind, caring, compassionate man? Yes, but he has also given the appearance of being cold and insensitive. In June 1992, Carling was due to attend a charity dinner in Scarborough which Wood had arranged, with his approval, to raise funds for a local hospice. Carling had promised to speak, but was forced to pull out because of unforeseen circumstances. Wood confessed his disappointment to others, but was stunned when a local newspaper ran the story the next day, quoting him as accusing Carling of gross discourtesy. The report must have found its way back to Carling and there has been no contact from the England captain ever since.

Wood, hurt and bewildered, confesses: 'It is a great sadness to me that that is the case. I can only hope it is because of a misunderstanding. Certainly, I do not understand what it is all about. To this day, I am his number one fan and have fond memories of our earlier association.'

It is sad to reflect that what may have been a misunderstanding about a speaking commitment, albeit exacerbated by a newspaper report, should ruin a longstanding friendship. It does, however, underline the idea, propounded by others here, that public criticism produces this sort of reaction from those with personality problems: silence as a defensive mechanism.

Ted Wood still recalls vividly that electric moment when he first witnessed Carling's exceptional talents. 'He was playing for Yorkshire schoolboys and it was perfectly obvious he was already an accomplished player. My big worry was that he might not come to Durham. I could remember one player impressing me as he did on that day, and that was Marcus Rose, who went on to be the England full-back.' Fran Clough was in the same category; Oti, too. They remain the most exciting players Wood has ever seen at Durham. Later, Wood was again moved by Carling's talent during a Cardiff v. Barbarians Easter Saturday match he saw on TV. 'It was before people were talking very much about lines of running. Will came in towards the ball which is ideal and then accelerated away on the outside. That made my hair stand up on end. He was still only twenty-one.'

It was the pace and the power, still his strongest points, Wood believes, which marked out Carling as so special. Intriguingly, Wood felt that the grander the stage, the more impressive the young man's talents became. This was truly the mark of the master – like a young Olivier negotiating with the assured calm of a veteran the transition from local rep to the West End stage. And bringing the house down on his first night. 'At University, he had both time and space yet he didn't look as good as when he was playing off the cuff at the higher level. When the distance and space closed down, he was faster and sharper,' says Wood. In fact, Wood shared Peter Dixon's concern that Carling was trying too hard to succeed, attempting the increasingly unrealistic, especially when he played at full-back for the university. 'He used to play around too much on his own, he was too adventurous. He used to run at the defence and take them on all the time.'

As his second year at Durham progressed Carling came to grasp the differing requirements of university rugby. By then, he was scaling the ladder again (five rungs at a time, given his abilities), playing for Durham in the County Championship. He had wondered whether to opt for Yorkshire, but Dixon warned him that they had a poor record for watching players not actually playing their rugby in the county. So he chose Durham, but his skills ensured an audience of those that mattered wherever he performed.

Yet not everyone could see genius in the making. Ted Wood recalls him reacting 'quite strongly' to the disappointment when he was not picked for an England Students team. He felt he had played well at the trials, but did not secure the place. 'It was hard for him to hide his disappointment and in fact he never was picked as a first choice for England Students.'

First impressions can be misleading, but Wood's thoughts as a result of his initial contacts with Carling were that the boy was ill at ease with himself. He did not know whether Carling was unhappy with himself, with the Army, or with something else. 'Personally, I think he was unhappy with university rugby. He needed his confidence building up. He is not arrogant: people forget he is very shy.'

The ordinary players of the north-east rugby clubs did not stop to conduct a detailed psychological study into whether Carling was a misunderstood young man or not. To the tough club men from Blaydon, Durham City, West Hartlepool, Westoe, Tynedale and Hartlepool Rovers, it was a simple issue of Town v. Gown. They piled into student lads like Carling, whom they regarded as the privileged ones, and if their target was able to get up, they gave him some more. Andy Mullins, now captain of Harlequins, recalls the intensity of those matches, against club sides that had been built around men who understood deprivation and disadvantage: 'Week in, week out we played those local club sides and it was always tough. Sometimes harder than ever. The West Hartlepool match was a jaunt for them; they were the biggest team we met and probably the best. But with every club, it was quite forcibly contested. They wanted to knock the students.'

If the student with the most exalted reputation was most frequently targeted, then quite plainly Carling was the one best able to handle the physical demands. His class shone at this modest level, a fact which did not endear him to the club players, but made his move to a higher grade inevitable. When the time came to find a club himself, his intention was to join one which would enhance his prospects of higher honours in the game. In Durham there was only one man to see about it, Mike Weston. If you had rugby business in the city, he was the man best qualified to ask. He was, after all, the England manager at the time.

Weston achieved some magnificent feats during a long career in English rugby, but perhaps the greatest was finding someone else to run ninety yards to score the equalizing try in the last minute of the 1965 Calcutta Cup match between England and Scotland! It was his pass which sent the Northampton wing Andy Hancock on his long, famous run into history, for the score which is remembered at Twickenham as vividly as Prince Obolensky's second try against New Zealand in 1936.

Weston was born in Durham, went to Durham School, and played for, among others, Durham City, Durham, the Barbarians, England (twenty-nine caps) and the British Lions (six Test caps). He probably possessed more contacts in the game than the Mafia in the Italian Parliament. 'Funnily enough, I had played against Will Carling,' said Weston, at his home high above the cathedral city. 'We used to go to Sedbergh to play them at cricket and he was in the school side one year. He was the talk of the place, but because of his rugby, of course. When he came to see me, I was in my second term as chairman of the England selectors. He said he would probably be going to London when he finished at Durham, and asked my advice as to which club he should join. There were several centres at Wasps – Simms, Lozowski, Davies – and he would have been about fourth choice. So I rang up John Currie, whom I'd played alongside for England at the start of the 1960s. He was chairman of Harlequins at the time and said he'd get their club coach, Dick Best, to make contact with Carling.'

Best, never a man who could be accused of not having his ear to the ground for the valuable intelligence which flows around the country's rugby circuit, already knew of Carling's reputation. He got in touch, and one of

England's finest prospects became a Harlequin. This involved the tortuous process for Carling of catching the train south from Durham on Thursday afternoons in time for training at the 'Quins Stoop ground, across the road from headquarters at Twickenham. Best would meet him at King's Cross railway station and the pair would battle the rush-hour traffic through London, in time to reach the ground for the start of the session. When the training session was over, Best would drive the youngster back to King's Cross to catch the sleeper to Durham, where he would arrive early the next morning for a lecture. Either that same evening or the next morning, Carling, who was by now in his second year at the university, would return by train to London for the Saturday match. Just occasionally, he would stay down in London.

Neither Carling nor Harlequins were very keen on the idea of him representing Durham, except in the prestigious UAU tournament. He was also, at this stage, a member of the North of England side, which had been put together for the Divisional Championship, a tournament given life by the Rugby Football Union with the purpose of providing the ultimate, pre-international rugby level, test for players. The Midlands, astutely coached by Alan Davies, won the inaugural tournament in 1985, but the following year the North won the competition with some handsome rugby in which the young Carling received his normally downbeat comment of 'outstanding'.

The twentieth of December 1986 was a unique day in the history of English rugby, although few of the people present at Wasps' North London ground for the Divisional Championship game between London and the North were aware of it then. The North trounced their opponents 34–6 (six tries to one), but two names from the team-sheets that day were to play a major role in rugby during the following years. London had chosen the former Cambridge University blues Simon Smith and Mark Bailey ever since the tournament had begun, a year earlier. But a 11–0 defeat by the South-West at Bath the previous week, and an injury to Smith, had forced changes. On to the London right wing came a player whom very few people outside Rosslyn Park's ground in Roehampton Lane, London SW15, knew anything at all about – Martin Offiah. In the North side, the uncapped Will Carling lined up at centre for only his third match at Divisional level.

Offiah scored London's only try in the match before coming off injured. There were some disparaging remarks about him afterwards by some of the North officials, which proved to be notably wide of the mark when he finally turned professional. 'How long have you had the break dancer on the wing?' one North official asked an astonished London man, adding, 'Someone tackled Offiah and he went off.' The reality was that Offiah was class in the making. The mouth-watering thought of what Carling and Offiah might have achieved in partnership for England is one for discussion beside a winter log-fire with a good cognac at hand. They played for the same side, the Barbarians, twice on the 1987 Easter tour to Wales, against Cardiff and Swansea. Alas, Offiah was a gem belonging to a country that never knew it possessed one, and he departed for a career in rugby league before he had even won an England cap. His loss to the amateur code was incalculable.

For Carling, the North's triumph in the Divisional Championship was quickly followed by more success.

Within three months his inspired play had helped Durham win the UAU Championship, with a 15–6 victory in the final at Twickenham over a Bristol side which included Jonathan Webb. Carling, by now a player of stature on every stage, made a magnificent break soon after half-time, yet Durham's only points came from their fly-half Canning, who kicked five penalty goals to Webb's brace of goals.

This was taking the golden touch ridiculously far: first, success for his Division among club players regarded as the élite of English rugby, then a title for his university. Andy Mullins, the captain of Durham that day, remembers Carling's valuable contribution: 'We were leading only 12–6 when Webb cut through our defence and was away to our posts. But Will caught him up, tapped his ankle and pulled him down ten yards short of our line. It was the match-saving tackle. Then we kicked a penalty to settle it, but that would have turned it if Webb had scored.'

It was the old story. Carling's speed and strength had once more underpinned his all-round contribution, whether it was in attack or defence. But Mullins was not terribly surprised: he knew class and quality when it stood before him. 'Will was in a different class to our other backs. He always had good power when he ran and was very quick off the mark. His basic ball skills were high and his outside break was terrific. He was able to do the same things whatever level he was playing at. He could cope. Always. No matter how much better the opposition. He played full-back for a while and some people tried to persuade him to stay there. He didn't mind in the short term but he always wanted to be a centre, long term.

'He and I both played for Durham County but when

he was chosen for the North, too, he was rather taken away from the university club. We were trying to play twice a week but he didn't want to play that much and it was disappointing. But then if I had been offered the chance to play for the North, I would have done exactly the same. When he joined Harlequins, other people just did not understand the commitment he had to make to do that. He just came across as arrogant.'

But Carling didn't help himself in the latter respect, either. Mullins remembers an incident prior to a UAU game one day at Durham. 'Will turned up and said, "What's the game plan, then?"' There was a stunned silence: this was, after all, student rugby, not First Division club level. When no one volunteered chapter and verse on the best attacking options available and the weaknesses on the left side of the opposing right centre, Carling produced a somewhat lofty reply. 'He said: "It's so different at 'Quins. When you get there for training you talk about opposition weaknesses and what they favour. It's all completely different."' This, of course, went down in student company like the proverbial lead balloon. 'It was perceived as arrogance,' Mullins added.

No wonder. Unintentional, perhaps; on the other hand, maybe not. Perhaps the acclaim, the plaudits, the growing swell of applause, had gone to Carling's head. His opinion of himself had never been exactly derogatory, but in moments like this, in front of his fellow players and students, these insensitive remarks reeked of haughtiness and were much better thought, not said. By expressing his opinions publicly, Carling demonstrated a gift for straight talking which he would underline on many future occasions. The trouble was that when similarly frank opinions were turned in his direction, they were by no means welcome.

Andy Mullins is a wise judge of his friend's complicated make-up. 'He is quite a complex character. He can be in tremendous party mood one evening and the next day he is very quiet and contemplative. At times he is very private. If he doesn't agree with what's being said and what's going on, he will voice his opinion to start and if it doesn't go his way, he tends to withdraw. That is his character. He is shy socially. He will have a conversation with anyone, but he won't open up. I can understand people saying they didn't really know him. I guess I don't know him that well.'

But if the personality remained baffling, the talent was bursting gloriously into flower. Like all the finest blooms, it had been judiciously cultivated and nurtured with care, but it flourished principally because of its innate quality. Will Carling now had the loftiest stage on which to perform. But all the pressures associated with years of schoolboy adulation and student promise would be as nothing compared to the spotlight now about to be focused upon him.

6 A Destiny Fulfilled

'The triumph of hope over experience.'
Samuel Johnson

Nineteen eighty-seven, *annus mirabilis*, was a year of extraordinary events. Or, in the case of English rugby, non-events. A hurricane blew down most of the trees of south-eastern England, reducing much of the countryside to scenes reminiscent of the Vietnam war. In rugby union, it was World Cup year. The tournament, long dreamed of by the nations of the southern hemisphere, had at last become reality as Australia and New Zealand pressganged the conservative countries of the northern hemisphere and dragged them part of the way, kicking and screaming, into the twentieth century.

On the third day of the new year, Will Carling had appeared in an England trial, renewing his partnership with Kevin Simms from England Schools sides. Nor did their team, the Rest, do badly, England beating the junior side only 10–9. Just eight members of that England side from the trial survived a protracted selection meeting for the first international of the Five Nations Championship, five weeks later. They were to be the unlucky ones. Carling, although he gave a sound display, did not join those colleagues from the Rest who won promotion for their efforts that day, which proved to be a classic case of the good Lord looking after his own. England went to Dublin and were beaten 17–0 in a dismal opening to the season. 'Considering hopes were so high, this was possibly the worst performance by England since the war,' said *Rothmans Rugby Yearbook*. The new dawn had quickly proved illusory.

England had had some grim times ever since the rump of Bill Beaumont's 1980 Grand Slam side had broken up, but given the extensive preparation of the team coached by Martin Green, the former Cambridge University player, the defeat in Dublin plumbed hitherto unknown depths. Those who sought to defend England's performance, if such it could be described, complained about the weather, claiming that all the preparations had been concentrated upon an attacking approach, assuming good conditions. But anyone who goes to Dublin in January and expresses surprise at wind and rain is either naïve or plain daft. Green, in fact.

Carling, the proud possessor of a sure talent for the future, was well off out of it, and this went for the entire season, really. Defeat in Ireland was followed by a home defeat by the French at Twickenham 19–15. Then came another defeat by Wales in Cardiff, 19–12, in which the fighting and bitterness between the sides was a disgrace to the good name of the game. Only a 21–12 victory over Scotland at Twickenham on the final day of the Championship offered England any solace.

Inspiration and organization seemed to be disturbingly absent for most of the season, and, following the troubles at Cardiff, four players were omitted from the next England team by order of an outraged RFU committee. It was not a happy ship. Given the fact that the World Cup was due to begin on 22 May, the party must have travelled to Australia with about as much confidence as the First Fleet of colonists heading there in 1787.

While all this was going on, there was an ideal test of young Carling's resolve and ability to handle all aspects of the game. The B international between England and France was held at Bath on 20 February, the night before the senior international between the countries at Twickenham. 'B', in this case, stood for brutality; it was hard to recall a tougher match at any level. French club rugby is, by tradition, often more akin to street mugging. Acts I have witnessed under the guise of rugby football on a French rugby field would earn the perpetrator on a British street a healthy six months' hospitality at the hands of Her Majesty's jailers. David Hands, rugby correspondent of *The Times*, wrote after one French club final in Paris: 'One felt bruised simply watching it from the press box.'

The French arrived at Bath intent on mayhem. Players demonstrating scant concern for their own safety by going down on the ball received the sort of fate normally reserved for animals straying into the path of country buses. Shirts were torn, skin shredded and ripped off, eyes attacked by punches and fingers. As an example of the attraction of rugby football, it was simply horrendous. England, at first appalled but then typically inspired by the rogue boots and flailing fists, gave an outstanding exhibition of powerful, controlled rugby football in the face of intimidating odds. Players like Andy Robinson, Mick Skinner, Jeff Probyn and Will Carling established their international careers with their bravery that night. The tackling by England was crushingly effective, strangling the life from French attempts at creativity. England won 22–9, and by the end of the evening some gutsy players had marked the selectors' cards, very firmly and emphatically.

Peter Williams, the Orrell fly-half who played that

night and later went on to turn professional after winning four caps, recognized the establishment of a real talent for the future on that wet, murky night in the west country. 'It was obvious then Will was going to make it. He was very confident and had all the attributes to succeed at the top. We had a lot of good ball with which to work and we used it. French rugby has always been a lot worse than the English game for the physical stuff. But Fran Clough was never bothered about being pushed about and Will Carling is the same type of bloke.' Williams noted the key characteristics of Carling's appeal: speed off the mark, solidity in defence and technical proficiency. 'Both centres destroyed the French that night. Clough also had a really good game and they complemented one another. Will had a good footballing brain and could read the game well. The nucleus of the side which was taking shape played in that B match.'

The emergence of leagues had already started to improve English rugby at that time, according to Williams. 'The Divisional structure helped and the leagues assisted, too. You were starting to get a fully professional attitude to an amateur game.' Williams believes that Carling's talents were such that he could have succeeded in either code of the rugby game. 'He has the strength to play and succeed in both union and league. Will would have done very well in rugby league and would have benefited from joining a really top club. But he stayed with union and showed that we were right; all the talent really had been there.'

If anyone had thought Carling's ball skills were his sole claim to fame, that match at Bath would have changed their opinions irrevocably. Together with Fran Clough and Peter Williams he erected a midfield barrier, ably assisted by the breakaways, which not even a French team containing those wingers of punishing pace, Patrice Lagisquet and Patrick Estève, could break down. It was hugely impressive stuff. Such a display enhanced Carling's hopes that he would make England's first-ever World Cup squad. The portents seemed good. Three days before England's final match of the Championship season against Scotland, the Barbarians played, and were annihilated by, the New Zealand Barbarians. It was a fitting scoreline for 1 April: a 68–16 defeat for the home side. The England centre Kevin Simms, poor chap, played in the match at Cardiff and suffered a traumatic experience. Would it influence the decision on whether he went to Australia for the World Cup with England?

Will Carling had gone to South Wales to watch that match, and afterwards gave Simms a lift back to Cambridge. On the long journey, Carling poured his heart out. 'Will was very, very disappointed not to be in the squad at the time,' said Simms. 'His head was down and he didn't really know what to do. He said someone had promised him a place and let him down. He joined the after-match celebrations that night but was pretty upset. He felt very much overlooked.' When England announced the names of the twenty-six players who would represent them at the World Cup, Carling's name was missing. Disappointment closed in on the youngster. It would be a gathering of the world's greatest nations and finest players, yet Carling himself would not be there.

Looking back, with the considerable advantage of hindsight, it was, as Kevin Simms properly describes it, 'a blessing in disguise'. There was a notable precedent for the misfortunes of a team totally undermining the career of a fine young player. In 1984 England had chosen another centre with an impressive reputation, Steve Burnhill, a month or two after his outstanding performance in assisting Loughborough to win the UAU title with a comprehensive victory in the final over Nottingham. England left for a seven-match tour of South Africa two months after that UAU final and they selected Burnhill as a player of considerable promise for the future. He was not thought likely to win a Test place but the experience, so it was argued, would be invaluable. In the event, these could not have been less prescient words. England had an atrocious tour, struggling even against the weaker opposition and suffering Test defeats by 33–15 and then 35–9. Burnhill, exposed too early at that level in an unstable environment, disappeared off the face of the international rugby earth and was never seen again.

Over the years, England had proved themselves notoriously ham-fisted when it came to selecting young talent and developing it for their future. Thus the omission of Carling from the squad to go to the World Cup three years later began to be seen in a different light only when the expedition started to degenerate into chaos, loss and recriminations.

The eighth of June 1987 was a day destined to enter the same dark passages of English rugby history as 7 February, the day of the defeat in Dublin four months earlier. England had to meet Wales – a sadistic swing of fate this – for a place in the semi-finals against New Zealand. They were overwhelming favourites, for Wales were beset by injury difficulties before the start in Brisbane and then lost the inspirational Norster during the game. They played much of the match with fourteen men. No matter, England misfired and spluttered hopelessly. At first blinking in disbelief at so sub-standard an English display, and then with a growing confidence which made every Englishman on the ground seethe with frustration, Wales somehow emerged in some style, which brought them three tries.

For those England players tainted with the brush of failure, it was a time of desperate disappointment. Two of them, Jamie Salmon and Peter Williams, never played for England again. Stephen Jones, rugby writer for the *Sunday Times*, said later: 'When they [England] lost to Wales they set in chain a process leading to the departure of the management and half the team ... For England, it was a disaster.'

Speculation may be the occupation of the idle, but it is appropriate to contemplate what might have happened to the young Will Carling had he become embroiled in such an ultimately depressing experience. For he might well have been there: 'He was pretty close to being included,' says Mike Weston, the England manager on that trip. 'But he was regarded still as a rookie. There were several players in the pecking order: among them, Salmon, Simms, Clough, Halliday and Carling. Halliday messed about a bit and then decided he was not available and finally we chose only three centres, not four. Will was next in line to the first three, all of whom went. At that time, there was this question of whether he was a full-back or centre. That didn't help him in the selection for the World Cup squad, it muddied the waters somewhat.'

Simms, who did go, and who played in the débâcle against Wales, believes Carling was infinitely better off out of it. He, like others, had been captivated by the young man's high level of simple but essential skills. He knew England had a rare talent in their hands, but it was like allowing your children to carry the finest cut-glass decanter into the kitchen; you always wondered whether somehow they'd wreck the thing. 'I remember when he first got into the North Divisional side. He was playing for Durham at the time. Five of us were looking for the two positions at centre: Bryan Barley, Fran Clough, John Buckton, Will and myself. In his first game he was outstanding. He did things. That is his main strength, he tries things. And of course he was always very solid in defence.'

Simms, who had been at West Park, St Helens, knew Carling from his early days with Yorkshire Schools. He had played alongside him for England Schools, he roomed with him for the North in Divisional Championship matches; he was even to be his co-centre when Carling won his first senior cap. 'I had quite a nice relationship with him. But he has his friends and takes time to get to know people. He is very wary of people.'

England's failure at the World Cup in the summer of 1987 was a watershed in the history of the game in this country. It meant that the new season, 1987–8, offered bright prospects for many of the talented young players in the country. League rugby was introduced for the first time that season, transforming the national game in organization and establishing a proper system which rewarded progress, rather than the pedigree of a club. There was a new manager of the England team, Geoff Cooke, and a new coach, Roger Uttley, replacing Mike Weston and Martin Green. John Elliott was appointed a co-selector. England were using not merely a new broom to sweep away the long years of disappointment and failed potential, but a whole array of cleaning instruments and personnel to get the place shipshape. Nor was this before time.

England's record in recent years, 1980 excepted, had been a miserable catalogue of under-achievement. That a wealth of quality players had been available was undeniable, yet successive England officials and players had presided over a sprawling desert of failure, stretching back as far as 1963. Not a Grand Slam in all that time, 1980 apart – not a Triple Crown nor even a share of a Championship. For a nation with such numbers playing the game at its disposal, this was a shocking indictment of the lack of organization, player selection, a suitable structure for talent to emerge and an ability to instil in those players who were chosen for matches sufficient confidence to succeed.

Even a country like Ireland, with its strictly limited playing numbers, managed to assemble a record which put England in the shade. The Irish had won or shared the Five Nations Championship in 1974, 1982, 1983 and 1985, winning Triple Crowns in 1982 and 1985. For England, with all its vast riches of players, to have so poor a record that it could not hold a candle to the Irish was a tragic waste of resources. It was time for a long overdue recovery.

Leagues, it was felt, might help improve the picture. Club matches which had no relevance were contests without credentials. How could players expect to adapt to the highest level of international rugby if they were playing friendly games every week of the season, apart from a few decent tough affairs with the likes of Cardiff, Pontypool and Llanelli? It simply wasn't tenable. But the introduction of league rugby could be only a first step. Almost certainly it would take time for its importance to be felt. The Divisional Championship, started in its modern form in 1985, had offered the selectors a proving ground of sorts for aspiring internationals, and promised to weed out some of those plainly ill-equipped for tougher challenges at a still higher level.

Into this changing environment stepped the man most recently charged with making silk purses from sows' ears. Geoff Cooke, whose work for the North Divisional side had been noted in higher circles, was quickly head-hunted in the light of England's abject failure at the World Cup and Mike Weston's resignation as manager. Those in authority sensed that there *were* players of sufficient calibre spread out across the country – what was required was someone who could make sound judgements, put into place a long-term strategy and work towards that goal. Where disorganization had existed, they wanted a structured system; where lack of faith in players had been damagingly omnipresent, they sought loyalty; where panic had been apparent, they required a calm hand; and where misjudgement had proliferated, they demanded prudence and common sense.

Cooke had coached Bradford, Yorkshire and the North. At the time of his appointment he was the principal sports development officer for Leeds City Council. The man he wanted as coach, Roger Uttley, had an impeccable lineage as a player, both with England, for whom he had won twenty-three caps, and with the British Lions, for whom he had played in all four Tests on their outstandingly successful tour of South Africa, in 1974. Although Cooke insisted he would be a tracksuit manager, not one who remained behind office doors at Twickenham, he was a man steeped in experience on several sides: physical conditioning, the requirements of fitness at varying levels, and the planning of strategies for club and Divisional sides. Uttley could offer far more experience from the playing side, which Cooke had never known at the higher levels, but the combination of the two seemed promising.

Events had conspired to place before Geoff Cooke a kind of initiation period which would have persuaded even the boldest of men to take a pace backwards. His first international as manager would be against France, in Paris, and if that and the remainder of the Five Nations Championship season were not enough, England were then scheduled to embark in May on a month-long tour of Australia. There, they would play two Test matches (plus New South Wales and Queensland, which really made it almost four Tests, given the strength of the States) and another against Fiji on the way home.

Nineteen eighty-eight was shaping up to be a monumental year for Geoff Cooke, Will Carling and many other figures in English rugby. But first there was the Divisional Championship to study for the in-form players, and for likely performers of the future. It was the third year of the tournament but it proved a crushing disappointment in almost every sense. The North won it, winning all three matches but without ever establishing the control one was entitled to expect from the leading team. Carling was chosen at centre with John Buckton, the Saracens player; the youngster was sound, rather than spectacular, but the whole competition seemed still to be afflicted by uncertainties over its precise value, and by the on-going problem of motivation. So, with the new selectorial minds clearly unconvinced, it was decided to hold a national trial. This was played on 2 January 1988. When the teams were known, there was the surprise that Carling was paired at centre not with Buckton, colleague from the North's Divisional side, but with Kevin Simms, who had been unable to win a place anywhere for the North that season.

True to the form of that time, the outcome simply blurred the horizons even further, the so-called reserve side (or 'England B', as it was known) beating an 'England XV', supposedly the first string team, 13–7. The cards had been turned over and shuffled everywhere. The new regime of selectors would have had every justification for tossing the lot into the fire.

The French, Grand Slam champions the previous season with a pack of forwards who had overwhelmed (some word that, given their opponents) the touring New Zealanders in a game that had become known as the Battle of Nantes, were a formidable opposition to be faced in their own backyard, just two weeks after the inconclusive England trial. There was scarcely time for anyone in the England set-up to draw breath. When the side was announced, it was revealed that three new caps had been chosen; thirty-year-old tight head prop Jeff Probyn, blindside flanker Micky Skinner and centre threequarter Will Carling. The star turn of so many schoolboy matches, the young man in whom so much hope had been invested had at last ascended the ultimate stage. He was just twenty-two.

The team England chose had a startling preponderance of players associated with the North. Every one, from scrum-half further out down the back-line, had firm links with the North either at that time or in the immediate past. Four players had been born in Yorkshire: Mike Harrison, the right wing and captain, Rory Underwood on the other wing, and the half-backs, Les Cusworth and Nigel Melville. Of the others, Jonathan Webb, the full-back, had been educated at Royal Grammar School, Newcastle upon Tyne, Will Carling had been schooled at Sedbergh and represented Yorkshire Schools, and Kevin Simms was a Lancashire boy.

Cooke was going back to basics, relying on those he knew best to lay some kind of foundation on which he could help England construct a more convincing future. The choice of Carling and Simms as the centre pairing – one an untried novice at this level, and the other hardly an imposing bulwark of a player with whom to take on the strong French centres – was a gamble. Particularly in Paris. But for Will Carling, selection was the fulfilment of every dream – it was the climax of his ambition, throughout his formative years, to play rugby for England one day. He had delivered what his talent had always promised, a full cap for his country's rugby team. The circumstances had allowed him to fulfil his destiny, but then the perceived opinion had always been that he would emerge at some stage. The only uncertainty had been when.

Dave Robinson, who had been coach with the North Divisional side during Cooke's time as manager, considered the selection decisions taken for the match to be about right. 'The Yorkshire backs in the North side – Harrison, Carling, Underwood, Melville – were very good and well balanced. They had been together a while, too. Carling fitted in well; he was very compact and strong. I had first seen him play for Durham in the 1985 County Championship and you could tell as soon as you saw him, he was good enough. He was an excellent tackler, and was well balanced; always steady, with a real change of pace in attack.'

But immature. North officials remember Carling as the boy at university still playing sixth-form pranks. They recognized that he liked some fun, but found such schoolboy humour somewhat misplaced among the men of the Divisional Championship side. 'He did nothing wrong for the North all the time he played for us,' said one. 'But I used to think he was still very much like a schoolboy with his practical jokes. He never struck me as the right sort of guy for a future captain. He was too much of a loner for that. He was clearly never going to be a leader like Willie John McBride or Bill Beaumont, hugely popular guys everyone acknowledged. But then maybe it's an advantage if you detach yourself a little.' Nevertheless, Carling excelled as a player at Divisional level. 'He blossomed in the North side. In 1986, when we beat London so well, Carling and Underwood really clicked that day,' said Robinson.

Yet Robinson, like the scientist forever experimenting with shapes and forms, thought Carling would make an outstanding full-back. Part of his reasoning was derived simply from the logistics of the situation. 'England had some very good centres at that time. John Bentley of Sale was emerging, Bryan Barley was around, there was Kevin Simms, John Buckton, Simon Halliday and a couple of others. I thought Will would have more to offer as a full-back, too. He was a strong runner, good fielder of the ball, had a hell of a boot on him and could read a game which is invaluable for the full-back looking to counter-attack. I felt for the balance of our side at the time, it would have been an ideal situation for him to be at full-back. But Will wasn't keen on playing there.' Is hypothetical speculation as to how great his value might have been at No. 15 worthwhile? Robinson says: 'When a guy achieves world status, as Will has now, you cannot say whether he would have been a better full-back. All you can say is that he has proved conclusively he always had the talent to succeed whatever the opposition.'

Kevin Simms had been chosen for his footballing abilities; Carling for his undoubted promise and strength. He was regarded as the blocking centre beside the deft skills and lighter touch of the diminutive Simms. An interesting combination to set against the two power-house French centres chosen for the match: Philippe Sella of Agen, known as the Locomotive for his ability to keep going whatever the circumstances or impediments, and Marc Andrieu of Nîmes, a tall, strong centre with a punishing hand-off and no little speed.

If England have ever travelled anywhere more in hope than expectation, it was that journey on which they embarked on Thursday 14 January 1988. On a wing and a prayer, truly.

7 An Afternoon in the Parc

'In quietness and in confidence shall be your strength.'
Isaiah 30:15

A cavernous bowl, a Saturday in January. Fifteen players in blue jerseys appear, to a cacophony which reverberates around the stadium like the roar of a lion through the jungle. Then they play. To the accompaniment of cheering, jeering, roars, groans. But also to a saxophonist, trumpeters, drummers and other musicians in the renowned Dax band, who perform throughout the action. There is a trace of Hemingway at Pamplona in this music-filled, carnival atmosphere. Behind the goalposts at one end of the ground, in front of a backdrop of waving flags, a cockerel struts disinterestedly. It is the quintessential Parisian rugby scene.

The Parc des Princes is not the most awesome stadium in the rugby world, but for an atmosphere of intimidation, a cauldron of noise and excitement, it can strike fear into the hearts of visiting players like few others can. Only a short hop across the English Channel it may be, but it is a world removed from the sedate, quietly genteel playing-fields of Eton, Harrow . . . or Sedbergh.

They had lined up the new boy, the lad of just twenty-two, for his official team photograph before the start of the France–England match. The intensity is revealing: a studied expression, his face set, hair cropped quite short and a determined manner about him. No one knew, still less could guess, that weekend in Paris in January 1988, how Will Carling's future career would unfold. But though breaths might be held in Sedbergh, at a small school in Cheshire, in college rooms at Durham University and even back in London among some Harlequin players and officials, it was quickly apparent to Carling's international colleagues that this was very far from the traditional nervous youngster in the days and hours prior to his first cap for his country. Same situation many others had known, vastly different reaction from W. D. C. Carling, the young centre whom England hoped would come of age that day.

Of his potential, there was no doubt. But plenty of others blessed with potential had been this way before, and had failed; quietly, but utterly. Because anyone thrown in at this particular deep end had to be a great deal more than just proficient to survive. They had to adapt, instantly, to the culture shock of international rugby. It is faster, altogether more hyped-up, inestimably more intense. It is the supreme physical test even for the supremely physical; it is performed at a pace for which no one can be properly prepared. You dive in and swim: if you are good enough, you stay afloat, if not, you sink without trace.

The classic case is well documented. The new cap shakes with such uncontrolled emotion he can hardly hold his morning cup of tea, let alone a fast pass under pressure. He has slept fitfully the previous night, has desperately attempted to kill the minutes, let alone the hours, and is drained from the entire experience of the build-up, even before the kick-off. Will Carling's preparation was quite different. The usual scenario was unknown to England's new centre threequarter. They whisked him off to Paris, a boy of twenty-two among men in their early thirties, who stood back, mouths sagging in disbelief at his calmness. It bordered on effrontery. No sooner had he arrived at the England squad's pre-match headquarters, the Trianon Palace Hotel in Versailles, than he announced, once training was completed, that he was off to Paris to see a friend. Nothing wrong with that, but it was contrary to every script ever drafted for the new boy in any sporting side. Normal, nervous débutants cling to the body of the team like young children to their mother. But then this was no ordinary player elevated beyond his station to the international rugby theatre.

Carling had an assurance about him, a confidence to his gait. He offered the world an impression of complete control, both of himself and of the situation. Nerves undeniably existed, but they were contained. One didn't show one's feelings, anyway; that trait had been acquired from the earliest days. He had dinner, quietly, with his colleagues. Then, around eight o'clock, he went off for a walk, a stroll alone around Versailles; the prince and heir to English rugby greatness, inspecting the former king's palace. 'He said he wanted that time alone to collect his feelings,' said Kevin Simms, his room-mate on the trip. 'He was quite quiet that Friday night, often listening to music on his own headset. He was out walking for about an hour and a half. The rest of us tended to sit around for a chat after dinner. It was certainly different to have a new cap out on his own.'

The new boy was different the next day, too. 'He wasn't particularly nervous on the morning of the game,' said Simms. 'He didn't ask for any advice beforehand. He seemed to have it all formulated in his own mind. He didn't need me. I wasn't surprised. I had got to know him from school through to the Divisional side.

He had taken everything in his stride and I wouldn't have expected anything less. But it is most unusual to be able to drop straight in like that. When we got to the ground and the match started, straight from the start he just did things the way he still does them. He had a go at people, he took them on. Sure, he made some mistakes but then had another go again. To do that in your first international is quite something. Especially in the atmosphere of Paris.'

Carling was even able to disregard a potentially traumatic early moment. Almost from his first touch, he streamed down the right with a two-man support outside and the French cover as threadbare as old carpet. England had a glorious opportunity for an early try but the new boy erred, mistiming his pass and allowing the chance to slip away. But if it was a split second of anguish, it scarcely showed. He made his tackles with determination and fortitude, and he ran and supported strongly in attack. This was proving to be no slaughter of the innocents, as some had forecast, but another illustration of little David getting one over on Goliath. Well, almost. England led 9–3 and threatened the grandest upset in the Championship for years, a toppling of giants. Alas, Berot kicked a penalty to make it 6–9 and England failed to quell just about the only potent French attack, launched inevitably by Blanco. Rodriguez, the grizzly, powerful and determined No. 8 from Dax, seized upon the loose ball deep in English territory to dribble over and score, with two minutes remaining.

France had won 10–9 and England had discovered a cruel lesson about the need for precision and a killer instinct when opponents are stumbling. But only 10–9? Even the England manager Geoff Cooke had feared the worst. 'Simon Halliday and John Buckton were the two centres we had our minds on for that match. But they were injured. There was a worry about playing Carling so soon. After all, he was still a student at Durham University and everyone thought we would lose by 40 points in Paris. We wondered whether he would be able to cope. But he had shown himself to be a quite remarkable talent. As soon as he went into the North side, he made an impact. He could attack, defend and he had an awareness of things. He was in control of himself and his game. Often when players are running at pace, they lose their vision and awareness. But Will always retained that.

'He did very well in Paris. With his first touch he made a nice little run and could have brought us a try. It was a 3 on 1 situation; if he had timed his pass we would have scored. He didn't. But it was still obvious, long before the end, that here was a player for the future.'

England were not short of ability that day in Paris. They had a young hooker, Brian Moore, who was to develop into a world class player, an outstanding back row of Micky Skinner, Peter Winterbottom and Dean Richards, powerful line-out presence in Wade Dooley and a scrum-half, Nigel Melville, in the classic mould.

So the French crept home, with almost as much uncertainty as from Moscow. They did at least get a win this time, but England were surely entitled to raise a glass or two in celebration of a performance that bore practically no relation to what had gone on the previous year. Or so some of the younger players felt. But on a cold Saturday in Paris, the new caps received from an old cap a little schooling in the harsh realities of international rugby. Peter Winterbottom had known the worst of times with England. He had arrived in the side two years too late for the 1980 Grand Slam and had now played five seasons in the Championship, without a sniff of a title. Defeat, for Winterbottom, hurt; the fact that it was by a single point was irrelevant. As the party developed and a couple of the new caps laughed and drank, 'Winters' turned on them, snarling with aggression. 'If you think losing by a point justifies celebrating, then maybe you will never play for England again,' was the gist of his words. The laughter stopped.

Nigel Melville remembers: 'The lads that had been there before, in the sense of that situation, were absolutely mortified we had lost. We should have won. The older lads were upset and perhaps felt the young lads had let them down. After all, Will Carling had done something wrong early on, on the pitch. And Kevin Simms threw a pass when he was about to be tackled but finished up over the French line. Had he held on to the ball, he would have scored. "Winters" certainly wasn't too impressed.'

A verbal mugging from a player of Winterbottom's stature never did anyone any harm. The 'straw man', as he became known on the 1983 British Lions tour of New Zealand because of his straw-coloured hair, which seemed to be everywhere, was brave and committed. He had a complete disregard for his own physical safety on the rugby field and, like all such men, earned a deep and abiding respect from his opponents. Besides, Carling could take it. So could the other newcomers, men like Skinner and Probyn. Certainly Melville, who had known all about young Carling's inexorable rise to fame, was not surprised to see him handle every aspect of his first international weekend with a quiet aplomb. It befitted the boy from the school, he reasoned with a smile.

'At Otley, my club in Yorkshire, we get a lot of

Sedbergh boys coming down to join us when they leave school. They all come with that air which is perceived as arrogance. They are brown stocking boys! When you first meet them, they are always pretty loud, pretty confident. That is what Sedbergh School does for you. I used to wish I had been brought up in the public school system, rather than the comprehensive where I was educated. Most of them certainly have a presence which you never get from the state school system. People talk about the public school network and it certainly exists. They are different. Even those at twenty-eight or thirty have Sedbergh, the school, written all through them.' Like a bar of rock. Melville continues: 'They are very, very proud of their school. And rugby is the sport they are proudest of. They are coached well – you don't get any duff players coming from Sedbergh.'

Melville, born in Leeds and now living in the city, first saw Carling when he was still at Sedbergh. 'I played for the Luddites against Sedbergh's 1st XV when Will was in their side. Peter Winterbottom played that day for us, too. It was quite obvious Will was the outstanding player in their team. He was not the sort of player in a normal team game who would strike you in the way Rory Underwood might with his exceptional pace. But Will looked a hard, solid, dependable, strong player. He looked a Bryan Barley type of player. He wouldn't score twenty tries a season but he would help the wing outside him do so. When he came into the senior level, he was a very quiet boy. Not at all arrogant. He was quite unassuming, a polite lad.'

Good judges watched and digested carefully the performance of Carling in Paris. He had been written and talked about by so many people that his was already a reputation to reckon with. At Harlequins, the club he had joined the previous winter, no one was enormously surprised that the boy stepping out into a man's world had proved himself perfectly equal to the task. 'There had never been any question of his ability,' said a club colleague. 'They should have taken him to the World Cup the previous year. It was between Clough and Carling for that trip and they went down the safe road, with Clough. But Carling was playing well enough and he should have gone for the experience. Everyone else was taking a punt on some youngsters. For a young guy who had never played on the club circuit, it was refreshing to see his confidence when he joined 'Quins.'

Les Cusworth was also impressed. Recalled to the side for the match in Paris, Cusworth recalls the new, raw recruit coming into the England team at a very difficult time. 'It was unsettled and no one knew quite what to expect,' said the former Leicester fly-half. 'But you could see Carling always had the confidence in his own ability on the field. I think that match in Paris was something of a damage limitation exercise, in that the new selectors wanted to see how we could play. You could see Cooke and Uttley were very well organized and astute about what they wanted. There was immediately more structure to it all, more organization.'

There was also, according to Cusworth, who had been in the international rugby wilderness for four years, better line-out preparation and greater awareness from the whole team of what was required in all situations. England got their reward; the line-out was particularly effective that day, and they emerged with a solid platform, a base on which to build their aspirations for the future. Before that, there had been only darkness. Cusworth believed the selectors saw him as a stop-gap to settle Rob Andrew into the side eventually. He was right, too; after one more game, Andrew replaced him and Cusworth's stop-start international career, born as far back as 1979 against New Zealand and then resurrected, albeit briefly, ten seasons later, finally ended. The greatest indictment of the England system through those lost years, 1980 excepted, was that so skilful a player as the little Leicester fly-half should have won just twelve senior caps. With the knowledge and vision of a solid coaching system in place, Cusworth was the kind of quality player around whom England could and should have built a team to enjoy years of success.

But at least he saw things changing before he finished. He quickly spotted Carling's cool confidence in a potentially difficult situation. 'When he went off to visit a girl from the Foreign Office in Paris the day before the match, you could see he was a confident, pretty single-minded sort of bloke. Throughout the years since, he has got better and better as a player and I believe his experience from those early days has been valuable. He's a very strong, compact player, a very well-balanced runner. A very gifted lad.' With a few other qualities, too? 'Certainly. He's a bit of a loner. But look at all the top sportsmen, they have all had that little swagger about them. Besides, I think if you don't know a guy that well you should use the phrase "single-minded" about them.'

England came home from Paris, with something of a spring under their step, to face Wales at Twickenham three weeks later. Alas, it didn't last. A new regime, a new exciting young centre they might have discovered, but some things never changed – Wales beat them 11–3. The Welsh, extraordinarily, fielded a side containing four genuine fly-halves: Mark Ring, Bleddyn Bowen, Tony Clement and the official holder of the position,

Jonathan Davies. This offered them the sort of creativity England lacked, and a disappointing display for the home side contained just a single penalty goal by Jonathan Webb, late in the match. If Paris had been a harbour of hope, this was plainly a port of poverty for English rugby.

The management decreed that changes were required, so out went the captain, Mike Harrison, who had led England in the World Cup, Kevin Simms and Les Cusworth. None of them ever played for England again, such was the finality of the decision. Harrison was sacked by his fellow Yorkshireman, Geoff Cooke, a decision which the England manager regards to this day as one of his toughest ever. 'We had inherited Mike as a captain but I knew him well, he was a great friend of mine,' says Cooke. 'It was the worst decision I have had to make in rugby affecting a friend. I found it daunting in my first year as England manager.' Melville was made leader once again. Carling survived, though, as Chris Oti, Simon Halliday and Rob Andrew were drafted into the side. Halliday, a highly gifted player whom England, true to type, had failed to utilize to his utmost thus far, had played international rugby on and off since 1986, Andrew since 1985. Cooke was determined that England would finally discover whether either was really to play a fulsome part in the revival he sought for the national side.

That revival of sorts began in the Scottish capital, Edinburgh. But it was a match made memorable only by the late-night antics of two players, the Scot John Jeffrey and England's Dean Richards, who decided that the famous old Calcutta Cup, made originally of silver Indian rupees, was just the thing for a game of football in the streets of Edinburgh around midnight. The old pot was quite badly dented, although not as much as the image of the game after a desperately poor spectacle that afternoon. England won 9–6, two penalty goals and a dropped goal to two penalty goals. It would be stretching the truth to say that England floated out of Scotland the next day on a tide of Bollinger. However, a win was a win and those charged with bringing to life the corpse known as English rugby regarded it rather as a down-and-out reflects on a bad meal at a charity hostel – it might have tasted shocking but it must have done some good.

Three matches had now been played by England that season, and the grand total of points achieved, twenty-one, had comprised a rivetingly entertaining five penalty goals and two dropped goals. Not a try in sight. The last match of another dismal season for England was against Ireland at Twickenham. This was a High Noon shoot-out to avoid the dreaded Wooden Spoon, and when Ireland led at half-time through a single dropped goal to nil, many felt it was time to uncork not the champagne but the cyanide capsule. What followed did almost as much damage to the central nervous system, but in a rather different sense. England ran in six tries in the last forty minutes of the season, with the demonic air of escaped convicts raining blows on the heads of their long-time tormentors. It was essentially an exorcism of frustrated, troubled souls, a kind of cleansing of the long years of failure. Ireland, it has to be said, offered some tackling which would not have deterred a competitively minded Under-11 side, but England swept through them like an uncontrollable spring flood tide.

The finish to Rory Underwood's final try, his third, seemed somehow to epitomize the mood of all English rugbymen. The celebratory dive over the line spoke volumes for the widespread sense of relief. He felt it, his colleagues understood it and an entire nation experienced it. A final winning margin of 35–3 was England's biggest win in a Five Nations Championship match since they had beaten France 37–0 at Twickenham in 1911, seventy-seven years earlier.

There was one sad aspect to the day: Nigel Melville, who was leading England and winning his thirteenth cap, was tackled so heavily into the touchline fence that he suffered injuries which ended his international career. This was to have a considerable bearing on the international future of Will Carling. Since Christmas, the young Durham University student had experienced astonishing progress in his sporting fortunes. He was now playing regular first team rugby for Harlequins, and had secured an England place. He returned to the university after each international widely known and, not surprisingly, found the mundane requirements of his psychology degree altogether less invigorating a subject than discussing and pondering England's last match.

The most revealing factor in the huge win over Ireland had been the fact that England's wings, for years the lepers of the international rugby world, had scored five of the six tries. This owed much to the enhanced creativity inside them, and the centre partnership of Carling and Halliday was plainly responsible. For Geoff Cooke, Carling's performance throughout the season confirmed all the positive vibes he had felt about the youngster as far back as his first sighting. 'I had gone to watch him play for Durham against Yorkshire in the County Championship. "This boy is special," someone had told me, just as they had done on countless other occasions about a great many other players. Some were fair, others not so good. But then there was Carling. I was pretty impressed straight away. His vision, understanding and awareness of what was happening around him and his basic skills were all so good. We pulled him into the North side as soon as possible and I had pushed the England selectors to take him to the World Cup in 1987. I thought he was just what they wanted.'

Why? 'He was better than any of the other centres they took. He had just got it. You see some players and they have got something that is a bit special. Yet, with hindsight, not taking him to the World Cup might have been the correct decision. Maybe it would have been too meteoric a rise for him to have gone. It hasn't done him any long-term harm not going.'

So the talent was there, and it was bound to emerge. So given that enormous ability, captaincy was a logical development – right? No, wrong. Fate needed to take Carling emphatically by the hand and lead him towards his destiny in the game.

At this time two factors surfaced as major influences upon the future of England's national rugby team. First, Geoff Cooke, the newly appointed manager, took charge fiercely determined to squash one habit indulged in by most selectorial panels in the past: changing the teams incessantly. In their first campaign, Cooke and Uttley used only nineteen players, against twenty-four from the previous season under the control of Weston and Green. Continuity was a policy Cooke insisted be strictly adhered to: he simply could not comprehend how selectors expected players to produce their best form if they sensed the close proximity of the axe. Second, on the day they overwhelmed Ireland, England had potentially an outstanding captain in their ranks. At almost thirty-two, Mike Harrison had plainly not been a long-term investment as leader, but in Nigel

Melville, who had led England on his international début back in 1984, they had a player technically and motivationally capable of taking them right through to the 1991 World Cup. In 1988, when he faced Ireland in what was to be his final international match, Melville was twenty-seven and could have anticipated his four best seasons at the summit of the game spreading out before him. Had that scenario been fulfilled, as it almost certainly would have been had it not been for the horrific injury which prematurely terminated his career, it is very likely that Will Carling would never have captained England. Or certainly not for many years, comparatively late in his career.

Geoff Cooke says: 'I have always been dismayed at the inconsistency of selection policy in English rugby. It is so important to have consistency in that area. You can't possibly pick a player one week and say he is the best in England, but the following week drop him and say he is not. Unless you are admitting you made an absolute howler in the first place, you have to expect a guy to take time and that means giving him a run, and the chance to develop. You have to get your first team virtually right, because if you don't, you are chopping and changing thereafter. We have done this in England for years and it has been our biggest single failing; we have been dreadful at it. We have a terrible history of one-cap wonders.'

There was one more international for England to play that season in Europe. It was, ironically, a re-match against Ireland, to celebrate the millennium of the city of Dublin: the Dublin Millennium Challenge, as it was somewhat grandly titled, abbreviated in Irish colloquial terms to the altogether more succinct 'Aluminium match'. It was largely an April romp in the spring breeze,

England winning 21–10. Refereed by the Frenchman René Hourquet ('Walk Away René', as someone had once dubbed him, in memory of the old Four Tops pop group hit record, after he had failed to spot copious knock-ons and other infringements in a match), it had a somewhat unrealistic tone. But at least the Guinness tasted as good as ever that night once the match had been got out of the way.

One week later, there was a match of altogether greater complexity and importance. For Carling, it was another taste of the rugby high life, the cream offered only to those at the top table. By now he was here to stay, a talent which had emerged miraculously quickly out of the ashes of the World Cup disaster.

Harlequins, his club, had traditionally been regarded as something of a joke in club competition. The right club to join if you wanted to win a cap, or get a good job in the city, but not in the same street as Bath or Leicester, or even Gloucester, when it came to success at club level. Two men on the playing side decided it was time to render this widespread perception obsolete. Dick Best had once been a chef at ITN in the West End and clearly knew how to concoct a decent soufflé. But now, as Harlequins' coach, he began to show that he could cook up a pretty appealing dish on the rugby field. His team surprised the rugby fraternity by demonstrating muscle as well as magic, in winning their John Player Cup fourth round tie 17–4 at the physical west country junior club Berry Hill. In past years, this might have been a journey too far for 'Quins. Like the soufflé, they never travelled very well, it was said, disparagingly. Best was intent on showing otherwise.

Waterloo were buried 37–4 in the quarter-finals, but a semi-final draw at Wasps did them few favours. The

North London club had appeared in the last two Cup finals and anticipated that a home match with the dainty 'Quins boys would be ideal preparation for another trip to Twickenham for the final. But Harlequins' steel and will emerged again. It was 16–16 at the end of full time, but Harlequins, bristling throughout with determination, scored first in extra time to win the tie 20–16.

Best had emphasized to his team what he expected, long before kick-off. At their final training session before the game, he put his forwards through a physically shattering seventy scrums. Forty lashes might have seemed far more pleasant. But it induced a peak condition and a mental hardness and discipline which were to prove crucial. Moon's try in extra time put Harlequins through to their first-ever Cup final, to meet Bristol, who had negotiated smoothly a semi-final at the Midland club, Moseley, 34–6. 37,000 people, quite the biggest crowd ever seen for an English Cup final, went to Twickenham for the match. They were to be served the finest dish of the entire English season.

If Best had been instrumental in altering attitudes as coach, then Jamie Salmon had contributed mightily as a player. Salmon had been a good enough player to be capped by both New Zealand, where he had gone to live as a young man, and England, when he returned to this country. A change in the International Board player qualifications facilitated this unusual situation. Few people play for their country; to be capped by two countries and recognized by the All Blacks, especially, was a mark of Salmon's quality. As for England, although he was to win twelve caps, it was another illustration of a fine player not earning the proper recognition of his talents. At twenty-eight, the strong, hugely experienced centre threequarter would have been an outstanding choice as captain of England, after the World Cup débâcle. Instead, for some mysterious reason, he was never chosen again, a shocking waste of a highly tuned rugby brain.

Espousing the theory that fortune favours the brave and bold, Best had decided that all-out attack was the way to beat Bristol, the winners of the competition five years earlier and beaten finalists the following season. The Harlequins' style was a blaze in the darkness which had permeated every corner of English rugby for so many years. They flew at Bristol's throats like demented animals from the start. For Will Carling, the Durham student in their centre, it was a stunning illustration of how the game could be played even at this level.

Harlequins' brilliant, adventurous approach earned them an 18–0 lead before Bristol, toiling like porters behind a passenger in a hurry, had started. The west-countrymen were swept imperiously aside with a rare flourish of pacy, inventive play. Harlequins ran the ball from every position, even those of apparently dire danger. Attacks beginning deep in their own 22 became commonplace; Bristol huffed, puffed, chased and tried vainly to play catch-up rugby. Their big, powerful forwards found it about as pleasing an experience as a spell on the rack.

Carling, young, still learning but already a good enough reader of the game to put him in the critical position at the vital moment, scored after only six minutes. He finished off a counter-attack which had started when Bristol missed touch, Everton Davies running the ball back and the forwards supporting before Ackford put Carling over. Salmon, overlooked all season and not even good enough in the judgement of the national selectors to earn a place on the forthcoming

England tour of Australia, then looped in the centre to put Harriman over. Salmon, with some authoritative goal-kicking, landed a conversion and penalty goal, Thresher doing the same, and 'Quins were away at 18–0. It was good enough to make the spine tingle.

Bristol retrieved three points by half-time, and then, with their opportunity to use the wind, began an impressive attempt at salvation. They got it back to 13–18 before Harlequins added a penalty to lead 21–13. That had become 21–19 with fifteen minutes left, before the try of the match, perhaps of the year, undid Bristol once and for all. It was scored, from 85 yards range and as in all the best schoolboy comic stories, by W. D. C. Carling, the discovery of the English season. It still ranks as one of the finest he has scored in his entire career.

It began yards from the Harlequins' own line, with Thresher hurling the ball out to Davies. The wing's pass aimed at Harriman was X-certificate, a shocker which could have lost Harlequins the match. Instead Harriman, one of the most graceful players in English rugby and one of the fastest, picked it up off his boots, one of countless instances of high skill in a classic match, and swept away downfield with his blistering pace. Salmon was in support, and outside him, ready and poised, his rugby brain having again read the situation like a book, was Carling.

The movement had been stunning, though a try was by no means certain. But it was inevitable once the youngster had cleverly swivelled his hips, turning an opponent first this way then that, and then powered past another with a strong hand-off. His strength took him to the line and he scored with an *élan* which had hallmarked Harlequins' approach. People stood up everywhere, and stayed on their feet; the pumping adrenalin from witnessing so outstanding a try was simply irresistible. At last, English players had shown just what they could do given the right preparation, motivation and opportunity to employ their talents. The draining experience in the World Cup the year before was forgotten in an instant.

Will Carling had scored two of Harlequins' three tries, and played a major role in their triumph. Yet, revealingly, the shy introverted young man was the only one not to lift the Cup when it was presented. But he listened carefully as Jamie Salmon, referring to the panache of the Harlequins' play, told a TV interviewer: 'It is what this country needs; guys to have the confidence to take people on.'

So ended the 1988 season in the northern hemisphere, though there was still the matter of a scheduled England tour to Australia and Fiji, beginning in May. For Carling, there was a problem: his final exams at Durham clashed with the dates of the tour. His request to the university authorities to delay the exam until he returned was refused, though they did agree to allow him to take the papers a few days early so that he could get to Australia, albeit late. Sam Stoker, principal of St Cuthbert's, the house for day students at the university, remembers the cloak and dagger operation the university mounted to make this possible. 'It was agreed that if he was met outside the exam room and taken straight to Newcastle airport and put on the London plane, he could sit his exams a few days before the rest of the students. I picked him up, and when he reached London he was met there, too, so that he would not pass on any information.'

Presumably the Durham authorities believed they had a spy of Oleg Gordievsky proportions on their hands, a man who would stop at nothing to feed back information on the examination papers to his waiting colleagues! By putting him on the first plane to Australia without so much as a telephone coming within his reach, they felt such a monumental risk could just about be taken. Poor Carling seems not to have been given the benefit of any doubt. He joined up with the England squad in time to play in only the last three games. England had lost the first Test in Brisbane 22–16, after which match Simon Halliday returned home. Neither he nor Carling had been able to make the full tour, Halliday for business reasons, but England suffered the inevitable consequences of disruption because of the unusual arrangement. Indeed, they faced a powerful New South Wales side soon after Halliday had gone and before Carling had arrived and become acclimatized, with the ludicrous result that Rob Andrew was pressed into playing at centre. England were hammered 23–12, and Geoff Cooke resolved there and then that no such nonsense would ever be allowed to occur again.

Carling finally appeared in the straightforward win over New South Wales B and was in the England side which lost the second Test 28–8 to Australia in Sydney. It was a disappointing English performance, but it underlined to England the yawning chasm in class between the two hemispheres. It was all very well to have a party at Ireland's expense in the Five Nations Championship, but such a record did not impress anyone much in Australia, and the scepticism of the scoffing, hard-drinking Aussie rugby fans was justified as the English wilted in both Tests.

There was a consolation, of sorts, with a 25–12 win over Fiji in Suva's steamy heat, but even here, the back-line stuttered like some old jalopy on a pot-holed

Fijian road. It had been, as *Rothmans Rugby Yearbook* concluded, 'a highly demoralizing tour'. Cooke was moderately satisfied with Carling's play in the last three games. 'He did all right under difficult circumstances. It was always going to be difficult for him joining the tour half-way through.'

England returned home with their playing fortunes at something of a crossroads. Carling, too, was about to embark on a new path.

8 A Lieutenant Exits, a Captain Emerges

'The harder you work, the luckier you get.'
South African golfer Gary Player

The British Army has made some monumental cock-ups in its long and intermittently distinguished history. Allowing the politicians to let it become embroiled in the chaos of Northern Ireland, where Protestant against Catholic makes Gloucester against Bristol look like a tea-party, would rank fairly high in that category. But whoever made the decision to accept William David Charles Carling's resignation from the Army after he had left Durham should be consigned to the guardhouse forthwith, and detained there indefinitely.

An international sportsman with the high profile of Carling should have been manna from heaven for the Army, who had put him through the basic tests comprising essays and lectures at the officer selection unit at Westbury. Carling was credible, intelligent. Earning a cadetship to Durham meant that, in the Army's words, he had to be quite good. Those securing that privilege are 'fairly rare animals', I was told. An Army uniform in the wardrobe might seem to have its advantages. When a girlfriend named Sophie decided that Will was no longer her favoured beau, Carling is said to have been dismayed. He came up with the idea of sending her a personal photograph of himself dressed immaculately – in his Army uniform. Alas, the young lady was not moved by such military dress. The love remained unrequited. But when Carling returned to England in the summer of 1988 from the national rugby team's tour of Australia, with seven caps to his name even though he was still only twenty-two, there occurred a mysterious parting of the ways between the military and the son of a military man.

He had represented the Army only twice in the Inter Services Championship. In the 1987 tournament, Officer/Cadet Carling played in the Army side which lost to the Royal Navy 21–10, but it was his only appearance of that Championship season. The next year, 2nd Lieutenant Carling helped the Army beat the RAF 26–3, again his only game of the competition. Then came the break-up. The official story goes that Carling was told he would not be able to play representative rugby. But that tells only half the story. Certainly, Carling was heading for a six-month intensive course in which new recruits are physically and mentally intimidated, day and night, night and day. Having a game or two of rugby in the middle of this mind-testing, physically exacting, prolonged examination is not quite the normal routine.

Lieutenant-Colonel M. J. Dickinson, the Army's representative on the Rugby Football Union, says: 'Will discovered his rugby programme didn't quite match with the Sandhurst programme.' Which was true. But was the intensity of the Sandhurst training course a factor in Carling's decision to come out? Dickinson admits: 'The first part of the course is very, very physically demanding. The idea is to break them down completely [the new recruits] and then build them up again. To start with, you have raw material. You are joining an Army; you cannot pussy-foot around. Will had never been through that course and it is essential that everyone does go through it. It lasted six to nine months in those days although it is now a year. But you cannot pop in and out of it.'

The latter point answers neatly whether Carling might have been allowed some special dispensation. He was, after all, likely to play for England. But the Army said no. And perhaps Carling was secretly relieved. Was he really suited to a life in the services? The son of an Army man, yes, but so what? Some sons of military men end up as New Age travellers. Carling, by universal agreement, was a shy, vulnerable young man. He could be moody. Were these the qualities for a young man entering a gruelling training course in which the first casualty is one's softer side?

Some souls fit like gloves into the brutal world of Army discipline and training. They revel in the harsh environment, which chews up and spits out its sensitive recruits like orange pips. Will Carling was not like that. He could be deeply wounded by personal criticism. He often found it hard to communicate with others; he was far removed from the kind of gregarious character which usually excels in an environment like the Army. I can think of few with qualities less suited to such a life, and the realization almost certainly also dawned on Carling himself.

If the rugby career was a convenient diversion, a smokescreen to blur the guidelines, the Army should never have become confused. A mere youngster he might have been, but the Army needed Carling far more than the young man needed them. The value of a leading sports personality to one of the services these days is inestimable. Just how many column inches of wonderful, positive newsprint Rory Underwood has secured for the Royal Air Force during his long and distinguished career as an England rugby player is impossible to tell. What is certain is that the RAF could not have bought such valuable promotion of its service had it lavished hundreds of thousands of pounds in straightforward advertising.

In our modern world, the image is everything. The sight of a famous, handsome, intelligent young man dashing down the wing for England at Twickenham, and indeed all over the world, is an outstanding advertisement for any of the services. The feature-length interviews abound when the sportsman is as successful as Rory Underwood. It comes to the point where it hardly matters just how good the sportsman actually is at his job – the picture painted is sufficient. In Will Carling, the Army had in its grasp potentially the most valuable source of self-promotion for decades. To allow such a huge advantage to slip through its fingers was an appalling indictment of the decision-making at the top.

Somehow, whatever the method, a suitable compromise could and should have been found. Carling was certainly distracted by the imminent arrival of the Australian rugby touring team that autumn of 1988 and the Five Nations Championship season after Christmas. The prospect of the British Lions tour to Australia the following summer was probably on his mind, too. This was all pretty understandable. The Army insisted that the Sandhurst course could not be interrupted. But even Army commanders sometimes have to compromise, and had they done so, those in authority would probably be bathing nightly by now in the pink gin or champagne supplied by a grateful colonel-in-chief. Nobody could have given the British Army a higher profile than Will Carling.

'There cannot be any short cuts in that course,' reiterates Lieutenant-Colonel Dickinson. 'They must do the training. But if it had been twelve months later, it would have been different.' Indeed so. By the time they realized the catastrophic cost of their intransigence, the Army had lost their man. But when Tim Rodber, another good rugby player who was to win international honours without ever approaching the same level as Carling in terms of class or exposure, explained to the Army that his rugby interests might prove difficult to arrange, he was accommodated. 'Perhaps the Army had learned their lesson,' a serving officer told me, a shade sadly.

The news from young Will that he wanted out was received within his own family with all the enthusiasm which doubtless greeted Prince Edward's 'I quit the Royal Marines' announcement at Buckingham Palace! But the opposition in the Carling household came surprisingly from Will's mother. 'Oh, no, you're not,' she is said to have replied. Bill Carling took a more philosophical line, promising to discuss it later with his son. But the boy was not for turning. It may well have cost as much as £8,000 to buy him out. Within a matter of months, the Army's disastrous decision was seen in an even worse light. Ex 2nd Lieutenant W. D. C. Carling was made captain of the England rugby team.

The long saga of the captaincy had bothered the national side for some seasons. Captains had been used like sticking plasters, one coming off and another being put on. Since Bill Beaumont had been forced by injury into premature retirement midway through the 1982 Five Nations season, England had been captained by eight different men in six years: Steve Smith, John Scott, Peter Wheeler, Paul Dodge, Nigel Melville, Richard Hill, Mike Harrison and John Orwin. None had ever hung around for much more than a season, and the lack of continuity was maintained right up to the autumn of 1988.

Geoff Cooke understood that there was an inherent problem. 'When we left out Harrison, Nigel Melville took over again as leader. Then when he got injured against Ireland, John Orwin was made captain and took the squad to Australia in 1988. But John was not a long-term prospect and I felt we needed someone who could hold the job perhaps right through to the 1991 World Cup, three years away. But here we were, about to start the 1988–9 season, and we thought, who are the candidates?'

Rob Andrew was their first choice. Andrew, a bright, communicative, well-presented and eminently approachable former Cambridge University student, fitted the bill in every respect bar one – he was not certain of his place. His international career had begun back in 1985 and by this time he had won twenty caps, which gave him as much experience as any other candidate, and a great deal more than some. But doubts were still being expressed, volubly in some quarters, concerning Andrew's right to be in the England side. His confidence had wavered between sound and unsure; it was not until he joined the 1989 British Lions as a replacement in Australia, and came under the coaching influence of Ian McGeechan, himself a former international threequarter, that Andrew blossomed.

'Rob was the obvious candidate in 1988 but he was struggling with his game,' says Cooke. 'Had we given it to him, he would have had the captaincy, the goal-kicking and his own game to worry about. It would have been far too much. We needed someone who was virtually certain of his place for the next few years.

Someone who had leadership qualities and who we thought could develop as a captain. Increasingly, Will Carling became a fairly obvious answer.'

But not to Geoff Cooke's colleagues. When he suggested Carling to his fellow selectors, there was a stunned silence. 'They thought I was crackers,' says Cooke. 'We talked it through for hours. But he had a degree of arrogance, confidence too. Arrogance as a player and he had obviously been a captain. He was a very astute guy who very quickly latched on to people. He was very good at assessing people and adapting his behaviour to how they responded to him and the needs of the situation. But it was very much embryonic rather than proven leadership.'

Very soon after his appointment, Carling made an early telephone call to one of his predecessors, Nigel Melville. 'Will was panicking a bit,' says Melville. 'He phoned and said, "They have made me England captain – what do I do?" Arrogant people do not do that. He realized people thought he was arrogant but I think he is self-confident and people mistake that for arrogance. It was quite obvious he was the outstanding player in the side. It certainly wasn't a big shock to me that they chose him. People like Winterbottom didn't expect to get it; he wasn't that type. Rob Andrew wasn't certain of keeping his place. He would have been the ideal choice at the time, for he had some caps. But there wasn't any certainty he would be around for very long. As I say, I wasn't surprised he was chosen; he was the obvious choice. My only reservations were his age and his immaturity at the time.'

Roger Uttley confirms that Carling was not the first choice. 'He came to the captaincy completely fortuitously. Had Rob Andrew come on earlier and Nigel

Melville not got injured when he did, it would probably all have been different. But we needed to give Rob time to rediscover his confidence. And Nigel was out of the running, finished.'

That often short but crucial period when momentous decisions are made remains in Uttley's mind concerning the decision taken by the England hierarchy. 'We raised Will's name and Geoff said to me, "What do you think?" I said, "What do you think?"' They swallowed hard and opted for the youngest man to captain England for fifty-seven years. P. D. Howard of Old Millhillians, in 1931, had been the previous holder of that particular record, though P.D. doubtless assumed the role for rather different reasons from W.D.C. Uttley adds: 'He was confident enough to disappear off into Paris on the Friday afternoon of his international début. That struck me as the act of a very confident young man. We felt he must be very cool and confident.'

The English management invested much time and thought in the process of settling in their new captain. He was invited not only to join the selectors over their deliberations on team selection, but to comment on individual players, their capacity to integrate and their potential. Once the season was over, he was to be asked to give his views to the RFU committee on England's performances. These were new planks in the system. For any England captain, this was uncharted territory – the inner sanctum had hitherto been barred to all outsiders. There was, possibly, an argument in favour of informing the RFU committee of the captain's views of the season as a whole. After all, anything which developed closer links between the players and those at the top of the tree was to be welcomed. Some mechanism for expressing the thoughts, the wishes, the frustrations and the

Proud captain of Terra Nova Junior School First XV

An early winner. Holding the Junior Water Polo cup at Sedbergh
(Sedbergh School Library)

The burst through, the jolting hand-off: Carling breaks the London defence; and the North clinch the Divisional Championship, 1986 *(Colorsport)*

Power play for Durham, the winners, against Bristol in the 1987 UAU Final
at Twickenham *(Colorsport)*

Overleaf
Big boys' league. Carling, caught in a
pincer movement, scored two tries as
Harlequins beat Bristol to win the
1988 John Player Cup final
(Colorsport)

Wallabies block Carling on his debut as
England captain, but he led his team to
a rare victory over Australia. England
28 Australia 19, Twickenham, 1988
(Russell Cheyne/Allsport)

The day English rugby touched perfection. Carling dives in for his side's
third try to complete a 26–7 rout of the French, 1990
(Russell Cheyne/Allsport)

grievances of the players was long overdue; rugby's authorities had kept this particular door barred for far too long.

Asking the captain to sit in on selection and give his views was another matter entirely. Traditionally the captain had only been involved in selection on tour. Bill Beaumont helped choose England teams when he led his country to the Far East in 1979 and to Argentina in 1981. He had also contributed some opinions, after being asked to do so, prior to the selection of the 1980 British Lions tour to South Africa, which he had known in February of that year he was to captain. But here were England asking a twenty-two-year-old who he thought would fit best into the squad or team. Beaumont believes the idea was quite wrong. 'I do not believe a captain has sufficient knowledge to name the correct people,' he says. 'If I had been asked, I would have probably ended up suggesting all my mates. That was because they were the players in the area where I was playing, the North-West, and were therefore the ones most familiar to me. At that time, leagues were not in place and so you played a number of local matches. I would not have known if there was a brilliant young centre coming through at Wasps, because I don't think we played Wasps, or if we did, we only saw them once a year.'

Under the league system, Carling did have a slightly better insight into other teams. But still, he could hardly have given a complete opinion on a player. Trying to assess a rival lock forward or No. 8 in a league match in which you are playing yourself is difficult enough. But you could never see him more than once a season, and forming impressions from that single meeting alone could be grossly misleading.

Still, the selectors put their faith in Carling from the

off. They gave him a nice gentle starter, too: Australia, at Twickenham. It was his first match as leader and he was the youngest player in the England side. And the match was on Guy Fawkes Day, which invited all sorts of ribald comments in the tabloid press about an explosive start for the ex-Army man. In fact this was plainly a below-strength Australian squad, for they arrived at Twickenham for the Test match with three defeats from their first six matches.

London Division had undermined their confidence at the first hurdle, out-running them in an orgy of attacking rugby masterminded by Dick Best, the same coach who had plotted Harlequins' Cup final success by similar means six months earlier. London, scoring three tries to one, were too fast for a surprised Australian side which had broken up after the 1987 World Cup and was missing such familiar names as Lynagh, Slack, Lawton, Poidevin and Tuynman. The North then beat them at Otley and the South-West quickly followed suit at Bristol.

Part of the cavalry had since appeared over the hill for Australia, Michael Lynagh flying in after injuries had left the party short on numbers and, more critically, on class. But the beach at Noosa, just outside Brisbane, is a whole lot different from Twickenham rugby ground in November, and not even Lynagh could acclimatize sufficiently quickly to prevent England winning the Test, 28–19. No matter, it was the manner of England's success which proved so invigorating and generated such optimism for the future. Taking their cue from London, they ran the ball at the Wallabies in a bold gambit, and, with most of the possession, for once made use of it. The number of days in recent times when England's rugby team had produced a performance to instil hope could have been counted on the hand of a chainsaw operator down on his luck. But this was manifestly one of them. Carling, who had been slightly concussed in a heavy collision, made the half break which put Simon Halliday away for the last English try. The new captain was then forced to retire.

The shock of losing to England, for renowned Pom-bashers, proved so instructive that Australia promptly swept through the remainder of their tour without another loss. They dismissed Scotland 32–13, and then overwhelmed the Barbarians 40–22. David Campese, the great sorcerer, picked up the tour by its lapels, scoring a brace of tries against both Scotland and the Barbarians.

A fundamental strut in their youth policy for the future, England had introduced the Harlequins lock forward Paul Ackford against Australia. He would be thirty-one early in the new year! A first cap it might have been, but Ackford played at once with a power, a command and an assurance which made one positively lament his long, lonely years in the wilderness of English club rugby. Everyone enjoys unearthing diamonds but it is quite difficult to do so if you are standing on them in hobnail boots and with blinkers over your eyes, which England had been doing for the better part of twenty years.

So English rugbymen wore their party hats at Christmas time and quaffed their champagne, confident that 1989 was going to herald a bright new dawn. Why not? The mighty Wallabies had been sent packing from the land, kangaroo tails firmly between legs, and there was an exciting new captain at the helm. Surely nothing could go wrong now? Which is doubtless what they said to the man on the bridge of the *Titanic*.

The reality was that England needed only until 18 March of the new year to demolish such notions with the impact of a sledgehammer. In that time, the span of the season's Five Nations Championship, England contrived to squander home advantage against Scotland, prevent France scoring at Twickenham for the first time in thirty-six years, and then commit hara-kiri once more in their biennial disaster journey to Cardiff. It was a season of alarming fluctuations in fortune, and the new captain must have wondered, quite rightly too, what sort of an old tub he'd taken command of.

The Scottish match dispelled, abruptly, all the myths about an English renaissance. It was a dour struggle, England snatching a 12–12 draw because Rob Andrew and Jonathan Webb kicked four of their eleven attempts at goal. Scotland scored the only try of the match, a suitably messy, fragmented act made possible by Webb spilling Chalmers's high kick. Jeffrey hoofed it on over the English line and just won the frantic race for the touchdown. Of such deeds, legends are plainly not made.

If England seemed to have tumbled all the way back to square one after that miserable performance, then Ireland, in Dublin, restored hope. 'This was a performance of character by England,' *Rothmans Rugby Yearbook* was to announce. Dooley and Ackford in the line-outs, ably assisted by Teague, Richards and Robinson in the back row, established a hard core on which England built their success.

Two weeks later, the unbeaten French arrived at Twickenham half-way to another Grand Slam. They left, like the Australians, humbled by the commitment, the determination and especially the discipline of the England side. An 11–0 victory was emphatic; and yet the last match of the season, from which a victory would have given England their first Championship since 1980, proved to be another exercise in the puncturing of self-belief. Wales were hopeless – they had lost their first three matches of the Championship and were desperate to avoid the ignominy of a whitewash. England, in terms of ability and skill, had the clout to wash Wales once and for all right out of their system. But once again, they lacked the nerve. Admittedly, the weather assisted the Welsh, incessant rain turning it into a dog of a day. Wales were somehow lifted from the gutter of complete failure by the hands of two men: veteran lock forward Robert Norster, one of the finest practitioners of line-out play seen in British rugby for twenty years, and scrum-half Robert Jones.

The latter was Carling's old nemesis from the attempt of the England Schools side in 1983 to win the junior Grand Slam. That day, just up the valley from Cardiff at Pontypridd, Jones and his colleagues had thwarted English aspirations with a narrow victory. Now, at the National Stadium, Norster's complete dominance of line-out possession and Jones's astute employment of it – a series of high kicks which hung, death-like, above and behind the English defence all afternoon – were sufficient to win the match.

Even then, it required a try which plainly was not touched down properly, by the Welsh centre Mike Hall, to win the game. But as at Twickenham at the start of the season, the try was created by an English aberration: Underwood hurled a slippery, soggy ball at Webb who promptly dropped it, this time allowing Emyr to kick ahead (just as Jeffrey had done at Twickenham) for the crucial score. For the first, but not the last time at Cardiff, English eyes burned into

Rory Underwood's back long after the moment had passed.

The complete season had been a learning process for the new captain. He had leaned heavily on the experience of those around him: men like Dooley and Andrew, who had been there since 1985, Underwood, a year longer still, and Richards, a colossus for his club. You could glimpse Carling's anxiety at times, the frowning expression searching for an answer, like an anxious mother looking for a child. But that was to be expected, given his youth. Captaining England Schools is one thing, but leading the senior national side before a Twickenham capacity crowd requires, well, a strong will. It was no detriment to his brand of leadership; indeed, it was the way the England management had seen it happening. 'We never expected him to be a perfect leader from the word go,' said Roger Uttley. 'But if he maintained his form then he was the man for us.' Geoff Cooke agreed. 'He started off with that *Boy's Own* comic strip victory over Australia. The crowd took to him because of his part.'

Well, partly. The fact was that England rugby followers shared the mood of the nation in the dark days of 1940. They were desperate for a victory, any sort of victory. How it came about was largely immaterial; spirits were so low that no matter the narrowness of a win, it would be remembered simply as the day England won. When the Australians were beaten at Twickenham, the collective sigh of relief was sufficient to launch a hot-air balloon.

Those allied to English rugby had endured long years of frustration and failure in the relationship; now they yearned for a change in their fortunes. Anyone would have been welcomed royally had he delivered a victory.

Carling, of course, was not the instigator of this revival in the national rugby team's fortunes, but he presided over it on the field. That brought him a kudos when England won and initially, when they stumbled, an understanding through his palpable lack of experience and obvious youth. In a sense, he could not lose.

Supporters had become virtually immune to the pain of defeat. Wales were regarded as well nigh unbeatable, particularly at Cardiff. This was all very well when Welsh teams took the field with the likes of Gareth Edwards, Barry John, J. P. R. Williams and Phil Bennett among their ranks. All the Welsh forwards had to do, assuming they were good enough, was win the ball and just run towards the half-way line from where the match would re-start, after an outstanding score scripted by the brilliance of their backs.

Even when Wales fell from eminence, some of their representatives during the 1980s being no more than a weak shadow of the former giants, still the legend lived on. In English eyes, at least. Everyone else began to beat Wales; Ireland qualified for the freedom of the National Stadium after winning there in 1985, 1987, 1989 and 1993. On their other visit, in 1991, they drew. Scotland beat them seven times out of eleven from 1981 to 1991; the French had won every single match between the nations, home and away, since 1982. Most have been public floggings. For England, it was different. So the 1989 defeat was seen in a more placatory light. Defeat had been disappointing, or so the official line ran, but at least England had only been beaten once all season. Furthermore, although the Championship was close, sufficient progress had been made to dull the memory of an opportunity that had slipped away.

The more realistic, brutal assessment was that

Carling's side had let slip their first chance of a Five Nations Championship title by losing to the worst team in the tournament. By only three points, admittedly, but this was to set a pattern for near misses in the coming years. At work at its root was the English philosophy of accepting defeat in the right spirit of the occasion. French supporters at Parc des Princes welcome opposing sides like the mob, Louis XVI and his acolytes; the Welsh have a raw, gut expectation of victory. The rise of Scottish nationalism in recent years has elevated expectations to demands for a home win at Edinburgh, and the Irish have suffered long adversity in the fortunes of their national side with a phlegmatic air. English rugby is still filled with, and supported by, legions of honest folk who can enjoy victory but accept defeat in a philosophical manner unknown in Paris or Cardiff. It's part of the English way. If England win, it's jolly nice and you feel better. But if they lose, well, it's nothing unusual. People will still turn up next time.

Attempting to cast aside this attitude, which tolerated moderation and rarely castigated good losers, was the chief task facing the Cooke/Uttley regime. Their will to win had to be carried on to the field by every player, not least their captain. In part, Carling's inexperience was responsible for the loss of a Championship in 1989; another captain, sensing the course of events with a wiser, more knowledgeable eye, might have altered the tactics. The alternative view is that England, still a new side in creation, allowed itself to be dragged down into a Welsh dogfight. The hype, the myth – everything got to them. Their inexperience was critical. And all season their captain had been struggling with a secret injury.

England sides of old had prepared for the Championship on the Friday night before the first game over a couple of gin and tonics and a four-course supper. Nowadays, such antics are as redundant as the British manufacturing base. The idea prior to the 1989 Five Nations tournament was to spend some days in the warm weather of Portugal, going through physical tests and laying careful plans. Training in warmer climes lessened the risk of muscle strains or pulls at that time of year. But the plans threatened to come rapidly to grief when the new captain felt a stab of pain in his left leg after a running session. It was to be diagnosed as a shin splints condition, and although he managed to get through the Five Nations season it then flared up and cost him the British Lions place he had earned for the tour of Australia that summer. Jeremy Guscott, who had announced his glorious talent to the wide sporting world when he replaced Carling for the match against Romania in Bucharest that May, took his place in the British Lions tour party.

Carling, forced to remain inactive at home, unwisely agreed to accept an offer as a TV pundit when the BBC beamed coverage of the Test matches from Australia. It was a crass mistake. Clearly, and quite rightly, he did not want to criticize colleagues and friends in public. But in accepting such a role he should have realized the necessity for adverse criticism, where appropriate. Had he not wished to be critical on occasions, he should not have become involved. The compromise position he sought to adopt was pitifully embarrassing and served no purpose to anyone.

Chris Rea, host of the BBC TV coverage at the studio in London, says: 'I never wanted to go for Will in that role. Only because I think it is unfair to put players in that position. I do not blame Will for seeking to avoid criticism of colleagues. He did relax more when he did the job for the second and third Tests but there was a positive story to tell from those games because the Lions won. In the first Test they were appalling and should not have escaped criticism. But that put Will in a very, very difficult position and I sympathized with him.'

The story did not end there, however. One national newspaper rugby correspondent, who was in Australia covering the tour, somehow acquired the quite erroneous impression that Carling had been critical of the Lions players, and promptly wrote the story. Both the Lions and, especially, Carling were extremely upset. When the hack realized his mistake he immediately offered his apologies to Carling, both publicly and in private. But he received in return a coolness for some time.

The bitter irony for Carling was that the Lions turned the series around, after losing the first Test, when they introduced a pack of Englishmen into their team for the second Test. Dooley, Teague, Andrew and Guscott had all missed the first international for different reasons, but now they were to play highly influential roles first in levelling the series, with victory in Brisbane, and then in winning it, albeit narrowly 19–18, in the final Test back at Sydney (Dooley excepted by then, due to injury). Eight of the side which won the vital second Test were Englishmen; just three were from Wales. Such a statistic underlined the difference in ability at that time between the two nations and further emphasized the calamity of England's Championship-influencing loss to the Welsh four months earlier.

For Will Carling it should have been a Championship to start his captaincy. There was a sorrow in his reflections. But if the opening season of his leadership had come within an ace of ultimate triumph, with all the accompanying frustration and anguish, what was to follow was a journey into dark days such as he had never known in his entire sporting life. It was to leave scars which would take years to heal.

9 Grand Slammed!

'Only those who dare to fail greatly can ever achieve
  greatly.'

Robert Kennedy

We're at the end of the runway, and BA flight 4833
starts to roll for take-off. But it's not the familiar feeling;
no quickening of the pulse, no anxious look shot out of
the window at either side of the 757 aircraft. No nervous
expression on our faces. Just nothing. We bump through
some low cloud as we climb away, but nothing registers,
there is no message from our minds.

They come to offer champagne, white wine, red wine.
But we fob them off, as quickly and briefly as possible.
Conversation is the last act we wish to conduct. We feel
like victims of a mugging – wanting to be left alone,
hoping fervently that no one will raise the subject. But
then, as we descend for London, someone does. It slaps
us in the face with the impact of a cold, wet fish. 'Ladies
and Gentlemen, thank you for flying British Airways
tonight. To those of you who were at the match today
at Murrayfield, let me say "Well done" to Scotland.'

There it is. Laid before us, so that none can escape
its torment. The Scottish passengers emit a loud roar;
the English, to a man, bury their heads and contemplate
the darkness below. Scotland 13, England 7. It doesn't
sound too dramatic, outlined simply in letters and
numbers. It could mean anything, really. To those who

inhabit the world outside sport, it might be some sort of code. But to those who filled Murrayfield on the afternoon of 17 March 1990, it is a bald scoreline they will never forget.

Time, they say, dulls even the sharpest of pain. But the disappointment remains. For those of us at the match, partisanship is virtually impossible to avoid. The followers of victor or vanquished would say precisely the same. Officials, writers, supporters from England all felt the wrenching dismay of failure. For those involved, especially the England captain, Will Carling, defeat and the loss of a confidently anticipated Grand Slam was the bitterest of blows. 'Carling,' said a close colleague at Harlequins, 'was affected for over two years by the memory of that defeat. Because of all the criticism of the defeat and the fact that he knew he had made some poor decisions.'

We fled Edinburgh in a manner reminiscent of the exodus from New Zealand after the final Test of the 1983 British Lions tour. Once the All Blacks, their notorious efficiency crushing the demoralized, weary Lions 38–6 in the fourth and final Test in Auckland, had completed the execution, the competition devised by some members of the British press corps swung into action: who could catch the first plane out of the place. It was a variation on *Challenge Anneka*. The winner lifted off from Auckland airport, bound for Fiji, from where he would file his Sunday newspaper story, within ninety minutes of the tour's last whistle. It would have been an almighty story if the plane had crashed. First Eden Park, Auckland; now Murrayfield had induced the same kind of desire for flight. No point in hanging around, best to get home – always better to handle one's grief in private.

Had it really been only a game? Not to the hordes of fanatical Scots, some of whom even now mocked us as we prepared to touch down once more on English soil. That slow, sinister walk from the tunnel at Murrayfield by the Scottish team before the start, every step a dagger of intent, thrust coldly, deliberately into the heart of each English intruder in the ground. Until that moment, it had seemed likely to be just an extension of England's season so far. What a season. Fiji had been swatted, like some irritating, irrelevant fly, 58–23 at Twickenham in November; the Irish had been dispatched by 23 points without reply (a Carling try included), and by universal agreement, England had not played especially well. Perfection followed, in Paris. The first half, by the end of which Carling's coolly commanding men led 13–0 in one of the most one-sided forty-minute spells of international rugby I could recall, was peerless. 'England's first half performance was as close to perfection as one can come,' I wrote in the *Observer* the following day. It was marvellous to watch.

It ended 26–7, France's finest destroyed on the rugby field like some of its city that day by the killer gales. It was, beyond dispute, one of the best England performances in living memory. It was Carling, diving through the broken ranks of the French defence for his side's last try, who provided a fitting testimony to the greater pace, the superior alacrity and verve, which had hallmarked England's win. 'The side that day really put the 1980 team in the shade for the first time,' said Roger Uttley. He was qualified to make such an assertion: he had played in Bill Beaumont's Grand Slam winning side ten years earlier. He added: 'This is the next great England team.' So it seemed.

The gourmet feast was not over yet. Wales, for so

long the cruel tormentors, were invited to Twickenham and then tortured before 60,000 witnesses. All the long years of failure at the hands of the Welsh were banished from the subconscious as four tries, three of them converted, and four penalty goals were hammered into the Welsh body like a stake through the heart.

Scotland, then, were the last lambs destined for the English slaughterhouse. And surely a slaughter it would be. The Scots had trailed Ireland in Dublin for most of the match, before slithering home 13–10 winners. A poor French team fell 21–0 at Murrayfield, victims chiefly of their own indiscipline, for lock Alain Carminati was sent off. Wales, 9–10 behind for a time in the second half at Cardiff, bluntly dismissed any notions of a Scottish triumph over England when their opponents could prise out only a 13–9 win at the National Stadium.

So for the first time ever, two unbeaten British sides met for every honour, mythical and actual, associated with the tournament: the Five Nations Championship title, the Grand Slam, the Triple Crown and the Calcutta Cup. The two camps could not have been more different: Scottish sobriety, practicality and pride against English dash, elegance and expectation – especially the latter.

Ian Wooldridge summed it up in the *Daily Mail*: 'England burst on to the field like an SAS hit squad. Scotland came out in measured single file, ominously self-possessed, an invisible Piper Laidlaw VC at their head. Whoever dreamed up the theory of body language was vindicated. The tension was numbing and not a ball had been kicked yet. Readers not privileged to be present may think it absurd to write thus of a mere football match. But this was not a mere football match. I am nonplussed to define precisely what it was but it certainly embraced ancient history, modern politics and the constant personas of Anglos and Celts.'

The English camp had been confident. 'We just did not anticipate defeat,' the English fly-half Rob Andrew was to say, much later. Nor did his colleagues. For it was England who had played all the great rugby of the season, eleven tries rattling past the bewildered, puffing defences inadequately assembled by Ireland, France and Wales. Would they do it? Of course. It was just a matter of by how many points, wasn't it? When England breezed through training twenty-four hours before the match, the portents were alarming for Scotland. Carling was to write afterwards with a touch of obvious pride: 'Our last training session . . . went very well indeed. I don't think there was a ball dropped in forty-five minutes of really good work. Our moves were neatly executed, and everyone was concentrating to the full.'

Alas, matches are won on match-days, not at the final training session. England lost at Murrayfield for one principal reason. They under-estimated Scotland. It was Bannockburn revisited. There was an air of complacency, induced by the comfort with which they had moved to the brink of a Grand Slam. No side had troubled them for twelve months; the passage of time had allowed them to become complacent. Even in the defeat at Cardiff, they were plainly the best side on paper. For two seasons, apart from eighty minutes in Wales and now eighty minutes in Scotland, no side had been comparable with Carling's team.

But there were plenty of sporting precedents for failing to 'show', as the Australians call it, on the big occasion. Ken Rosewall, that marvellously talented Australian tennis player, contested – and lost – four

Wimbledon men's singles finals in his career. Greg Norman, the possessor of one of the world's most exciting golfing talents in the last fifty years, had won just a single 'major' in his long and distinguished career by mid-1993. His failures, when the temperature of competition was searingly hot, cost him a US Masters title, a US Open title and another Open Championship.

This ability to experience the heat of competition and prosper despite its ferocity divides the great competitors from the good. No better illustration of the former category exists than Nick Faldo, who drew on raw courage and determination to haul himself back from the depths of depression at imminent disaster to win the 1992 Open Championship title. Nor was that the first time Faldo had demonstrated that he possessed such an arrow in his quiver: in America, at the Masters, he had emphasized the point conclusively by shutting out the hugely popular challenge of the veteran US player Ray Floyd, amid the jangling nerves of a play-off.

It's the same with the greatest teams; they can 'front up' to adversity, staring it in the face without blinking. And by doing so, they emerge, drained certainly but justifiably fêted, in the halls of sport where only the supreme stroll. Manifestly, England blinked first at Murrayfield. The passion of the Scots caught them by surprise; they reacted like animals, prodded by the electric stun gun. There was instant uncertainty, a disorientation which their enemies exposed to the utmost effect. Scotland were all over them, like a rash: tackling, taunting, ribbing, niggling – above all, competing. The glorious wide open spaces the Irish, French and Welsh had offered England now vanished. There was a photograph used on the cover of the next *Rothmans Rugby Union Yearbook* which conveyed perfectly, without the need for a single word, the story of Murrayfield. Carling is caught by David Sole from the front, by Derek Turnbull from the rear; Tony Stanger bars his path to the front, Chris Gray stands behind, set to pounce. The pincer in which England's captain is caught was England's plight for eighty minutes. No room, no space, no time, no chance for thought, no opportunity to break the pattern. No hope.

Challenge flared from every Scottish nostril, fire from each mouth. The sacrifice of bodies for the national cause was always a more natural function to Scottish minds than to English ones. Politicians, sitting in judgement at Westminster, might do their worst in blighting Scottish lives; the swaggering English might have come sure in the knowledge of triumph. But proud Edward's army had been sent packing once; now it was the duty, the honour, of every Scot on the battlefield to vanquish this modern-day English challenge.

Teams under this sort of pressure begin to implode. England did not challenge convention. Now their young captain revealed all his comparative inexperience, his lack of a wise, experienced head, as his team began to fret and fray at the edges. He failed to grasp that single points in this kind of tight contest were like sandbags against the rampant river; perhaps just one extra would prove crucial in the final analysis. Certainly they would prove psychologically valuable. For that reason, the decision to run a series of penalties close to the Scottish line in the first half was fatally flawed. This was a policy of inadvisable adventure, an elegant flourish of the sword when all that was required was a short stab.

Carling tried to defend himself afterwards, amid a welter of accusations and charges. 'A major talking point has been our not kicking at goal when we had penalties in the right-hand corner in the first half. Some have said that Brian Moore overruled me – that's not true. I wanted to run the ball. The only question was how we ran it. Then, later, we opted for scrums on the line, when we might have got three points through a kick at goal. Well, it would have been a hard kick from the right-hand side, into a strong wind. We were only 6–4 down. We had a pressure position.'

This argument was shot through with inconsistencies. First, the view that Carling was in full and complete charge of his team was not shared by those watching from the sidelines, nor by the Scottish captain, who was even closer at hand. Terry O'Connor, then rugby correspondent of the *Daily Mail* and the most experienced of the English pressmen in attendance, wrote pointedly: 'While the Scots played to the referee's command, England were petulant and undisciplined and conceded penalty points as a result. Often they bickered among themselves and at times it seemed there were three captains on the field. Carling's ability as a centre of world class is without question, but there must now be doubts about his captaincy ability. His forwards repeatedly took the wrong options without reprimand.'

David Sole, recalling his proudest day as Scotland's captain, remembered that single-file walk on to the pitch in his lively autobiography, *Heart and Sole*: 'For Will and his boys the emotional torture was only just beginning.' And, more revealingly, he wrote: 'A couple of hours beforehand, she [his wife Jane] and the other Scottish wives and girlfriends had been in the foyer of the Carlton Highland hotel in Edinburgh with their English counterparts. Jenny Ovens, Scott Hastings's then girlfriend, now wife, had said in a spirit of camaraderie to the English girls: "Good luck. And may the best team win." "We will," had come the reply from the English wives' party. They had obviously digested the pre-match hype in the same way as had done, I suspect, their "better halves".'

Sole added: 'England had been given a number of penalty chances but with Brian Moore and Will Carling apparently in some disarray as to who was calling the shots, they opted to run or scrummage them rather than taking shots at goal. I think the no kick decision by Will and/or Brian was wrong. Had I been in their position I would have kicked for goal. The wind wasn't too bad and we now know that Simon Hodgkinson was more than willing to have a shot.'

Witness for the prosecution, No. 2. Steve Bale, writing in the *Independent*, said: 'Carling preferred to run penalties at Scotland into the wind, but the moves were executed at such tortuous speed that they played into the hands of the Scots' voracious defence. The psychological effect was overwhelming. The decision not to try for goal with the score at 6–4 to Scotland suggested complacency, and its complete failure meant that England derived nothing from a protracted period of first half pressure.'

Mick Cleary, in the *Observer*, also indicted them: 'Twice in the first half they [England] spurned kicks at goal from only twenty metres, electing instead to rumble at the line. Confidence is one thing: cockiness another.'

No accusation here that each correspondent seemed to be watching a quite different game.

Robin Marlar, in the *Sunday Times*, employed a historical analogy. 'Did England really think if they threw themselves at the Scots from a tapped penalty they would carry all before them? Thus, in their wisdom, did English generals murder a generation in the First World

War.' And Stephen Jones, rugby correspondent of the *Sunday Times*, added pertinently: 'Nor did they [England] help themselves by electing to run four kickable penalties in the first half alone. They were playing against a stiff breeze and Simon Hodgkinson is not a long-range goalkicker. Nevertheless, he should have been called up each time, and on several occasions it seemed that Carling was having trouble wielding his authority.'

The truth was that England had no authority in their play that day, from their captain or from anyone else. We were into the headless chicken syndrome. Carling's contribution as captain was ephemeral, lightweight. Furthermore, his apparent lack of faith in Hodgkinson, his side's goalkicker, was curious coming just six weeks after the same player had kicked brilliantly at Parc des Princes, landing four penalty goals and a conversion in a swirling gale. The wind in Paris had been ten, perhaps twenty times stronger than at Murrayfield. To emphasize his value to the side, Hodgkinson had then kicked another four penalty goals and converted three of his team's four tries against Wales. If this was insufficient as a c.v. to get the job at Murrayfield, then heaven knows what sort of qualifications Carling was looking for.

The fact that eluded Carling, for three years a student of psychology, was that the psychological damage to the Scots caused by England leading at half-time, even by a single point at 7–6, would have been enormous. Scotland had enjoyed first use of the wind; to have reached half-time trailing, with that advantage gone, could have broken their spirit. With Scotland leading 6–4, it was essential that England get points on the board. That fact and the psychological impact of the kick, if successful, putting them into the lead, was completely overlooked by the England captain. For the son of a military man, the strategy was sadly awry.

Clearly the experience hurt Carling deeply. 'Then we had to endure the criticism afterwards, one of the most painful experiences in sport,' he wrote later. 'Trying to come to terms with the public perception of our defeat is one of the most difficult things I've had to go through. It's been a harrowing two days.' And it was to be a harrowing two years, looking further down the track. The sore festered, refusing to heal. Another of Carling's remarks demonstrated vividly the wound to his pride. 'It has been said that if these two sides had played ten times, England would have won nine times.' It was the classic retort of the petulant schoolboy, knocked flat in a playground fight and getting to his feet, bloodied, to bleat at his assailant: 'I'll get you next time.'

Murrayfield, 1990, was where Geoff Cooke's audacious decision to make a twenty-two-year-old his captain for the long-term future failed. When England ruled the roost, as they frequently did in the early days of Carling's captaincy, there was no problem. The boy could learn the job and no one was sufficiently mighty to throw a spanner into the smooth-running England machine. But when someone did manage to do just that – and the Scots did it extremely effectively at Murrayfield – the vehicle stalled.

Cooke defends his captain by attempting to apportion the blame. 'We made it very clear to the players the captain does not carry the can for all the decisions made on the field. There were a lot of experienced players out there. In terms of altering tactics during a game, that is never down to one person. Others should be seeing things, recognizing what is going well and wrong. That is why we were able to defend the position in Scotland. If tactically we were felt to be naïve, don't put it all down to the captain. Others had lots of input. There was no guarantee Hodgkinson would have kicked the goal. All these things are easy with hindsight. The crucial part was the second half, where we had total domination of the game. Scotland never got in the England 22 with the ball in hand. But Scotland defended like tigers and we made some poor options: we had only ourselves to blame.'

But come on, who's kidding who here? Captaincy isn't like that. It never was. Listen to Clem Thomas, rugby correspondent for the *Observer* for years and a former captain of Wales who also skippered the British Lions on a couple of occasions. 'I remember leading the Lions once during our tour of South Africa in 1955. We were playing Natal and were in some trouble. One of the Irish lads in the team came up to me and said, "We must change and do it this way." I said, "Shut up, this is what we are going to do." I wanted a high kick hoisted to the Natal line. We drove in hard after it, won the ball and scored. If I'd listened to that idiot who wanted to do something completely different, we'd have lost. You have to make strong decisions as captain. The moment a captain is undermined by people around him, he is in trouble. You have to be very tough as a captain: it's a hell of a burden. One guy only can captain a side, not half a dozen.'

The trouble with a policy of collective leadership concerns what happens when there are dissenting voices in the heat of the battle. No time for a debate, and whose view prevails? If others are to be prey to a general indictment should things go wrong, then why not let their opinion be the one which decides? But captains – real, authoritative leaders – never ruled by consensus. They might ask for an opinion, but the decision was always theirs. The US 3rd Army did not sweep through Europe in the Second World War, smashing aside all German opposition, with General Patton, its commander, holding a debate at every road junction as to the best way forward. Nor did his lieutenants either make decisions themselves or take the rap if things went wrong. He was in command, he made the decisions. The buck stopped at his doorstep.

Cricket is a completely different sport, one which allows more time for reflection. But Mike Brearley epitomized the art of firm leadership when he captained England. An opinion might be quietly proffered, indeed sought. But the final word was the captain's; quickly, when required, and decisively. Will Carling was twenty-four when he led England at Murrayfield, 1990, in the Grand Slam encounter. Few young men are worldly, decisive leaders at twenty-four. As Senator Lloyd Bentsen said, witheringly, to Vice-President-elect Dan Quayle during a US vice-presidential election debate in the 1980s: 'Senator, you're no Jack Kennedy.' Will Carling is no General Patton.

Geoff Cooke calls it 'the first major crisis of Carling's captaincy'. He adds: 'The criticism got to him then.' So deeply, in fact, that Carling reacted dramatically. He pondered seriously, and at much length, whether to relinquish the captaincy – and came close to doing so. It had all built up, like a queue of angry customers in front of a shopkeeper. Carling was faced with criticism in the media, grumbles from disenchanted England supporters and whispers from fellow players. Was he good enough? Could he captain effectively? Look at the mistakes he'd made under pressure at Murrayfield; when would England actually win something? The dejection of ultimate failure after the elation of earlier successes was hard to bear. Carling pondered every angle, every course of action. It was a desperately unhappy time for him. That old silver spoon suddenly seemed badly tarnished.

Cooke confirms: 'He had some thoughts about giving up the captaincy. He got tired of the constant media interest. He was under the spotlight: the blue-eyed boy. Everyone wanted him, but then of course that created jealousies and envy from others. Being English, being confident, the Celtic fringe got into him. He is not easy to get to know; quite a private sort of person. But we talked about it and he came out of that.'

A close colleague at Harlequins confirms that Carling considered quitting. 'It is true he wanted to give up the captaincy. Several days after the defeat at Murrayfield, he was still considering it. He was morose at the time.' It was not just the disastrous outcome to a season in which England had played some outstanding rugby that persuaded Carling to question whether he wanted to continue as leader. There had been rumblings of disagreement over a period of time between the RFU and representatives of the England team, over the vexatious matter of rewards for players. At the heart of this debate lay some long-enshrined rules which divided generations.

The elders, those who saw their role as the guardians of a game they had known and admired all their lives, stood shoulder to shoulder against change. Waving the banner of rebellion were the modern generation, the current players, who saw themselves playing a sport which had changed out of all recognition, so that to continue to call it amateur risked charges under the Trade Descriptions Act.

One simply could not draw any kind of corollary line between the game played years ago and the one played now. The best players, like Will Carling, were professionals in all but name. They did not receive a wage for playing, but they embraced every other element of the professional code each day of their lives. They trained virtually daily, they sought counsel on what they should eat, they avoided drink and they went to bed early whenever a match loomed. It was more like a monk's life than an amateur sportsman's, and when players began to be rebuffed in their requests for some minor rewards, hackles rose. Not unreasonably, either: a big rich cake was being divided up, and the administrators were gorging themselves. The players, whom everyone had come to see, were not even being offered crumbs.

None of them wanted money. They were not as crude as that. Carling stated his own views emphatically in his book *Captain's Diary*, published in 1991. 'I never want to be paid for taking the pitch. I still play because I enjoy it . . . But I think the RFU will have to relax the rules in other areas. I don't see any harm in a few players being able to make pocket money out of endorsements. The sums won't be large, and it'll only affect a handful of players at the top.'

This seemed a perfectly moderate viewpoint. Any sober-minded, neutral observer living outside the world of sport would not have understood the fuss. Most onlookers were bewildered that even such minuscule 'rewards' could be denied to players who contributed so generously to their club and their country. To suggest that any concession of that nature would irrevocably end rugby's unique spirit was to talk gibberish. It wouldn't make a fig of difference. Would people really refuse to attend future England internationals if Will Carling was receiving a few thousand pounds for promoting a clothes range? Would the sponsors walk away from association with a sport which had elevated their company's name into orbit in the commercial world, just because Rob Andrew might be advertising a particular motor car? Hard as it is to believe as we stand on the verge of the twenty-first century, these views are still seriously propounded today in some quarters. Carling was not alone in wondering whether he needed so much hassle from people who were simply out of touch with reality.

Such talk from England players, and especially from the England captain, seen traditionally as whiter than white, was as welcome in the RFU committee rooms as a petition to abolish the monarchy. The views of the committee were expressed, firmly and resolutely, to Carling. 'Someone at the RFU had had a go at him. It was to do with the promotion side of things,' said a close friend at Harlequins. 'He was told that unless he shaped up, they would get rid of him as England captain. That shook him. It had been taken out of Geoff Cooke's hands. It was because of the things he had said about the way the players wanted to organize some promotional things.'

Carling's old uncertainties emerged once more, the insecurities crept back into his subconscious, as he pondered whether to quit the captaincy – an act which he must surely have known would create an explosion of publicity. Losing the Grand Slam in Scotland had been the greatest setback of his young and almost constantly successful life. That he considered quitting at the first major reversal underlined emphatically his fragile confidence. This was hardly the action of the archetypal rugbyman, empowered by self-confidence, disregarding adversity. On the contrary, it showed the very different characteristics, the enormous sensitivity, which lay behind England's young rugby captain. He was truly a man apart.

According to Uttley, Carling would have preferred Halliday to Hodgkinson in his side. Hodgkinson possessed an extraordinary ability as a goalkicker, his fourteen caps between 1989 and 1991 producing for his country an astonishing 203 points and winning for England several matches they would otherwise have lost. But Carling had tried to persuade Geoff Cooke and Roger Uttley to choose as full-back Simon Halliday, the Bath player who was his long-time friend. Carling's reaction to the selectors' refusal of the idea revealed to Uttley another part of the young captain's make-up.

'Will had the idea of converting Simon Halliday to full-back,' says Uttley. 'We went to see a match somewhere and then had a committee meeting afterwards. The idea was well discussed but it was out-voted. Will didn't say a word after that for a time. Then he said, "I have been let down." It was as though he felt personally slighted that we hadn't gone along with his idea. He thought he knew best. That was the first time I saw another side to him. He had only ever been successful. When you are used to going out and achieving things it is hard to understand why people might be reticent and are not particularly enthusiastic for your ideas. I wouldn't criticize him for that. He had no experience of being thwarted; he was in the spoiled child syndrome.'

An increasingly disillusioned child, too. By now, W. D. C. Carling had become so high profile that his every move, on and off the rugby field, was being minutely dissected. He was imprisoned in the goldfish bowl with the world staring in. Events in the summer of that dramatic year, 1990, were to offer him little respite.

10 Pain in the Pampas: An Overture for Triumph

'He has gained every point who has mixed practicality with pleasure.'

Horace, 65–8 BC

Ten years short of the twenty-first century, international rugby union players were in trouble. They had been hijacked, perfectly legally, by the game's administrators, and manoeuvred into a situation where, in the words of the erudite former Australian coach Alan Jones, they had become 'mobile banks'. This was a charge hard to repudiate. Run-of-the-mill international matches were now grossing sums in excess of one million pounds for the host unions, an extraordinary figure that reflected the explosion of interest in the sport. Attending major matches, until then an activity most people could take or leave, became *de rigueur*. The West car park at Twickenham, with its hampers, its car boots filled with bottles of wine, Scotch and champagne and the commercial tents operated by companies such as Guinness, had become as fashionable as the lawns at Wimbledon or the riverside at Henley. Whole stadiums were being transformed at vast expense purely through the efforts of thirty unpaid sportsmen, whom thousands flocked to watch and countless others sat crouched around television sets to see. Had shares been available in this growth industry, huge over-subscription would have been certain.

For the authorities, this was a wondrous scenario, the answer to their every prayer. The old stadiums in which they sat began to disappear, section by revamped section, and swish, contemporary new edifices rose in their place. Out went the old wooden benches, the splinters-in-the-bottom specialists; in came new plastic tip-up seats. Officials who had been confined to working in cramped, old-fashioned offices deep in the bowels of the old stadiums now sat back in softly padded chairs and surveyed plush, roomy, individual offices into which the sun poured. And all this because one major winter sport became infested with the hooligan element, causing thousands silently to desert it, and rugby suddenly woke up to the fact that self-marketing might actually pay dividends.

The outcome was good for everyone – well, almost everyone. Treasurers of the Home Unions in Britain and Ireland saw their balance sheets transformed, first by increased ticket revenue but then, more propitiously, through the sponsorship support of large international companies. Spectators enjoyed better facilities at the cathedrals of the sport in the northern hemisphere, and officials were able to invest more money in updating facilities for corporate hospitality, media requirements and other associated needs. The money continued to flow in. A small detail: in 1988 it was possible to purchase a match programme for an England international for 60 pence. By 1994 it cost £2, a rise of 223 per cent in just six years – some inflation. Only the salaries of the privileged élite, the chairmen of privatized industries, could match that level of increase.

There was, however, one group which did not benefit:

the players. The ones who actually put bums on seats received no tangible advantage whatsoever. True, they could now invite their girlfriends or wives to an international weekend, and the authorities would pick up the tab for accommodation and the meal on Saturday night. But the women still couldn't sit in the same room as their menfolk for dinner. They had to be partitioned off in another area of the hotel, presumably so as to avoid infecting the main event of the evening with talk other than rugby. Curiously enough, this quaint, monolithic practice had long since been abandoned in the country where the macho male is supposed to rule like a medieval king – Australia.

Modern players, almost to a man, long for such a radical innovation to be tried in this part of the world. Rather than collecting their women at around eleven o'clock after they had dined alone, most wish to share their company for the whole evening. But that would be a perk too much, an innovative step too great for those who wield the real power in the game. They regard theirs as a private club, to be shielded from outsiders. The fact that a straw poll of the players would produce an overwhelming majority in favour of inviting women seemed of no consequence.

Some on the Rugby Football Union would like the rule changed, and the Welsh might support them if the Welsh Rugby Union ever got past the stage of trying to agree among themselves what time of day it is. But that seems unlikely. The Irish are non-committal, but the Scots and French are totally opposed to allowing women into their dinners. Yet dinners for touring teams are mixed affairs: it is only the Five Nations evening which remains a no-go area for women. 'It is incredibly embarrassing,' said an England squad member. 'You have not seen your wife since Wednesday morning when you left home and went straight to join up with the squad that night after work. True, you had tea with her for a few minutes after the match in the Rose Room at Twickenham, and then went together to Central London for the dinner. But you are not even allowed to stand with your wife in the same area where pre-dinner drinks are served. It is archaic.' However, after the England–Wales Five Nations match in March 1994, women were invited to the dinner for the very first time after a championship game. This was at the instigation of that year's President of the RFU, Ian Beer.

These individual factors combined to create a greater discontent; players believed themselves to be leaned upon, to be exploited. There was a mass of evidence to support such a view, for demands on the leading players had multiplied as fast as rabbits in a remote warren.

When the criticism from a stunned nation began to crowd in on Will Carling in the aftermath of England's Grand Slam defeat and second successive failed Championship campaign, a summer of solitude must have seemed essential. But there was just one problem – England had arranged a seven-match tour of Argentina, beginning on 14 July. This was a momentous date to down-trodden folk: on 14 July 1789 the French peasants had stormed the Bastille, triggering the French Revolution.

The tour had been the idea of the late John Kendall-Carpenter, rugby football's own Thomas Cook. Kendall-Carpenter was an interesting chap. At a time of life when most folk yearn for some time, peace and solitude with their family, his idea of fun was to spend his life in the first- or business-class compartment of an aircraft or the first-class accommodation of an anonymous hotel anywhere around the world where rugby was played. Sad, really, because you came to wonder whether he actually had a home to go to. But in his role as chairman of Rugby World Cup Ltd, he had the perfect outlet for such an expensive hobby.

Kendall-Carpenter simply could not understand why rugby players would not want to do precisely the same as him. He arranged the tour and left mentally and physically tired players to carry it through. Six top players – Rob Andrew, Rory Underwood, Jeremy Guscott, Dean Richards, Mike Teague and Paul Ackford – saw it as one trip too many and wearily hoisted the 'not available' flag. But 'not available' was not an option to Carling, the captain.

So England set off with a large collection of untried players, which was rather like fire-fighting in the Blitz with trainees. The big names were missed and even the players of proven international quality were below their best. Carling himself wrote later: 'I know Brian Moore and Wade Dooley were disappointed with their form.' It was, quite obviously, the wrong tour at the wrong time; England's best players needed to recharge their batteries, on a beach beneath a warm sun. Touring Argentina in the southern hemisphere winter was the last thing they needed, even if the intention had been honourable: namely, to re-establish good relations between the two countries in the wake of the Falklands War.

Through his high profile and by his astonishingly rapid rise to the peak of his sport, Will Carling had acquired enemies. This is the fate of all successful Britons. For a nation which attaches so much importance to sporting triumph, we are quick to condemn those we have placed on pedestals. And yet Carling did not help himself in this regard. If some thought him aloof and remote, suspicious and secretive, some of his actions were hardly designed to appease such doubters. One such incident occurred during the Argentine tour, and although it was successfully camouflaged by the rugby brotherhood at the time, its emergence now sheds revealing light on the England captain.

England had a rough passage in Argentina. Most of the younger players they had taken along to be groomed for the future did not measure up, either on the field or off it. Carling, who set himself the highest standards, became ever more disenchanted at the antics of some of them off the field and the performance of most of them on it. It became an increasingly unhappy tour. Three of the four first matches, against provincial opposition, were lost, an astonishing reverse for the country which had cleaned out the French, Irish and Welsh just a few months earlier with some wonderfully attacking, compellingly entertaining rugby. The first of two Test matches against Argentina, both in Buenos Aires, was faced with some trepidation, but England returned to the basics of howitzer power up front and siege-gun-accurate goal-kicking, Simon Hodgkinson again emphasizing his value as a match winner with 17 of England's points in their 25–12 win. There was a huge sense of relief afterwards.

But if the English thought they were out of the wood, they were to be confounded. They squeezed home, unconvincingly, 15–12 against Córdoba and then prepared for the final Test. But before it was played, Carling managed to pour petrol on already volatile waters by an extraordinarily insensitive act concerning the coach. Since his appointment, Roger Uttley had done much commendable work with the forwards. He was not a man of great hyperbole; he preferred to let actions speak louder than words. He was that way as a player, too: a tough, no-nonsense, craggy individual who undertook and completed the essential donkey work which is to a pack of forwards as oil is to an engine. He remained true to type, as a coach.

Uttley's methods may have missed a beat when placed against the brilliantly innovative motivation of an Alan Jones; he could not compete with Jones's finely tuned intellectualism. Describing the effort and industry of his Australian players on the 1984 Wallabies' Grand Slam tour of Britain and Ireland, Jones had called it the Gucci factor. 'Long after you have paid the price, you remember the quality.' One did not expect such magnificence at the press conferences held by Messrs Cooke and Uttley.

But Uttley was a sound, solid performer who knew the game backwards. Certainly he felt he did not deserve to have his position challenged by Carling, who, mindful of the difficulties of the side throughout the tour, now sought to introduce another coaching brain into the side's preparations. This was seen to be extremely insensitive.

Dick Best was in Argentina at the time with a party of rugby supporters. He was employed by a Twickenham travel agency, Edwin Doran Travel, and frequently escorted overseas tours by clients. He was still Carling's club coach at Harlequins. Best had turned up at one of the England training sessions, purely to enable his group to see England train and collect some autographs. There was no hidden meaning in his presence; he was, after all, the coach of the England Under-21s and the B side and his club had contributed six of the players to the squad. If he wanted to, he was perfectly entitled to check on their progress. Carling thought that Best's input would help the touring team. No one actually used the words at the time, but the unspoken message was clear – Uttley's role as coach was in question.

All this was doubtless a manifestation of the pressure to which the young England captain and his team were now subjected. He had made the tour without some close and valued friends, colleagues like Rob Andrew and Rory Underwood who were important members of the England captain's coterie. Shorn of such players, England had stumbled badly on a tour which it was assumed would reveal the depth of talent just ready and waiting to emerge in the English ranks. After all, England should have won a Grand Slam at home only four months earlier, for they were, quite obviously, the most talented team of the Five Nations Championship, Scotland included. They had got it disastrously wrong, in a psychological sense, on the big day at Murrayfield, but few, apart from Scotland's strongest followers, seriously challenged the view that Carling's team was liberally laced with class and skill. Now, just sixteen weeks later, it was being beaten by run-of-the-mill provincial teams in lowly-ranked Argentina. Carling, as captain, naturally felt the let-down more than most.

Geoff Cooke says: 'Everyone was under pressure. We had lost at Murrayfield and things were not going well on the tour. It was a difficult time.' Roger Uttley recalls: 'Will missed the support of certain people who weren't included in the tour party. We went to have a look at the next layer down really. But it was a difficult tour; some of the accommodation left a lot to be desired in the sticks, training facilities were poor and some players underachieved.

'I felt as though Will was taking this out on me. We had been losing matches, but . . .'

Uttley collected his thoughts again. The journey from Harrow School, where he teaches, to South America might be intimidatingly long but the memory remains vivid. 'Geoff and Will came up to me after the end of one particular training session. The idea was put forward that as "Besty" was on the spot and in view of the dire situation we were in, we should make use of his services.

'My reaction was, if things were felt to be that bad I might as well pack my bags and clear out immediately. I know my limitations as a coach and I was aware that I wasn't performing particularly well but neither were a lot of other people! I intimated that I would not be happy working on that basis and the idea was not pursued. Will thought this course of action was necessary at that time; the end result being the only thing that mattered. For me, having not felt at all well and struggling to get the playing side right, this request was very nearly the final straw. Some things are not on, I thought. The sooner I can get home the better. I can do without all this trauma and aggravation. I had nothing to prove to myself or anyone else.'

Given the climate that had been created by these disagreements, the sequel to the tour was probably inevitable. The final Test was a messy game, penalty kicks puncturing it like markers in a map. Argentina had not lost two Tests in a home series since 1976, and now the goal-kicking of their wing Vidou kept England under constant pressure. England led 10–9 at the interval, only to fall 12–10 behind. Hodgkinson's penalty goal then followed his earlier try and conversion, squeezing England ahead again at 13–12. But a shapeless game was decided when Vidou landed his fifth penalty goal, giving Argentina victory by 15 points to 13.

'It would be nothing short of a disaster for England to lose this game,' Geoff Cooke had said before the match. So it was official – England had suffered a disaster. As his side failed to pull clear in the second half despite the ascendancy of their forwards, Uttley sat in the stand at the Velez Sarsfield Stadium with a wistful expression on his face. Was he longing for home? Maybe. If that was the case, he had reason to feel melancholy.

Uttley returned home bitterly disillusioned. England had twice come within touching distance of the Five Nations Championship title and each time had been thwarted. Now they had been beaten by Argentina, and by general consent the tour had been a failure. Uttley was a family man who had considerable commitments in his teaching job; now he sat down and considered quitting. 'I actually discussed the thought of jacking it in then,' he admits. 'After that tour I was at a low ebb. I discussed my decision with Kris, my wife and thought it all over. Did I want the job enough to go on? That sort of question was at the front of my mind. Will Carling might have felt threatened by me because of what I represented. By that, I mean a mixture of my achievements in the game and ability to get on with people. But I do not understand why.'

Uttley was no paid coaching supremo: he did not collect a £40,000 salary for his role. He fitted it in as best he could around the commitments of his work and family life. The latter certainly suffered, and he began to question the price he was paying to sacrifice time with his wife and children.

But the mood for change among certain players had not been dispelled by the ending of an unhappy tour. Not very long afterwards, Carling and some playing colleagues asked Cooke outright to change the England coach for the new season. They felt they had gone as far as they were going with Uttley; it was their opinion that a new face was required. Uttley's fate now hung in the balance; if Cooke sided with the players, the coach would be left with little option but to resign.

But England's manager quickly demonstrated his loyalty to Uttley. He pointed out, decisively, to those seeking the coach's head that a closer examination of their own failings might be rather more appropriate than calling for someone else to take the blame. He remembers: 'One or two players certainly were looking for excuses other than their own performance for the disappointments. Of course, it is always easier to do that. We discussed it but felt that there were no really valid reasons for a change of coach. As far as Roger was concerned, it was a question of reinforcing his belief in his own ability. You do start to doubt your own ability when you have a protracted period without success. My view was that it was too easy to say things are going wrong, get rid of Roger. But even if we had, there was no guarantee that would have altered things. I have never believed in that sort of approach to man management generally.

'I had a lot of faith in Roger's ability and felt it was just one of those crisis periods teams go through on their way to achieving their potential. Suddenly, it had become a minor issue that developed into a minor crisis. It came about because of a loss of confidence. People were looking for someone to apportion blame to. They felt a new coach would have the effect of introducing an injection into their own performances. But that wasn't the situation at all in my view. I saw it as a question of everyone saying, "Let's look at where we have been going wrong, what we are good at and how we can identify best those areas.'''

Uttley agreed to remain at his post only once it emerged that Cooke had given him strong support. They had joined the team together and Cooke intended that the partnership should see the task through. His backing crushed the rebellion utterly.

Thus the overture to the new 1990–91 season had hardly exuded serenity. Nor did the first movement possess much harmony: Carling found himself dropped from the London side for a Divisional Championship match. By now, a mass emigration from north to south had altered decisively the power base within English rugby. The Northern Division selectors had decreed that players not attending every training session would not be considered for selection. Given the fact that several of the players, including the likes of Carling, Winterbottom and Andrew, were by now playing their club rugby and working in London, it was wholly impractical to expect them to trudge the length of the country twice a week for training sessions. So, perfectly understandably, they switched to London.

The effect of this change was dramatic. London began the 1990 Divisional Championship by hammering the North 43–8, the side containing nine players from Harlequins. Carling was injured in the game and missed the next match, a 25–24 win over the Midlands. On the Thursday night prior to the final match, against the South-West at Gloucester, the players assembled for training. The cry quickly went up: 'Where's Will?' Carling had not appeared.

Twenty-four hours earlier, it had been the England captain's twenty-fifth birthday. He had been in Glasgow on business but had inexplicably failed to telephone

Graham Smith, chairman of the London selectors, to put him in the picture. Smith and his coach Dick Best were left to juggle with an acutely difficult situation. Certain other players, their love for Carling hardly renowned, pressurized both men with questions. 'What are you going to do? What's happening? What's going on?' Smith and Best knew decisive action was required. They promptly announced that because he was not there, Carling was dropped, England captain or not. When the press got wind of it, there was, in Carling's own words later, 'a furore'. Carling later conceded: 'I can see I handled things poorly.'

Graham Smith, RFU committee member and London Division team manager for five seasons, was another to encounter Carling's inability to handle criticism. His involvement in the decision to drop Carling cost him, he reflects, the friendship of the England captain.

Smith explains: 'The decision to leave out Will was not taken lightly. It gave us considerable heartache. But he did not arrive at training and no one knew where he was. We were trying to establish London as some sort of force: the credibility of the whole team was involved.

'I met him soon after and tried to explain it. I said we should not fall out over it for what I had done had been for the team. I thought the air had been cleared but I realize that is not the case even now. We don't talk any more. I understand he thinks I let him down and did not protect him. But this was almost four years ago. I thought I had a relationship with him and personally regret that incident very much. I thought we had resolved it but it seems not. I don't think Will can handle that side of things.

'I have found the situation quite upsetting on occasions: I have felt he has deliberately avoided me. I have been hurt by this. I know what happened over that incident and I had the support of everyone else involved: the coach and the captain, in the decision I took. We had no choice but to leave out Will. To have carried it on seems silly to me. And disappointing.'

London could only draw the match, 12–12, but it was enough to give them their third successive title. And when the clock at last ticked around to midnight on 31 December, Will Carling and a good few others associated with the England rugby team must have uttered a private cheer at the passing of a year which had seen a crushing deflation of almost every expectation. Three hundred and eight days had passed between the bitter ending of England's Grand Slam dream in 1990 and the opening of their next attempt at such glory, the following season. But the tactics which the England party formulated to achieve that final step this time were chosen as if the memory of Murrayfield, with all its inherent pain, had been as recent as the previous week.

England went back to basics in an attempt to nail, once and for all, the growing charge that they were forever destined to be the nearly men: nearly Championship winners in 1989, nearly Grand Slam winners twelve months later. Now, as the planning and preparation began for 1991, there was a steely inner resolve that a third failure was simply not tenable. Reputations were on the line; another near miss might even cost the management and the captain their posts. By now, England had won just a single Championship in twenty-seven years, a dreadful record which revealed a saga of abject failure, personal disappointments and inability to translate talent into achievement. Everything seemed ready for a change. Twickenham's towering new North Stand had just been completed, an impressive, lofty structure which was a revealing comment on the growing sums of money now rolling into the RFU coffers. The stand consisted of three tiers and had cost £15 million. All England needed now was a million-dollar team to put in front of it and dispel the tears of failure which had tended to flow too often of late.

On paper it seemed as though England would spend the first half of the Championship season engaged upon revenge missions. First they faced the journey to Cardiff to play Wales, followed a month later by the visit of their most recent persecutors, Scotland. One could hardly criticize the new season for starting with a whimper. In fact, it took scarcely an hour after the final whistle on the opening day of the International Championship for controversy to attach itself once more, leech-like, to Will Carling's coat-tails.

The omnipresent question of amateurism now rose up to overshadow the match as the talking point of the weekend. Unwisely, the England captain, coach and manager refused to attend the customary press conference after the match, preferring to leave the stadium with lips tightly sealed. Unappealing as this behaviour was, matters of greater long-term significance were involved. First, the players felt betrayed by the failure of the Rugby Football Union to put into place firm guidelines governing what they could earn from off-the-field activities. They sensed prevarication on the part of the authorities; the suspicion may have been justified. Second, there was a lingering disaffection with most branches of the media.

Carling had already alluded publicly to the increasingly strained relationships he had experienced in that direction. In December he had accused Chris Rea, rugby

correspondent of the *Independent on Sunday*, of speculation that he was going to resign. Carling wrote in his
book, 'I'm getting some pretty strange treatment from
Chris Rea at the moment . . . He announced last month
that I was going to give up the captaincy . . . I never
had any intention of resigning.' Geoff Cooke and one
of Carling's Harlequins colleagues shared Rea's view
that the England captain was contemplating quitting,
yet suspicion of the media had hardened into open
hostility in certain England players. Even Cooke
remembers: 'I was completely irritated at that time by
the whole media thing. We had had a fairly wearing
period and I was fielding fourteen or fifteen calls a day
from the press. People were ringing me at home, all
hours of the day and night. Then we got an arrogant
note from the BBC regarding interviews, almost saying:
"We are the BBC, you must do this." They more or less
demanded we do it. The players were fed up with the
BBC and decided they wouldn't give the interviews. I
said, "Fine, if that is how you feel." We reacted badly
at the time, it was a misjudgement. I admit it could have
been handled far better than it was, but people don't
realize the emotional involvement of that particular
occasion. None of us were thinking straight in the
immediate aftermath of that match.'

Somewhere, amid the fog which had descended like
a blanket to cloud the issue, there came the claim that
the players had allegedly demanded £5,000 from the
BBC for interviews. When this was refused, they withdrew assistance. Or so it was said. Jonathan Martin,
BBC Television's Head of Sport, confirmed: 'A fee of
£5,000 was asked for a range of services, including
exclusivity for the whole season. We went to clear the
whole thing with the RFU. Their advice was that normal

practices would continue.' But commercial agents had their sticky fingers in the pie by this stage. Steve Hamer, a spokesman for the players' agents, WHJ Promotions, a company run by the former England cricket captain Bob Willis and his brother David, said somewhat grandly: 'The players have made this stand because they want to know what they can and cannot do. It has to be resolved very quickly.'

This statement was received at Twickenham with all the enthusiasm of cold soup on the November night of the Lord Mayor's Banquet. Why did educated young men who had risen to the pinnacle of representing their country at rugby football require a commercial agent few had heard of to explain their position? Could Will Carling, as the captain, not have done a rather more eloquent and altogether more diplomatic job? Public sympathy might well have enhanced their cause, had he done so.

Three days later, Bob Willis came out against the players, a remarkable turn-around. 'In my view the players should certainly have attended the press conference after the match at Cardiff. And the captain should have given his immediate post-match reaction to the BBC. I would have advised that. No way did we tell the squad not to talk to the media. I regard it as unfortunate they didn't attend the press conference. It is not a positive thing for the players to get the press offside.'

This seemed like a public rebuke for Carling and his players. Carling had never been comfortable with criticism, so it was no surprise when the relationship between Willis's company and the England squad was eventually terminated. The squad's growing distrust of the media, particularly certain branches of it, was becoming blatant. This state of affairs had been the fault, to no small extent, of the media itself. It was World Cup year, and rugby football had become a fair target for certain pressmen and television crews who had previously never strayed beyond the soccer ground or the boxing ring. Reporters and individuals who hardly knew the difference between a ruck and a maul, and still less understood the intricacies of the game's old-fashioned adherence to strict amateurism, now descended on a sport which for many had been a quiet backwater, frequented only by a comparatively few devotees. Quite suddenly the masses had arrived, in the shape of ubiquitous correspondents who one day professed themselves to be as knowledgeable about golf as Arnold Palmer and, courtesy of a jet aeroplane forty-eight hours later, were greater founts of wisdom on rugby football than Will Carling, Dudley Wood and half the All Black team put together. This plainly irritated both players and officials.

One major casualty of this trend was the so-called special relationship, not between the United States and Great Britain (that had ended decades earlier, but the Yanks never quite had the nerve to tell us Brits), but between rugby players and rugby writers. It had always been one of the game's great strengths that players, or anyone else associated with the sport, could speak as liberally as they wished after matches and feel secure even in the company of pressmen. The unwritten rule was that even if someone 'said' something at the end of a long, uproarious night, you checked with them the next day to see if it had been intended for wider consumption. Sometimes it meant that a good story had to be buried; occasionally, it could be aired. But the understanding and trust inherent in such a relationship meant that players could talk freely without fear that their views would be misrepresented or sensationalized. For the pressman such an arrangement was (and to some still is) invaluable because players or officials would happily 'mark their cards', filling them in on background details which they would never cite directly.

The arrival on the scene of media representatives who had no inkling of such unofficial arrangements wrecked much of this, to the infinite loss of both player and pressman. Suddenly, suspicion and distrust replaced comradeship and cheer; it was by no means the sole fault of the players that this occurred. Whatever was intended by the players or their agents in invoking such a disastrous path at Cardiff, it was guaranteed to ensure only that confrontation, sensationalism and commotion resulted. The RFU hierarchy was incensed. Secretary Dudley Wood said sharply: 'We have a public image and players have to recognize that.' RFU President Mike Pearey, who had to make a formal apology for the team's silence at the after-match dinner in Cardiff, added: 'The players realize it was an error of judgement. It was discourteous to say the least.'

It was also baffling, bewildering. Men of such intelligence as wore England jerseys that day must have known the likely effect of such a controversial action. Unless they actively sought confrontation and positively revelled in the banner headlines and the way the incident completely overshadowed the match, their judgement was again proven dreadfully awry. The press, those whom they had sought to injure, had a field day at their expense. 'Whatever the players' true feelings may be, they are in danger of losing the support of some who work with them, let alone the media and the public,' wrote Norman Harris, in the *Observer*. 'This weekend England are giving the impression of being self-obsessed

Technical excellence: Carling retains the ball in the classic position, despite an Irish tackle. Twickenham, 1992 *(Gray Mortimore/Allsport)*

Two distinguished former England internationals who also became worthy
British Lions: Peter Dixon (top) unloads the ball while his colleagues hold
back the French and, below, Bill Beaumont, the inspiration behind
England's 1980 Grand Slam *(Colorsport)*

Notable players during Carling's career. *Above left* David Campese, the Australian whose criticism of Carling almost pushed his tongue through his cheek. *Above right* Rob Andrew, who would have won the England captaincy ahead of Carling but for the vagaries of his form. *Right* Gavin Hastings, who was preferred to Carling as the 1993 British Lions captain in New Zealand.
(Bob Thomas Sports Photography)

Winners at last. England clinch the 1991 Grand Slam by beating France at Twickenham. *Above* The management team that set it up – from left, John Elliott, Geoff Cooke and Roger Uttley. Note the crestfallen face of French coach Jean Trillo to the immediate right of Uttley. *Below* Carling emerges from the scrum of celebration, shaken but not stirred *(Colorsport)*

The story of the World Cup Final – England are denied by outstanding
Australian defence *(Simon Bruty/Allsport)*

The captain's half-time team talk *(Chris Cole/Allsport)*

A superb action shot of Carling piercing the Welsh defence, as England
secured their second Grand Slam. England 24 Wales 0, Twickenham, 1992
(Bob Martin/Allsport)

Was this his finest game? Carling keeps the ball free for onward delivery.
Bath 15 Harlequins 12. Pilkington Cup Final, 1992 *(David Cannon/Allsport)*

Ieuan Evans and Will Carling together after the England–Wales
match at Twickenham, 1994. England won the match, Wales the
Five Nations Championship *(David Rogers/Allsport)*

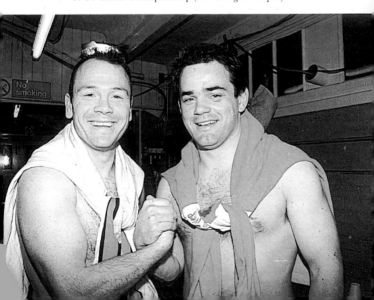

The pressure is off: the England captain in carefree mood
(Bob Thomas Sports Photography)

to the point of neuroticism.' That was one of the gentler remarks: the tabloids drew headlines of the size usually reserved for the juiciest front-page scandals.

The row rumbled on and on. *Daily Express* columnist James Lawton, contrasting the actions of sportsmen at Cardiff with those he had recently experienced in America at the 25th Super Bowl, talked of British sport's failure 'to understand the power and the goodwill it so carelessly tosses aside'. Lawton asked the highly relevant question whether it had all been worth it for the rather pathetic request for a pool payment of £5,000. Precisely. But if the players, the media and indeed the management had all been at fault, then the tardiness of the authorities, Leviathans in the eyes of some players, had hardly been conducive to peaceful change. Too many blocks had been placed in the path of the reformers. One did not doubt the sincerity of those who sought to defend the citadel against permanent and disastrous assault. Indeed, some of the absurd suggestions emanating from certain players at the time suggested that defenders of the faith were needed to save the game from complete disintegration into financial disorder. But by offering only intransigence, the diehard authoritarians, those without the wit and intelligence to seek compromise, risked confrontation. When they got it, few onlookers were terribly surprised.

For England's captain, it was another depressing illustration of his occasional gross misjudgement. The whole affair could and should have been handled better by someone of his standing. Carling claimed later that it had been nothing to do with money. The Head of BBC Sport had clearly gleaned a quite different impression from direct negotiations. Carling said that the players had been frustrated by the activities of certain pressmen ringing them up so often and banging on doors for interviews. He suggested media intrusion and said that he did not see why England rugby players should have to suffer such harassment. He also said that pressmen should not be trying to sneak into hotels to catch players off their guard. Fair enough – but the retaliatory action the players chose was no way to solve such a difficulty. It would only play into the hands of the populist element within the media, and intensify the pressures for interviews. Intelligent players should know from experience the pressmen they can trust. Granted, they may not always like what a reporter writes, but until England is ruled by a military dictator who decrees himself the sole arbiter of editorial content, they may have to accept that others have a different opinion from their own – that's democracy.

In 1983, the British Lions' management for the tour of New Zealand had called a press conference prior to departure and said that any press representatives wishing to conduct interviews during the tour would have to elicit approval by a member of the tour management before speaking to players. This left players and pressmen open-mouthed in astonishment. Here was a group of thirty players, many of them married and some with children, who included in their ranks doctors, dentists, solicitors, company representatives and holders of similarly important posts in life, being told not to speak to media representatives, some of whom they had known for years. They were to be asked to make critical decisions in the field of their sport for the next thirteen weeks, but the ability to decide the character and trustworthiness of media men was apparently quite beyond the scope of their intelligence. It was an insult to both the players and the media, and most simply ignored it for the irrelevance it was. But the management lost enormous credibility, not least in the eyes of its own players, by issuing such an absurd decree.

The vast majority of those who represent their country at rugby football are perfectly capable of making judgements about whom they should and should not speak to. They are people of knowledge and ability. It seems to follow that the England players of 1991 were equally able to decide whom to give interviews to and who would represent, fairly and faithfully, their views rather than distort them. Decisions such as these are the making of the man. To have taken so small a point to such astronomical proportions, with all the repercussions which followed, was a gross error.

There had been a match that day, too. England won it, or rather Simon Hodgkinson won it, with seven penalty goals in his side's 25–6 victory. It wasn't a great match to remember, but it fairly crackled with style, elegance and entertainment compared to the shoddy aftermath.

England then had a month off, to indulge in a variety of activities ranging from the celebration of their first victory over Wales in Cardiff since 1963 to the licking of self-inflicted wounds over the interview fiasco. But it was only a brief opportunity to pop their heads out of the pressure cooker; Scotland were due at Twickenham on 16 February and the prospect had the nation by the throat. Meanwhile the amateurism debate rumbled on, becoming as boring as the discussion of tax amendments in the House of Commons. 'There had been no end of fuss in the build-up to the game as the team and the RFU bickered about opportunities for earning,' reported *Rothmans Rugby Yearbook*.

Part of the pre-match training had to be done on an artificial surface because of the weather, but there was little phoney about the initial exchanges in the match. England played like women scorned, snarling their hatred and aggression for the Scots. That was all right – the feeling was perfectly mutual! England had settled on a game plan which revolved around the power of their forwards. The opposition might wish to move the play around the field at pace, dragging the English giants like Ackford, Dooley, Teague and Richards to exhaustion. But planning such tactics and enforcing them against a pack of forwards with the physical might and powerful excellence of this English eight was something else. Wales had failed completely to achieve it, and now it was Scotland's turn to succumb. The Scots were denied a forward base for launching their back-row men and half-backs. Meanwhile, Hodgkinson punished technical infringements with five penalty goals and the conversion of the game's only try, by Nigel Heslop. Chalmers replied with four penalties for Scotland in their 21–12 defeat.

You could tell what it all meant to England. As the final whistle sounded, the BBC TV pictures captured an elated, enraged Rob Andrew, normally a man of mild, calm emotions, leaping with delight and then furiously pumping V-signs, as well as mouthing remarks at the beaten Scots. I don't think he was wishing them a safe journey home. That image, conjured from the traditional end-of-match chaos on the pitch at Twickenham, spoke volumes for the hurt, the pain and the bewilderment that England had suffered at Scottish hands the previous season. The memory had accompanied them, as close at hand as a tie around their neck, through most of the following eleven months. Defeating Scotland, anywhere, by any margin, clearly meant a world of difference to a win at Cardiff, even if it had taken twenty-eight years to subdue the dragon in its lair.

The good ship 'HMS Grand Slam' set sail, a couple of weeks later, for Dublin. Here, it encountered none of the acrid feelings which had drifted, mist-like, across the ground at Twickenham. A few Irishmen might blow up the Brits whenever the opportunity arises, but others welcome them into their country and nearly kill them in another way – with their hospitality. For England it was time to stand and deliver: Dean Richards proceeded to do precisely that.

Deep into the last quarter of the game, Ireland led 7–6 and had 50,000 voices roaring belief into their very souls. They might have held out and denied England once more, but for Richards. The giant Leicester police officer, with hands the size of golf-ball buckets, simply picked up the match and decreed its fate by his own enormous contribution. His power enabled England gradually to suck the life out of the gallant Irish, as a mosquito sucks blood from its prey. When this process had been completed satisfactorily, the ball was moved wide and Underwood, spinning and slipping from the grasp of tacklers like a top wobbling out of control, eluded tired opponents to score the critical try. Teague then added another, and England were home, 16–7, for their first Triple Crown since 1980. There was a tipple or two sunk that night in hospitable Dublin.

Yet even amid triumph, a spectre was emerging to challenge England's supremacy. France had begun the season by dispatching the previous year's Grand Slam winners, Scotland, in Paris. The French then won in Dublin and, as England clinched the Triple Crown, they humiliated Wales 36–3 in Paris, by six tries to nil. They had one more match – England, at Twickenham. It meant that for the second year in succession, two unbeaten teams would conclude the Championship by colliding for the Grand Slam. High Noon time . . . Take Four.

France arrived, tugging a respectful forelock in acknowledgement of England's superior forward might. But that did not mean that their journey was futile: far from it. Not when you could score tries with movements which began behind your own goal-line. The cocktail of England's forward strength and France's sheer inventiveness in attempting to attack from all positions produced a marvellous, compelling spectacle. Saint-André's try under the posts, after a magnificent sweeping movement the length of the field, was the ultimate sporting pleasure. But there was a great deal else besides: the smooth, calm command of the English half-backs, the sheer grit and determination of every English player to see this one through to a successful conclusion, the delightful *élan* of the French play.

England were constantly threatened by French genius, but their quality prevailed. They had the strength, the character and the class to repel so spirited a challenge and duly won their country's first Grand Slam for eleven years, Hodgkinson's trusty right boot adroitly directing them towards their ambition with four more penalty goals and a conversion of Underwood's try. Hodgkinson had contributed 58 of England's 83 points in the triumphant season, a convincing statistic to justify his presence. Yet it was to be his last full international appearance in the Championship, for within less than seven months he had been supplanted as first choice full-back, never again to return – an astonishing rejection for the player without whom the 1991 Grand Slam might never have been achieved.

England won many admirers at Twickenham on the

final day of the season. Their moment of triumph was well deserved, for they had been quite the most consistent, the most talented and the best team in Europe for three seasons. Yet even at the moment of their triumph they faced painful accusations. Some denigrated the achievement by claiming that they had won only by the complete sacrifice of their glittering play of the previous season. It was, they condemned, triumph without glory. This was not altogether arrant nonsense.

Undeniably, their play of the previous year had contained a rhythm, a speed and a dash which had excited everyone who saw it. Even in defeat at Murrayfield, they had fashioned a try from the top drawer, the kind of score which leaves the watcher breathless. But ultimately they had been left empty-handed. To have maintained exactly the same approach the following year might again have been sufficient to earn victories in the majority of their games, for they had the forwards to earn copious quantities of possession against any side in the world. But would so brave an attacking style have brought them what every successful side seeks: its place in history?

The greatest sides, whatever the sport, combine elegance and the entertainment factor with an enigmatic practicality which can, at times, appear to dilute the other qualities. But it is an illusion: all that is being sacrificed is the perilous bravado which threatens the eventual reward. Few remember entertainers alone: it is the winning of prizes, the acquisition of trophies or awards which marks down the best. England recognized that, and to snipe at their rejection of an all-out attacking policy would be wrong. It is true that they watered down the outstanding attacking style, which was a pity. But they ensured, by slightly tempering that approach, that they would taste the champagne which had until then been dashed, dramatically and disastrously, from their lips.

The policy adopted by Geoff Cooke and Roger Uttley was justified in that England could not have withstood the trauma of another failure. The outcome to the season exonerated the firm step they had taken towards caution.

11 The Valentino Suit That Didn't Quite Fit

'I bumped into a Yank who'd never even heard of Australia. "Turn left at Honolulu," I quietly advised the bastard, thinking he'd probably end up in New Zealand which would serve him right.'

Sir Les Patterson

Waiting in the wings, in the wake of England's Grand Slam triumph, were the manifestations of the twentieth-century British media: the television chat show, the radio talk-in, the in-depth newspaper feature interview, the self-styled 'revealing' magazine cover story. All had a single common denominator – they failed completely to unravel even half the story of England's captain. As leader of a national team's sporting triumph, Carling was in increasing demand. Wogan waffled with him, newspaper men fêted him, others probed like surgeons at the operating table. They all clashed resoundingly against a shield, presented affably and often with a jocular aside. But a barrier, none the less.

It represented Carling's fear of total exposure, his unease that outsiders, furnished with all the facts, might start asking questions which would awaken dormant uncertainties within his mind. Concealed from public scrutiny, such misgivings could be controlled by their owner. But should others come to hear of them and perhaps attempt to bring them into the open, he might have to face them, indeed discuss them in public, a prospect he had never faced in his life.

So the watching world received an image which had the stamp of official approval. The subject chatted amicably, grinned selflessly, parried cleverly and said precious little. But no one especially minded. They had the portrait pictures, the front cover shots; they had secured the man of the moment. So the text was a bit banal – so what? How many punters really understood? Securing the Carling headline, with some good pictures of the photogenic young sportsman, was the main thing. His face beamed out from a variety of magazines: *Rugby World and Post*, *Rugby News*, *Gentlemen's Quarterly*, *Esquire*, business publications. The expression was genial, a shade self-effacing. The camera never lies? Don't believe it.

A more revealing insight was to be glimpsed at the joint launch of an *Esquire* magazine special sports issue and his own book *Captain's Diary*, published by Chatto & Windus. Some trouble was taken to make a suitable impact. Countless pages were given over to sport by a magazine which was usually far more concerned with style, fashion and general news angles and events. The book launch came at a potentially propitious time, just before the World Cup, and a London club was hired to make an appropriate splash. Executives of the magazine clad in expensive-looking Armani suits, greeted their invited guests. There to greet the guests too was England's rugby captain, the familiar, bashful grin firmly in place for all comers. The illuminating moment came when it was time for some short speeches.

A senior representative from the magazine made some introductory remarks, Eddie Butler, rugby writer for the *Observer*, was there to add some light-hearted thoughts, and eyes gradually turned to Will Carling, particularly those of the magazine's senior executive. The expression said simply, 'Can you say a few words when Eddie is finished?' Carling returned the invitation with a cold look and a curt shake of the head. It was, frankly, astonishing. To have the England rugby captain at the launch of both his own book and a magazine on which he adorned the front cover, trailing the major interview of the entire issue, and then not get a word or two from the principal boy, was mystifying. It was a situation made for the traditional rugbyman: a joke or two, words of thanks and an invitation to sup up and enjoy the hospitality. Butler, of course, carried it off with aplomb; Carling did not even attempt it. The bewildered expressions on the faces of senior executives from the magazine and the publisher spoke volumes for their view of this incident.

Carling's reticence in the company of others had been further fuelled by recent events in his rugby life. The critics, imaginary and actual, had begun to crowd in once more and insecurity ensued: it was a familiar picture. But the questions raised against England's style of play on their path to the Grand Slam had irritated not only Carling but many in his playing clique. The bruises such words caused were nursed painfully by those involved; they sensed criticism each time they turned a newspaper page, they suspected treason in every act of the reporter. David Campese, for example, wrote: 'England should not overrate their achievements. What was the big deal about running the ball? They were playing a bunch of nobodies.'

In Carling's case, the inner confidence had scarcely been bolstered even by the achievement of a Grand Slam. The win did not inject a potion that would ensure instant assurance on a grandiose scale. Nor did it dispel the fears, the fragile uncertainties which continued to haunt his mind. Those in the media who asked the 'right' questions and were either too uninformed or simply lacked the desire to probe deeper were welcomed like soulmates. This was especially true of the television team which was to cover the World Cup in Britain, Ireland and France later that year. With reporters who were hardly long-term observers of rugby or who had previously only read the news or acted as programme announcers, England's players sensed safety. They invited them into the camp happily and without reservation.

It was to be ITV's first shot at major coverage of rugby union, traditionally the preserve of the BBC, whose executives had been mortified at losing the decision on coverage of the tournament. But ITV were under pressure. No one could do it like the Beeb, was the word. How could rugby union be rugby union without Bill McLaren? With this in mind, making waves and stirring controversy of any kind during the tournament was simply not part of the ITV script. Making it all light and breezy, with the commentary team wearing silly clothes and doing daft dances at odd moments, was more their style. This lack of a newsy, cutting edge suited the England captain and his players down to the ground.

But this would come later in the year. Once the Grand Slam had been completed in March, Carling's attention turned back to his club, who were embarked upon a journey to the Pilkington Cup final. For Dick Best, it was to be the final club challenge before he took over from Roger Uttley as national coach, immediately after the World Cup final, in November. Harlequins had failed in the two years following their 1988 Cup final success, but now they won at Gloucester, never a bad assessment centre for a visiting side's credentials, and then beat Rosslyn Park and Nottingham (the latter only after extra time) to contest the final with Northampton. They needed another extra thirty minutes to complete the job, too, finally nailing the East Midlands club 25–13 after being held 13–13 at the end of eighty minutes. It represented the triumph of achievement through endeavour. The final on 4 May marked the end of a long wearying season.

Sixteen pressure-free weeks stretched invitingly ahead ... for all but England's best rugby players, as usual. The weather was no longer suitable for a winter sport in this part of the world, so the obvious answer was to cross the world to the southern hemisphere for some more rugby – just in case England's finest hadn't had enough here.

The excuse this time was preparation for the World Cup, which was scheduled to begin at Twickenham on 3 October with a pool match between the defending champions, New Zealand, and one of the host nations, England. But the insertion of this tour into the schedule meant that England's best players had now played the game during every season in both northern and southern hemispheres since 1985, with the exception of the northern summer of 1986. In May and June 1985, an England squad containing Wade Dooley and Mike Teague had toured New Zealand; in June 1987 the first World Cup had been staged in Australia. In May and June 1988 England had toured Australia and Fiji; in the summer of 1989 a British Lions squad full of the top English players (Carling excepted only because of injury) had toured Australia.

In July and August 1990, England had visited

Argentina. Now, twelve months later, England were to tour Australia and Fiji for the second time in three years. It was a ludicrous over-exposure of our top players to the demands of a game which requires enormous physical commitment. Add on to the touring schedule the usual Five Nations Championship campaign each winter season in Britain, with all its inherent pressures, and you have a programme devised by the insane. However, the management insisted that it was essential this time as a build-up to the World Cup. This, of course, was the carrot held enticingly in front of the suffering animal's snout. The trouble was that it kept on being moved ever further away.

Predictably, the venture crashed. New South Wales beat them, Queensland beat them, Fiji's second string team beat them, and Australia humiliated them, 40–15, in Sydney. On July winter days, Sydney can be one of the most delightful places in the world. A visit to a Paddington bistro for lunch, an afternoon rugby match in the winter sunshine, and a journey home by ferry across the harbour. It beats catching the 7.40 train to work and the 5.15 home. But even that mind-numbing activity probably seemed preferable to England's rugby élite as Australia, developing inexorably into the side which would prove so distinguished at the World Cup, put five tries past the English defence. The Aussies clearly enjoyed the taste of blood; they had butchered Wales 63–6 in Brisbane the previous week.

England followed the limping shadow of the Welsh home, their plans for the World Cup, beginning in little more than nine weeks' time, apparently in disarray. Once more, however, England returned to the most basic of playing strategies for a tournament which was to captivate the sports-minded world throughout its four weeks. A few months before the tournament began, Carling wrote: 'The one sure thing about the World Cup is that it will be very, very exciting, for players and supporters alike. And since we're lucky enough to be playing, we're going to make sure, win or lose, that we don't let the supporters down.' They certainly did not do that. But the tragedy of the 1991 World Cup tournament was that England carelessly tossed away their opportunity of winning it. The story is familiar enough – I see no point in labouring through a month of tries scored, penalties kicked and tackles made. The highlights do merit reflection: the delight of outstanding matches such as Australia v. Argentina in the autumn sunshine at Llanelli, the emergence on a national stage of the Western Samoans, the resoluteness of the Canadians and the gallantry of the Irish in defeat to Australia. What a night that was in Dublin! But even at this distance in time, it is England that one remembers.

Beaten by New Zealand in the opening match because they were stifled by a strait-jacket of tension, England knew that a long, hard path lay ahead after that single defeat at the pool stage. The runners-up in Pool 1 were destined for a quarter-final in France, followed by, if successful there, a semi-final in Scotland, assuming everything went according to the form book – which, ultimately, it did.

Long before the tournament had even started, Serge Blanco, that exquisite performer in the rarefied David Campese class, had prophesied England's demise should they find the trip to Paris on their itinerary. But rather than England yielding to the pressure at Parc des Princes, it was the enigmatic French, their emotions rarely under control on the day, who succumbed; on the field and off it. Blanco, set up for physical intimidation by Heslop's grossly late challenge, unleashed a flurry of blows which would have been better placed in the boxing ring. Heslop came off worse, in the immediate moment, but England profited eventually, the excitement and rampant emotion induced in Blanco impairing both his judgement and that of his team. When the fiery Basque, Ondarts, lost his cool late in the game, England knew they were on course for victory.

Their captain confirmed it, wresting the ball from the grasp of the French wing Lafond, who had caught a high English kick towards his own line but had then been driven back by a cluster of sweating, snatching Englishmen before Carling seized the prized 'pill' to dot it down for the decisive score, in injury time. That was appropriate; his perfectly delivered pass to Guscott had set up England's first try for Underwood, and the captain had one of his finest games for England.

Even then, the emotions were still fizzing. The French coach Daniel Dubroca was spotted in the tunnel leading to the dressing-rooms, grabbing New Zealand referee David Bishop around the collar. New Zealanders do not take kindly to 'having their collar felt' by anyone, but the two men were hustled apart to cries of 'Cheat' by the enraged and emotive Frenchman. It was a tragedy for Dubroca, a great man of rugby; it was to cost him his post as national coach, and it soured the image of a fine man. But it was also indicative of the pressures to which all those operating in the World Cup cauldron were now subjected.

England's performance had demonstrated enormous character and determination. But only half the job had been done; the Scots then had to be tamed in their own country, too, just one week later. Asking sportsmen, whatever their game, to 'peak' at such short intervals is the ultimate expectation. Even players more carefully prepared than ever before were subject to the physical reactions and requirements of their bodies. Some tasks are beyond the mere human frame, whatever the nature of the test devised for them by experts. England now faced uncharted territory, in that no English international had ever gone straight from Paris to Edinburgh for internationals within the space of seven days. The ramifications of the journey were immense, in a personal, collective, physical and historical sense.

What made the confrontation all the spicier was that it was England's first return to Murrayfield since their defeat there in the 1990 Grand Slam decider. So they were assured of the kindest, gentlest welcome going. After all, there was not very much at stake – just a place in the World Cup final!

The Scots had brought in their own cheerleader, the Princess Royal, for the occasion, and they had also invited thousands of kilt-clad natives to make their visitors feel even more intimidated. England, by contrast, had only guts and the bravery they stored in their kit-bags for generous application before kick-off.

It was never a classic match, but then few semi-finals are, in any sport. The anticipation of victory and the prize which awaits is too great, the sense of loss in defeat too catastrophic. Nerves are like fingernails, frayed and down to the quick; it is generally those who can cope best with such towering emotion who survive. Or those teams which make fewer mistakes. The tendency to clam up in such situations is legendary.

Two kicks were all that separated the two sides by the finish of a frantic affair. Gavin Hastings, whose two early penalties had given Scotland a 6–0 lead, lined up another with the scores level at 6–6, only eighteen minutes from the end. It was a cinch, a 'gimme' in golfing parlance; just to the right of the posts and about twenty yards out. The sort of kick he would put over with careless abandon in a club match – but which he carelessly gave away in a World Cup semi-final. As the kick slewed away outside the posts, Scotland sensed that a glorious opportunity, perhaps their best, had gone.

So it proved, when England's fly-half Rob Andrew calmly dropped the late goal which put England into the final by a 9–6 scoreline. To have survived the occasion was a meritorious achievement by the England players, but the criticism began flowing even while the champagne was still being poured. England had never opened up, never exploited their supremacy in key forward areas. They had won, yes, but had always been susceptible to a late Scottish raid because timidity had denied their use of a fast, potentially dangerous back-line. And so on and so on . . .

While Scottish bleats to this effect could be comfortably dismissed as sour grapes, there was more than a semblance of truth to the accusations. England did have a potent back-line, full of pace, purpose and, most crucially, penetration. The creativity of players like Guscott, Carling and Halliday, the latter by now playing out of position on the right wing, such were his footballing skills, not to mention the finishing power of Underwood, gave England as good a back-line as any in the tournament, and better than most.

Bob Dwyer, the inventive coach of the Australians, was a long-time respecter of the abilities of Carling and Halliday, in particular. 'I saw them, separately, when they toured Australia with England in 1988. We were all impressed with the ability of each man; I was glad they were not available together, for that tour. Carling's speed combined with his strength made him a very difficult customer. Then there were his running skills. He has a rare ability among centres to make an outside break and that is not very common. His ability to get on that channel and threaten defences is commendable and a rare quality. But of course since then he has come on a lot.

'By the time of the World Cup, he was a constant threat. I wouldn't know enough about centres like Jeff Butterfield from England teams of long ago, but since 1959 and the start of the sixties, I would rate him definitely with the best of the English centres. Probably better than any. Certainly, I'd put him above players like Paul Dodge and Clive Woodward. He would have to be the most complete player in England for twenty or thirty years. He has added a fair bit of star quality to the England team.'

During the World Cup, intriguingly, Dwyer had one notion concerning England's captain dispelled. 'We went to a dinner one night during the tournament, Nick Farr-Jones and myself. Will Carling was there and we were really impressed with the regard the English public had for Will. From watching him on TV, he is pretty arrogant, but at this dinner he came over as quite different. He was down to earth, perfectly opposite to the aloof character you see on TV. He didn't give the slightest impression he was arrogant. I thought "Here's a guy you would be quite comfortable with." Yet I always figure my first impressions are usually right. But as a player, he is a much more imposing character on the field. You are conscious of his presence all the time. Only a very dominant player can do that.'

So England had a captain whom even the Australian coach thought the world of. Many Englishmen thought even more of Jeremy Guscott, outside Carling at centre. Simon Halliday possessed outstanding talents, even in the unfamiliar position of right wing. Rory Underwood, on the left wing, had earned fifty-two caps by the eve of the World Cup final, and as long ago as 1989 had equalled the English try-scoring record which had stood unrivalled since 1907. Yet they remained largely moth-balled. The tournament had seen English play of stature, certainly, but of statuesque proportions, too. The backs had stood forlornly around, occasionally producing a little masterpiece of a score, then they would return once more to anonymity, frozen out by the powermen up front and the kicking half-backs. It was like owning a Valentino suit but wearing tatty jeans every day: when you occasionally brought the suit out, you looked a million dollars, but what a waste . . .

So England arrived at the World Cup final to meet Australia – with a game plan as elegant as the Valentino suit. Hoorah – except that they'd forgotten how to carry off the stylish outfit. They overlooked the fact that wearing it was only half the story; you had to become accustomed to its hang, feel comfortable with its cut. The game plan they adopted and tried to employ broke English hearts, because it certainly did not break Australia's defence. If they really believed that was the way to play, why on earth had they not followed the creed throughout the tournament? To change now, at the final step, was a bold, brave, hopelessly misguided policy which could only end in sadness. Attacking with the ball through the back-line, feeling comfortable in possession, is an art requiring cultivation. It cannot simply be picked up at will, and it was reckless to imagine otherwise.

The great tactical masterminds, the players of true eminence, understand this implicitly. Practice is required for any worthy achievement, but to break defences nowadays in international rugby by means of original play and skills outside the forwards requires immense preparation. It is not like the old days, when defences were so tactically unsophisticated that any quality play could expose them utterly. The modern-day game has taken on a rigidity, a pattern which threatens the contribution of the individual or the creative instinct. To defeat such well-rehearsed methods of defence, constant attention to fine detail is required by backs. What possessed England to believe they could throw overboard the fundamental reason for their presence in the World Cup final, namely, the might of their forward dominance, and simply plug in another system, is beyond comprehension.

The role of the media, convenient scapegoats in all times of ill, was scrutinized. Had they not berated Carling's men for their excessively cautious approach? Had not the criticism built up to a crescendo, a rallying cry which demanded greater consideration than hitherto? Maybe. But if it had, it should have been rejected out of hand. Besides, since when did the media influence England's playing policy?

It may have been no more than the obvious which persuaded England to throw their previous caution to the wind: the presence of the ultimate world stage, graced by Her Majesty the Queen, the myriad television cameras beaming the action to all corners of the globe, the hacks in a specially enlarged press box, quills poised above the pots of acid, ready to condemn the side which ruined the World Cup final as a spectacle. It was this awareness of the huge expectation, I believe, the feeling that the first final in the northern hemisphere at the close of a thrilling tournament that had gripped the nation could not be soiled by a grim war of attrition alone among the forwards.

We had conjured in our minds, by then, images of Campese in Cardiff and Dublin, of the flying Argentinian Terán at Llanelli; of Bunce and Lima for Western Samoa, of Lafond for France. Memories of great tries scored and enthralling attacking play. Would the world appreciate a final condemned to purgatory by English forward grind?

England lacked the courage of their convictions. It was all right to play a tough, tight game through the qualifying stages – that approach had been responsible for getting them to the final. However, it seemed England bottled it when it came to plotting the downfall of the Wallabies by similar means. But such methods were understood well enough by the purist; they did not have to be justified to him. He acknowledged outstanding scrummaging, the superb line-out work of Ackford, Dooley and their colleagues and the constant foraging of hard back-row men who did not know the meaning or consequences of the words intimidation or physical sacrifice. Such observers are to be seen studiously watching the finer points of English county cricket, such as the leg break bowler slipping in his googly or the cautious batsman grinding out a stolid half-century on a pitch of spiteful intent favouring all the bowling. But how many attend county cricket to marvel at such talent? The greater crowds are for the one-day game.

Millions of those switching on the TV for the 1991 World Cup final were drawn to their set by the spectacle, the hype, the build-up. These were no long-established followers of the game; rather, they were occasional viewers who enjoyed a classic contest. A great many among the 50,000-plus crowd at Twickenham were in the same category: cheerful onlookers who had no more idea of the qualities required for damaging scrummaging in the front row or the most productive lines of running by a fly-half than they had of the position of the fingers in delivering the chinaman on the cricket field. The disaster for England was that they probably took into account such folk in formulating their game plan for the match.

We could never have imagined it at the time but the taunts, not least from those wily Australians like David Campese, had stung Englishmen deeply. The desire to ram colourful words into Australian mouths which were seen as too big by half ran away with England's reasoning. The game plan they now adopted was undoubtedly audacious but excessively foolhardy.

By contrast, and with a biting irony, Australia now introduced a qualified element to their play which had not until then been seen – not even at so intensely pressurized a stage as the semi-final, in which they had defeated New Zealand with some glorious illustrations of Campese at his magical, bewitching best. Their ploy for the final was simple – eliminate errors, even to the exclusion of creativity, capitalize on any opposition weakness, and tackle until your last breath. Bog standard stuff, but mightily effective because it is so hard to play against.

The English approach was a throwback to the First World War: 'up and at 'em chaps' sort of stuff, every bit as brave and impractical as the charge of the young subalterns at Mons or High Wood, circa 1916. The effect was similar, too. Australia repelled them, not with chattering machine-guns, but with tackling which just made the teeth chatter, such was the impact. This was no susceptible cover, but a solid, compact, compressed line of humanity which barred the way to every human foe, especially once they had gone in front, and could sense the game's greatest prize awaiting them from the hands of the Queen.

England tried all they knew to shake this Australian resolve, everything, that is, except the obvious – a change of tactics to the old tried and trusted formula. Curiously, no one seemed to think of that in the heat of the moment, and certainly not Will Carling. All around him was a whirr of frenetic activity. Andrew linked, Carling powered, Guscott dashed, Underwood waited, poised for a sprint. The ball kept coming their way, courtesy of that magnificent pack. But what a waste of fine forwards. All their hard-won assets were squandered as the backs threw themselves in vain on the unrelenting green and gold line.

The lack of adaptability by England's captain was highly revealing. His play was beyond reproach; once more, courageous and compelling. But on the highest stage the game could produce, his captaincy once more looked flawed. The consummate player, but not the complete leader. The former Irish coach Mick Doyle, capped twenty times for Ireland and a 1968 British Lion in South Africa, said: 'He is naïve as a leader. And that propels men to do things without thinking. I don't think Will is that calculating: he doesn't hedge that much, which suggests he doesn't have a mental searching office in his head, before he answers. Most guys have that. He feels more a member of the team than a leader of it. His input is like that of a normal player. A very good player, but just a player, not a captain.'

The tactics employed in the World Cup final were condemned by David Kirk, captain of New Zealand at the first World Cup and afterwards an Oxford

University blue. It was, said Kirk, too late to use such an approach. 'Although they did run the ball around effectively, the last pass went to ground, the positioning wasn't quite right,' he said. 'There was too much pressure to start doing that. They should have done it in the second half against Scotland when they were dominating possession so much. Finals require precision. A few mistakes here and there, a missed pass, a dropped pass, a wrong option, wins and loses finals. Australia played the way they played throughout the tournament. England played a new style and it is difficult to be precise with a new style on the big occasion.' It was the hard, harsh truth, and it is fair to say that awareness of it has increased ever since that memorable November day, particularly among the England players.

But if you judged it on the tournament as a whole, the right team won. Australia had played some outstanding rugby; they had been as delightful as they had been devastating. The philosophy of their coach was as fresh as springtime, the ability of his players to carry through so entertaining and skilful a game plan, masterful. None could criticize their approach, either on the field or off it. Even against the mounting pressures which had taken so significant a toll on teams like the All Blacks and their reputation, the Wallabies had remained the great entertainers on the field and the perfect companions off it. Nothing had been too much trouble, even when the pressure was at its height. The courtesy, charm and simple approachability of Bob Dwyer was the cue for his players. As the New Zealanders disintegrated under the weight of expectation, certain members of their management included, the Australians handled it all with a calm control and smooth assurance. Importantly, the high profile adopted by the England captain had proved a factor of major motivation for the Wallabies in the build-up to the final.

'People understand I am a bit of a stirrer,' said David Campese, some time after the tournament. 'I like to stir Will up. A lot of people are not used to that. Don't get me wrong – Will is a good player but I don't like the idea of having Will Carling and the England team. During the World Cup, it was always Will Carling this, Will Carling that. He obviously doesn't hate that role, either. But there has never been a player like that; it was never Andrew Slack and the Wallabies, or David Kirk and the All Blacks. Fifteen players play in a team. But Carling was all over the papers during that tournament. Writing columns, dressed up in some flag [St George, actually!], sitting on a motorcycle in black leathers, posing in casual gear ... everywhere. We got tired of all that. The idea of Will Carling lifting up the World Cup while we stood and watched was too much for us. We were determined to win it and make him watch us receive it.'

There was more than a touch of the downtrodden colonist in Campese's words. Australians take to the image of upper-class Englishmen as happily as they do to warm beer. They often don't wait to find out what the bloke is about; judgements are made from appearances – as in this case. It suggested crass naïvety on the part of the England captain to adopt so leading a profile during the tournament, and especially in the build-up to the final. Either that, or a disregard for the philosophy of Australians. It did not take Campese's words to reveal that side of the Australians' nature to those of us accustomed to Aussies. They're a great people, vibrant, fun-loving, wonderful company, steeped in the values of friendship and exceedingly hospitable – but one thing, to a man, that they cannot stand is a Pom putting himself out blatantly as star quality. They will acknowledge talent in their opponents, but they will have no truck with those they see as the epitome of the English colonial class. A prim little English nose is a tempting target to put out of joint.

Carling's lack of judgement now played into Australian hands. No wonder they fought like tigers, defending their territory and their lead like females defending their cubs. On the ground which signified the heart of English rugby, Twickenham, with all the connotations of the public school inherent in that phrase, fifteen Australians sensed their opportunity to inflict the ultimate failure upon the mother country's representatives. What made England's handling of the situation so astonishing was that, by their actions before the match, they played so instrumental a part in their own demise. Death not by a thousand cuts, but by a thousand words.

12 *Win, Lose, Sweet Chariot . . .*

'The worst part of having success is to try finding someone who is happy for you.'

Bette Midler

England had come down again, maddeningly, at the final fence. Once more, winning post in sight, the team had stumbled clumsily into another barrier. Just as at Cardiff in 1989 and Edinburgh in 1990, Twickenham in November 1991 was consigned to history as another gallant failure. This was becoming costly: two Championships and a gold Cup wrenched from their grasp. The trainers were baffled – the preparation had been perfect. It seemed the team simply couldn't surmount that last hurdle, which begged the question: was loyalty still desirable or was it time for new blood?

Two players decided matters for themselves. Lock forward Paul Ackford retired, although he was to be lured back in dramatic fashion by his club six months later; and flanker Mike Teague was so physically broken by his commitment to the cause during a year of intensive rugby that he retired to his Gloucester home a physical wreck, unable even to return to work. The Rugby Football Union agreed to meet his claims for finance lost during his enforced absence from work, because he was self-employed.

The 1992 Five Nations Championship fixture list now played a cruel trick. England had to go back to

Edinburgh to meet Scotland for their first match, and four weeks later cross the Channel again to play France in Paris. This was like expecting successful escapees from a German prison camp, who had reached neutral Spain to go back and do it all over again. England, you could bet your life, would receive about as warm a welcome, too.

There were positive sides to the situation, however. England had a new coach, Dick Best, who had taken over from Roger Uttley immediately after the World Cup final. Best, given his devotion to attacking rugby and the success his teams had enjoyed with it, arrived with the reputation of a romantic, of throwing prudence aside in favour of all-out attack. Nothing could have been further from the truth. Best espoused the value of attack but it had to be within the right context. Players had to understand exactly their defined role in such a plot, and only through judicious selection of options could they hope to carry it through successfully on this kind of stage. Hard work, as the precursor of any successful operation, was the bedrock of Best's faith.

England replaced the Bath scrum-half Richard Hill with Dewi Morris for the match at Murrayfield. Martin Bayfield came in for Ackford and Tim Rodber won his first cap in the back row. Morris was the interesting selection. He had made his début against Australia as long ago as 1988 and given Nick Farr-Jones, not too bad a player as scrum-halves go, something of a dog's dinner of a day. The great Australian had nodded approvingly as England kept Morris in their side throughout the Five Nations Championship which followed that winter, but had then shaken his head in dismay as England put the scrum-half into the wilderness for the next three years. 'Given the fact that he was all over Farr-Jones like a rash in that 1988 England–Australia match, he ought to have been in the England side ever since,' said John Reason, rugby correspondent for the *Sunday Telegraph*.

Had Morris's fiery attributes been present in the World Cup final, it seems certain that the drift defence Australia employed so effectively that day would have been instantly exposed. Morris makes breaks, and he makes them with real purpose and intent. Flankers and No. 8s who automatically drift wide to cover an opposition back-line move get the shock of their lives when Morris darts up the blindside or crashes through off the open side of the scrum. England were sadly short of such a facility on World Cup final day.

But in Edinburgh there was a greater freedom, which the stifling atmosphere of a World Cup semi-final had never allowed. The England pack was by no means as dominant but the backs now emphasized all that latent talent, running in tries by Underwood and Morris and going close to others in a conclusive victory by 25 points to 7.

Next up, it was Ireland at Twickenham, and those slightly late coming out of the gents' missed Webb's first score, a try straight from the kick-off in twenty-three seconds. That set the tone, for Webb and for Ireland. The England full-back, whose crucial missed kicks had contributed to defeat in the World Cup final, now scored 22 points to equal an eighty-one-year-old Championship record for an England player. Fittingly, Webb is a surgeon; and the clinical method with which he cut up the Irish was a testimony to his skills. England scored six tries, two of them from Webb, who also landed four conversions and two penalty goals. Carling called it the hardest and most exhausting match he had played since 1988 and Australia.

But if England's leader felt drained by that encounter, the French match in Paris was to prove immeasurably more taxing. It finished France 13, England 31 on the scoreboard, and France 13, England 15 on the field. The usual old story in Paris: superior opposition team with altogether greater discipline gets up French players' noses, especially when the fingers in the hooker's eyes and sly punches don't succeed in sparking retaliation from the visitors. In fact, England's ability to ignore any incitement to riot had been commendable through most of Geoff Cooke's tenure as manager. They had concentrated solely on their own game, determined not to allow others to break up their discipline and concentration. Days of shame such as Cardiff in 1989, when mayhem ruled the roost, had become just a distant memory. That reflected creditably not only on the management but, more especially, on the players who had to ignore the antics of frustrated, inferior rivals on the field.

The French, by contrast, simply lost their heads. Then they invoked the conspiracy theory, though it was stretching credulity to suggest that a stressed Irish referee named Stephen Hilditch, who found himself in so unfortunate a situation, could have wished upon himself the trouble with which he was now faced. Lascube kicked a prostrate Englishman and was promptly sent off. The decision induced in Moscato, his front-row colleague, a reaction not dissimilar to that of a bull denied an acquaintance with a cow of its particular fancy. Predictably, his dismissal came minutes later. Everyone will be famous for fifteen minutes in their lives, Andy Warhol had written, but these seemed curious entries for the Hall of Fame. Sending off two Frenchmen in front of a

Parisian crowd was not exactly designed to win Hilditch the Nobel Peace Prize, but it could have put him in line for a VC, given such bravery. It wasn't anything out of the ordinary in Paris, though – just another little dent in the *entente cordiale*.

While most of France reacted with arm-waving gestures of contempt for all things non-Gallic, there were thankfully by now some officials inhabiting the corridors of power within the FFR, the Fédération Française de Rugby, who sided with reason and recognized the culpability of their own players. Bernard Lapasset, who had replaced the ageing Albert Ferrasse as President of the FFR, showed his mettle by accepting the challenge of cleaning up French club rugby, the breeding ground for such acts of violence on the international field. Lapasset's disciplinary colleagues handed out suspensions on both players until 1 September. This was appropriate action to deal with such miscreants who had besmirched the good name of the game.

Will Carling sensibly kept his England team clear of the fall-out. They finished the game runaway winners, testimony to their unflagging control. The French had been trapped in a vice of concentration and discipline. If 1990 had seen an outstanding display by an English team in notoriously difficult climatic conditions in Paris, the performance two years later was praiseworthy for its cool composure amid man-made storms.

Victory had put England on the verge of a second successive Grand Slam, a feat not achieved by any side since England sixty-eight years earlier. Wales stood in their path, poignantly, once more, but this was a new, untried, toothless dragon which had few roars within its wobbly frame. In truth, England had to play only moderately to secure their place in the sun. Wales arrived intent mainly on preserving some semblance of dignity in what was inevitably seen as another England win. How times had changed.

The Welsh resistance was good enough to restrict England to three tries. But tacked on to the twelve they had already scored in the Championship, this gave them an impressive tally of fifteen and cemented their right to another Grand Slam. England won 24–0, easing up. But was it a flawed achievement? Bill Beaumont was one of those who thought so.

Carling, said Beaumont, had been exceedingly fortunate. While his record was second to none and it would be churlish to say otherwise, the reality of the situation had to be examined. 'Will was given the captaincy for a great length of time. No one else has ever had that. The system is there and he has benefited from it. He has been extremely fortunate as a captain. As a player and captain of any side you are given the opportunity and it is up to you to make the best of that opportunity. He has made the best of it and I wouldn't take that away from him. But he has been a very fortunate young man to have captained England during the period they have had. English rugby has been on a high but the standard of the rest of the home countries during that time he has been in charge, has been poor. Lamentable, in fact, in some cases. His has been a great career but it has been at the right time. Who have England played? They have lost to any side of note.'

A harsh appraisal? Not when you study the facts. Under Carling, England lost two out of three matches to Australia and they fell to New Zealand in the World Cup. Amid the poverty of class in northern hemisphere rugby at this time, matches against the southern hemisphere's leading countries were the only true guideline.

Three defeats in four matches against those sides is a powerful statistic to support Beaumont's argument.

You have to make the point that England were in a class of their own in Europe. But what sort of class was it? Wales and France, the two countries which had won or shared the Five Nations Championship title every year from 1965 to 1979, apart from 1973 and 1974, had declined seriously. Ireland had fallen into an even more serious decline. Scotland were competitive but short of real class throughout their side, even though they won the Grand Slam in 1990. That was it. England, profiting to an increasing extent each year by the introduction of Leagues in their club programme, began to pull inexorably clear of all rivals. The French might have matched them, but after sharing the Championship in 1988 and winning it outright in 1989 the selectors sacked the architect of their success, Jacques Fouroux, and promptly paid the price. Fouroux was the man who, according to uninformed 'experts', had ruined French rugby. He might have tried some alarmingly innovative tactics, some of which clearly did not come off, but it was not until Fouroux departed that French international rugby came truly to understand ruination. The chaos which ensued, commensurate with the crash in standards over the Channel, was dismaying even to non-Frenchmen.

The humiliations endured by Wales and Ireland at this time were tragic. Welsh rugby had collapsed into a trough, plunged deeper by a series of defeats at the hands of the All Blacks, who beat them 49–6 in the 1987 World Cup semi-final and promptly repeated the dose twice more, 52–3 and 54–9, when Wales were daft enough to undertake a tour of New Zealand in 1988. That visit included not only two Test matches in two weeks but also fixtures against powerful provincial sides like Waikato, Wellington and North Auckland. It was undertaking a trip to the undertaker's. Even now, Welsh rugby is still struggling to emerge from the coma it induced.

Suffice it to say that Irish rugby was in arguably an even worse plight until a sudden thaw in the chill brought some smiles in the 1993 Five Nations Championship. At times during England's unchallenged run of success, you had to pinch yourself to remember that this was the same tournament once graced by the likes of Gerald Davies, Gareth Edwards, Barry John and Mike Gibson. Otherwise, England's capacity to beat up all comers was too much like beating up your old granny. About as satisfying, too.

This was not England's fault; after all, they had actually improved their standards. But for the others, kind words are difficult to find. However, it is possible only to beat those sides lined up against you, and Carling's team had done that consistently well since his first match as captain, against Australia at Twickenham in November 1988. From that match through to the end of the 1993 Five Nations Championship season, England under Will Carling had won twenty-six of their thirty-five matches, drawing one and losing the remaining eight.

Those eight losses are revealing, however. Australia defeated them twice, Wales twice, New Zealand, Scotland, Argentina and Ireland once each. The common thread was the number of times England failed in absolutely critical matches when the pressure was at its zenith. This happened six of the eight times: a statistic which suggests an important failing at the heart of Carling's team. The two games they lost to Wales cost them a Championship the first time and, in all probability, an historic third Grand Slam the next. Another Grand Slam slipped away to Scotland, a World Cup to Australia and an important World Cup opener to New Zealand. Finally, defeat in Ireland in March 1993 cost them a share of the title in last season's tournament.

But twenty-six wins from thirty-five matches made it positively a golden era, assessed against the constant failures of English teams through the greater part of the 1960s, 1970s and 1980s, three decades notable only for incessant disappointments from the England team, with the odd exception.

Alan Jones, one of the shrewdest motivators of rugby teams the world has seen in recent times and a highly articulate assessor of any sport, believes that England's claim to greatness is flawed, despite the statistics. Years ago, in 1986 in the far south of New Zealand's South Island, Jones's Wallabies lost a Test match to the All Blacks, 13–12. He complained bitterly afterwards: 'Why is it that when we meet these people, we go to pieces?' At the time, England might have asked themselves the same question, not just about facing New Zealanders but about fronting up for the major matches.

Jones has a deep respect for the members of the England team who were instrumental in their successes. 'Rory Underwood has been as good as there has ever been, Carling makes a very significant contribution, Guscott is a clever player. The centres are as good as anything you will get in international rugby, although Carling has to understand he won't score just by breaking through. Unless it is against Italy. I am talking about a Test match. Andrew has stood the test of time and is a good thinker on the game. Richards is a colossus, one of the best thinkers and players. Dooley has been a real servant, he has known how to play. Moore has been the brains of the forwards, and is one of the great organizers in world rugby. He has made an extraordinary contribution to this side.

'But how good was this England side? If they were a great side, they would have won that World Cup final against Australia. If you are a great side, you don't let the British press tell you how to play. They changed their game in the vortex of the fight and you can't do that. The England forwards were better than the Australians, the Wallabies lived off scraps. England should have won; they will never get that chance again. Playing a World Cup final on your home ground has to be an enormous advantage. But England were hoodwinked in the World Cup final and missed their moment in history by losing that match. If you don't play a goalkicker who does the job under pressure then you change your tactics at the eleventh hour. That cost them the World Cup for he [Webb] should have knocked a couple of goals over.'

What of the standards during England's record-breaking era? 'The quality of international rugby worldwide has subsided significantly,' says Jones. 'That is tied up in a way with the eclipse of New Zealand. But as for the Five Nations, the opposition is terrible.'

Was this then the grand illusion of England's triumph? Was the honest verdict that England came first two years running but the rest came nowhere? The England players, not unnaturally, defended their achievements fiercely. The critics were equally voluble in their denigration. The truth, as ever, perhaps lay somewhere in between, but the nagging memory from these times is irresistibly of a Five Nations Championship more devalued in terms of talent than perhaps at any time in its history.

There is always the capacity for an upset, self-induced or otherwise, in any international match. Teams suddenly play beyond their compass to confound expectation, or enjoy outrageous fortune during a game to influence the outcome. So to string together eleven wins from twelve matches in the Five Nations Championship years of 1990, 1991 and 1992 was still some feat. Perhaps not world-shattering in the context of standards pertaining in other corners of the world, but still commendably professional and highly successful in its own field.

But the absence of outstanding opposition tends to deny a team its peak performance. Only by being challenged by the absolute best does a side discover its capacity; the phrase 'bringing out the best in others' is used frequently to describe champion teams. England never had that challenge in the northern hemisphere, so when they did encounter it against the likes of Australia and New Zealand, they realized that they needed sterner opposition on a regular basis. Its absence undoubtedly cost them their opportunity of becoming the best in all the world, rather than just kings of their own domain.

Carling was by now the possessor of a mega-profile. He had nurtured it in its growth and was now reaping the dividends. It was not always appealing. The demand for his time was considerable, the sniping at his back omnipresent, but he had brought the full panoply of the media circus to his own door by frequent exposure for specially commissioned portrait photographs or probing interviews. It was no good complaining that the attention was too great – he had helped create it, and now he had to handle it. Some of the intrusions into his life were grossly insensitive. But there were benefits, like the estimated £30,000-a-year contract he was handed by the *Mail on Sunday* newspaper for an exclusive, 'ghosted' column.

The final act of a tortuously protracted season came at Twickenham on 2 May, when Carling set out to help his club, Harlequins, overcome Bath in the Pilkington Cup final. Twickenham was by now more familiar a ground to the England captain than the Stoop Memorial Ground, home of the Harlequins, just across the road. It was fitting that Twickenham should now witness a performance by England's champion player which remains to this day one of the finest in all his career – perhaps the best.

It was the perfect setting for such a player: a crowd of 57,700, a world record for a club match, crammed in to see a game between two sides that could boast between them a grand total of twenty full internationals. And the weather was perfect. In its way, the game was a classic. The total, unrelenting competitive urge demonstrated by Winterbottom; an extraordinary 'one-off' return to rugby by Ackford, who had been persuaded back only by the sendings-off in the semi-final of Skinner and Langhorn who were both therefore suspended for the final, but who dominated the line-outs with a matchless display; the pace and invention of the esteemed Bath back-line; the cunning, delightful combination in the Harlequins centre of Carling and Halliday, the latter playing his last game before retirement; all the ingredients were there.

For Harlequins, it was eventually a failure. They led 12–6 with eight minutes of normal time remaining, the formbook having long since been discarded by the astonished crowd, who had come in the anticipation of another comfortable Bath success. The west-country club, already the Courage League champions, hauled themselves back from the brink by scoring with minutes left, de Glanville touching down and Webb converting from the touchline to tie the scores at 12–12. Alas, Harlequins now imperilled their chance of victory by missing a series of drop goal attempts from excellent attacking positions, secured by their forwards. Bath survived through extra time and by the last minute neither side had broken the deadlock.

Another failed dropped goal attempt by Harlequins was cleared downfield, Bath for once won a line-out, and Barnes, the master tactician, calmly dropped the goal which won the Cup and the double, with the equanimity of someone putting out the milk bottles. Harlequins had lost 15–12 after extra time, but Carling had played probably the match of his life. From the first, his had been an awesome contribution, full of robust running, powerful breaking of the line, endless determination to create openings for others and strength in the tackle to allow continuity and flow in the movements. He had probed for the chinks in Bath's back-line defence and posed a perpetual threat to his opponents. His kicking out of hand was to remind many of the long, raking touch kicks Paul Dodge had used so effectively a decade earlier for England and the British Lions. Carling was ideally placed to launch the kicks downfield; one position further out into midfield, he had that extra second of time and space in which to clear danger or set up attacks. He used it with brutal effectiveness, constantly forcing Bath's forwards to turn and toil fifty or sixty yards back into their own territory. That he was to finish on the losing side was the cruellest of climaxes to a season of swaggering highs and morbid lows.

The World Cup had been lost at the final hurdle,

another Grand Slam won. Now the Pilkington Cup had been snatched away from Will Carling's grasp in even more dramatic fashion than the World Cup on the same ground six months earlier. But there was one good thing about the end of the 1992 Pilkington Cup final. It meant the close of the season and the first chance for Carling to take a break from rugby football since the summer of 1989, when he had missed the Lions tour of Australia through injury. From the start of that international season, when England beat Fiji at Twickenham in November 1989, through to the end of the 1991–2 season, Will Carling had played twenty-four internationals in the course of twenty-seven months.

Enoch Powell had once started a much reported speech, albeit on a rather different theme, with a quote from Euripides: 'Those whom the Gods wish to destroy, they first make mad.' Playing international rugby, with all its commensurate pressures both mental and physical, almost once a month for over two years, was guaranteed to reduce the career span of any top player, if not send him to the madhouse. Few can take that kind of acute commitment year after year and remain physically fresh and mentally sharp. Such figures are highly revealing and are a dire indictment of those in authority who administer the game world-wide with scant concern for the burdens carried nowadays by the best players. Mobile banks, indeed.

But still ticking away deep within Carling's subconscious was the craving for success: the second son syndrome, manifested again. Nor did it affect solely his sporting life: he needed to be an achiever in his work, to feel a success, every bit as much as in his rugby. After leaving the Army he had joined Mobil Oil, where he was trained in marketing, as part of the company's graduate intake. Mobil executives remember that he interviewed well, but he was to remain with them for little more than twelve months before doors were opened sufficiently elsewhere for him to strike out alone with the formation of his own companies.

The reason for this lay in the growing expansion of his sport. Rugby union was still, agonizingly, coming to terms with the explosion of interest it had created within its own game. This attraction declared itself in many ways, including, of course, attendances at matches. The players developed a profile which would once have been unimaginable and, given the fact that they now inhabited a world which was turned on its axis by money, financial reward for the best players, if it was done judiciously, seemed a short step away. But that proved to be a simplistic view.

As England captain, Will Carling was in pole position to benefit. He had courted publicity assiduously, and had all the qualifications as a target for major corporate interest. He was presentable, good-looking, articulate and, above all, highly successful in his sport. What more could the head of a company seek?

Geoff Cooke recalls the circumstances in which Carling started his own companies. 'We were moving into a totally different scenario. He was inevitably at the forefront of that. He was exactly the sort of person commercial people wanted. He was getting lots of requests and offers of money and was in a very difficult situation: it wasn't his doing.' The strict regulations governing amateurism stated that no player could make money out of rugby-related activities. The last three words were sacrosanct to the rules of the game, akin to the Bible's 'Thou shall not' laws. The writing of books and newspaper articles was brought in, under some

pressure for change, but the wall against which the
players continued to collide consists of the words
'rugby-related activities'. This is a major restriction
which denies them pecuniary advantage from their
involvement in the game. Dudley Wood, as defender of
the faith, would probably not leap to the mind of any
England player as his favoured friend in this particular
field. But Wood goes on pointing out, in his own quiet
but meaningful manner, the consequences of the law. It
is a continual frustration to the players, but as Wood
says so often, for those who seek money from the game
rugby league is an open option.

Nevertheless, by running his own companies, Carling
could benefit in kind. He was not making money *per se*
from rugby-related activities because he was not wearing
his England kit in advertisements, but everyone knew
who Will Carling was, and it seemed more than coinci-
dental that the mushrooming success of his companies
coincided with his high profile in rugby union. There
was nothing whatsoever illegal about this. But as Geoff
Cooke says: 'The Rugby Football Union were hell-bent
on stopping it. Will Carling had the impression of more
freedom from the International Board. People there were
making him offers yet this was totally counter to what
the hierarchy of the Rugby Football Union wanted. So
you had this clash. Will didn't know which way to turn.
He was trying to understand the political agenda, and
yet was being offered lucrative opportunities. He has
solved it by having his own business, but it still causes
some tensions.'

Cooke is critical of the format of the RFU committee,
which he regards as unwieldy and not terribly representative of modern views. 'The Rugby Football Union
committee is a very large body of people, you cannot

get unanimity. There is a group of people on the committee who totally understand the way the game is changing. But there are some that have had the opposite extreme view. They are resistant to change of any sort. Therefore, nothing will change them. In the middle you have a group with sway. That is the problem of the decision-making process we have got. But it was the International Board that changed the process, not the players. If only we [England] had played by the same rules off the field and allowed the players to do what they can, it would be better.'

As it is, says Cooke, England are continuing to get themselves into what he terms 'an awful knot'. He warns: 'We are now going down the most dangerous road. Now, we have large Leagues with enormous pressures on the leading players only because of money. Money is dominating the game. Clubs need to generate money and the more clubs do that, the more they will use players to buy people in to sustain their position. We say, "What is so wrong with sharing that money?" Can't some go into a players' pool? I don't know where it is going to lead. Increasingly, professionalism is an inevitable consequence of the structure of the game.'

According to the latest available figures from Companies House, Carling has interests in three companies: Inspirational Horizons Ltd, Insights Ltd, and Player-Vision Ltd. His fellow directors in the last two companies include Peter Winterbottom, Brian Moore, Richard Hill, Harlequins Chairman Roger Looker and his agent, John Holmes, all rugby associated. The latter is listed as a director of Insights Ltd, the others, named as directors, either are or have been part of the files of PlayerVision Ltd. For the year ending 31 July 1992, Insights Ltd declared current assets of £4,883, with current liabilities £87,975. A bank overdraft of £34,671 was included in this figure. Only abbreviated accounts for the period ended 31 December 1990 are available for PlayerVision Ltd.

William Derek John Carling is listed as company secretary of Inspirational Horizons Ltd. The figures available from Companies House in May 1993 show that current assets were £9,596, after deduction of liabilities of £25,121. Staff costs amounted to £46,000, directors accounting for £44,000 of that total.

Carling has organized his business affairs properly and professionally. RFU secretary Dudley Wood says: 'Will has had good advice along the way from Geoff Cooke, John Holmes and others. That has helped him. The pressures of being England captain are enormous. It is worse than my position. The expectations now are a consequence of the extreme popularity of the game nowadays. Anyone in a top sport has to face those pressures. It is hard on the rugby player because of the amateur aspect of the game. Pressure is a funny thing: others take it in their stride while others it gets to. Will Carling struggled in the early days but he has learned to absorb it now.'

Carling, Wood and John Holmes lunched together to ascertain precisely the fields where commercial advantages might be exploited by the England captain. Wood says: 'John wanted to get absolutely straight what was possible and what was not. He seems very good, a clever agent. He is keen that his people convey the right image. We ran into a bit of difficulty at one stage [with the England players] mainly because nobody knew what was permissible and what wasn't. I don't agree with players getting paid – it would destroy the character of the game. But because of the success of the game we can afford to look after them very well and I totally support that. I mean things like looking after wives and girlfriends – I am very happy about that. But if money is going to become the motivating force for players or administrators, we have lost it.'

There is no doubt that Carling's earning potential would be astronomical if the strict regulations on rugby union players were eased. But already he is benefiting considerably from the activities of his companies, none of which are exactly harmed by having England's rugby captain on their books. Inspirational Horizons is a company which organizes conferences, assisting businessmen in the fields of motivation by the use of leading sports personalities. Players like Gary Lineker, probably John Holmes's most famous client, and David Gower have been used in this area. Carling's company seeks to put the experience of top sportsmen before businessmen from a wide range of industry. Conferences and seminars can be hugely profitable, too. And the contacts are guaranteed. As Carling himself admits: 'I suppose one of the advantages of being England captain is that it tends to get me quick access to the people in a company who make the decisions.' Well, it would not exactly be an impediment.

This privileged opportunity gives a sense of unease in some sections of the game, explains Dudley Wood. Carling benefits because his profile is so high, says the RFU secretary. 'He is in a position of benefiting, others are not. But we never really had the right to prevent that. Why should the England captain not open a super-market? But there are a lot of rugby people around who don't like to see rugby players allowed profit in any way.'

It's the old conundrum: it translates into one scenario

for the glamorous threequarter, another for the gnarled old forward. Some problem that: for the tubby old prop can see few horizons, inspirational or otherwise.

13 Mickey Mouse and the Psychologist's Error

'Will has been shown to be fallible. A Test captain has got to be able to think on his feet.'

Wayne Shelford

So now we knew. It was official: we had Will Carling's word for it. 'England,' blazed the headline above his exclusive newspaper column, 'can win their third Grand Slam.' That was not all. It would be achieved, the heading continued, to ensure readership attention . . . 'with style'.

The naïve cheered such words prophesying glory, the cautious groaned at the incaution of it. In France, Wales, Scotland and Ireland they simply tore out, not their hair, but the appropriate press cutting and tucked it away purposefully inside their wallets. For in the sense of having a psychological advantage in the build-up to an international rugby match, this was currency. Clearly Will Carling had never heard the 1940 wartime phrase: 'Careless talk costs lives.' Or, in this case, internationals . . . The blazing out of such words and promises has become a powerful motivational force to opponents before a contest. Sport today involves a thousand methods of motivation, of stirring animation among its contestants, and few coaches have used this weapon more tellingly than the Australian Alan Jones. 'It will be dockside brawl stuff,' he said on the eve of the Wales–Australia Test match in 1984, in Cardiff. 'Wales will be dirty on Saturday. These people would hit you over the head with a bottle if they could.'

Target idea No. 1: Rattle your opponents, make them irrational in their mind and, consequently, ineffective in their actions. Target idea No. 2: Open the referee's eyes to what might occur. If you're the team attempting to play the rugby, you don't want to be diverted by foul play from opponents intent only on distracting and frustrating the classier side. Target idea No. 3: Say something which is almost certain to invoke a heated reply. You never know what they might say then. It could be that more words of motivation will be released.

The plot worked like a charm in Wales. National coach John Bevan, clearly incensed, retorted: 'Wales could beat the Wallabies nine times out of ten.' See how clever it is? Now Australia had another Exocet primed and ready in their armour, and Jones, the master strategist, used it ruthlessly. 'Can you believe the arrogance of these people?' he stormed, to his team. 'Just listen to what this guy said.'

David Campese wrote later: 'I would say that by ten o'clock on that Friday night, Australia had won the Test match at Cardiff the next day!' Before the Australian players went out to face Wales, Alan Jones had been to each member of his team and asked him a question, face to face, slowly and deliberately: 'Can your opponent beat you nine times out of ten?' Wales had been had for breakfast, lunch and tea by the masterful Jones. It was the use of the psychology weapon at its wiliest.

A more recent example of the technique was the 1993 University Boat Race. Oxford's crew contained the celebrated Matthew Pinsent, the Dark Blues' president and

Olympic champion oarsman. Every day, in the week leading up to the race, the press was charged with acquiring a Boat Race piece, a feature interview. Who was their man? No prizes ... Matthew Pinsent. By the end of the week, Pinsent, the gold medallist, was so great a God that he even ate three Shredded Wheat for breakfast. Cambridge were puking at the mention of his name. But now came the psychology. Every Pinsent feature was pinned on the Light Blues changing-room wall. 'By the time Cambridge got into that boat, they were ready to kill Matthew Pinsent,' said a Cambridge insider. The outcome – Cambridge, winners, by the proverbial country mile ...

Will Carling knew a thing or two about psychology. At least he should have done. But now, not for the first time in his career, he offered his opponents an enormous psychological advantage even before a match had been played. It was woefully naïve, and England's players would come to regret it. Carling could not even claim to have been misrepresented by a flamboyant headline out of context, for he said, in the *Mail on Sunday* article on 10 January 1993: 'There is winning, and there is winning with style and conviction. The England rugby team are drawn irresistibly to the second option as we embark on our mission to secure an historic, third consecutive Grand Slam. We believe if we play to 95 per cent of our potential in the four games, beginning against France on Saturday, we will win another Grand Slam. That ideal is not wreathed in arrogance. As a team, we feel that rather than simply aiming to win, we must aim to provide a quality of performance. To solely concentrate on winning, I think, lowers the expectation of the team, lowers the level of play.'

The arrogance, whatever Carling might have thought,

was breathtaking, impudent. Winning was no longer enough for England – they had to do it in the grand style. The inference was clear: this lot aren't in our class. Just beating them is no satisfaction, we want to embarrass them as well. Why, we won't even have to play at 100 per cent to beat them.

An astute captain would have used a low-key approach in every press conference and every newspaper interview. 'No one has ever won three Grand Slams on the run. That suggests it is a well nigh impossible task,' would have been the gist of his comments. 'Why should we think we can do it when every other side has failed? If we win two or especially three of our four matches this season, we will have done well.' The strategy might even have been stretched a little further: 'We are tired, the players are getting old, you can't expect them to go on for ever. I am not sure whether they can do it any more.'

Then the tabloid newspapers could have their fling. You know the sort of thing: 'Carling condemns his own players,' or 'You're too old – Carling slams his mates,' or even 'Washed up – my no-hope mates, by Will Carling.' 'England captain Will Carling last night launched an extraordinary attack on his fellow England colleagues, slamming them as too old for another Grand Slam' . . . and so on. And all the while, you would be telling your players in the privacy of the dressing-room: 'This lot aren't fit to lace our boots. We're the class act, they can't play. We can skin them. Let's go out and do it – NOW.'

Besides, was such enormous optimism justified, before a ball had even been kicked? England had won just once in Wales on their last fourteen visits; was this a record to inspire Churchillian confidence? After all, history was

littered with English teams who had lost to Welsh sides.
By a low-key approach, England might have drawn the
sting from the opposition. Certainly their opponents
might not have taken the field as though eighty minutes
of rugby were going to decide whether they could ever
hold their heads up again in their homeland.

Despite all his experience of the media, Carling has
never learned how to handle it professionally. His words
and actions before the World Cup final had got up the
noses of the Australians: now he was expressing a view
which was sure to fuel the charge of arrogance, particularly in countries like Wales and Scotland. Three years
studying psychology had apparently failed to teach him
the value of getting the media on your side and of luring
your opponent into a false sense of security.

The implications of so amateurish an approach amid
the ultra-professionalism which marked every other
aspect of England's pre-match preparation were
bewildering. Teams go to the greatest possible lengths
to prepare for international rugby matches these days –
nothing is left to chance. Managers fuss and pay intense
attention to the tiniest detail, lest it become vital;
coaches are schooled endlessly in the arts of readiness
and player motivation. Fitness, it goes without saying,
is of paramount importance. Yet the value of presenting
the correct attitude, the right words, to the outside
world is ignored. Players are allowed to make the most
outlandish statements, which have the effect of putting
a rocket of stimulus into the shorts of the opposition and
render all the advance preparation quite meaningless.

Public relations are of enormous worth today, not
only in presenting the right image but in conveying the
impression you want for general consumption. The
value of lulling opponents into complacency is over-

looked time and again by some. But not everyone makes this cardinal error. For contrast, listen to the interviews given by the 1993 British Isles coach, Ian McGeechan. Whether he is speaking as the man behind the Lions or Scotland, the former Leeds schoolmaster is a master of the spoken word. No one could accuse him of being beyond reach, of refusing interviews – he is freely available to all, and furthermore, meets the interviewer with a smile. But if you expect Ian McGeechan to start saying that his teams can win, and not just win but win in style, by playing to only 95 per cent of their potential, you must believe the moon is made of blue cheese. The same goes for Alan Jones. These men are simply not given to such guileless remarks. Nor are most New Zealanders.

The reaction to the selection of the Lions squad to tour New Zealand was highly instructive. Criticism, in varying degrees, greeted the announcement in British quarters. Those in New Zealand charged with planning the defeat of the Lions reacted quite differently. It was, we were told from across the world, a squad to demand respect. It had strength, power, experience and many proven world-class performers. It was a squad which would go down well, down under. This was all pure, undiluted Kiwi psychology at work: try to convince the Lions that they have the men to succeed, lull them into that dangerous assumption, then pick a team to combat the big, grizzly Lions forwards.

The world saw the result of Will Carling's words at Cardiff a few weeks later. Fifteen Welshmen, encouraged by 50,000 more, were prepared to lay down their lives to deny Carling and his England team their coveted third Grand Slam. Limited in talent they may have been, and distinctly short of the style to which Carling's England aspired, but the Welsh chased, harried, hustled and tackled like ... well, like fifteen Australians at Twickenham fifteen months earlier.

Carling's words had been hopelessly misguided and destructive. Other players wrote newspaper columns but resisted, either through advice or through their own wariness, any desire to rub opposition noses in the mire. England's approach ought to have been one-dimensional, namely to win the game – by a penalty goal to nil, if need be. If you want your place in history, you don't concern yourself unduly about riding the smartest bus on the road to get there. Besides, Carling had plenty of reason to take a completely opposite view. England had already played two internationals in the season before the 1993 Five Nations Championship began, and in both their performance had been about as unconvincing as that of the Chancellor of the Exchequer.

They went to Wembley to meet Canada because of building work at Twickenham, and managed a fairly leaden 26–13 victory. Some parts functioned, others didn't, on the day. But it was, after all, only mid-October – too early in the season to judge, was the conventional view, and fair enough, too. Then came the South Africans, international lepers for years but now riding a tide of emotion back to Twickenham for their first appearance on the ground since 1969. But their much-vaunted laager mentality was England's for much of the first fifty minutes, as the unfancied Springboks, beaten consistently on their tour of France, took it to their opponents. It surely could not last, and it didn't, although Botha's kicking kept it close for too long. England re-gathered their composure and romped away to victory. But a sense of unease prevailed.

France were beaten by a whisker, and then came the

defeat in Wales, and another revealing insight into Carling's leadership. With only a minute or two of the match remaining, Wales continued to hold tenaciously to the 10–9 lead they had taken into half-time. But then England were awarded a penalty kick. There was no doubt that the position was difficult. It was inside Welsh territory but close to the half-way line. Every Englishman raised his eyes to the distant Welsh posts and asked himself one question: 'Can he kick it?' He, full-back Jonathan Webb, thought not. It is too far out, was the view he communicated to his captain. Will Carling accepted it. The ball was kicked deeper into the Welsh half, Carling explaining later that assuming England won the resultant line-out, they still had time to get the score which would win the match. The fact that they had tried and failed to do just that for the last thirty-nine minutes did not seem to weigh very heavily on his mind.

So Webb escaped the crushing responsibility, but Carling, as leader, could not escape the judgement of history. Views are mixed on the subject. 'You cannot force a player to kick for goal if he is convinced he cannot do it,' one coach told me. But others saw it as Carling's inescapable task, his duty, to tell his goalkicker to attempt it. 'He should have been thrown the ball and told to kick the bloody thing, whatever he thought,' a former international player said. 'Maybe the adrenalin would have carried it over.'

International rugby has built its history on such moments. Back in 1966 at Cardiff, I had seen the French full-back Claude Lacaze line up a penalty goal chance which would decide the international of that year against Wales. It was from an intimidating distance, wide out near the touchline. But the time had come for the last act; Wales, holding a slender 9–8 lead, had conceded a penalty, but the referee's final whistle was sure to follow the kick. Lacaze could have turned down the chance, possibly preferring an up and under to the Welsh line and the hope of a try. But he went for glory.

Cardiff Arms Park was trapped, spellbound, as the little Frenchman ran up to kick. It was a superb effort, too. High and handsome it soared towards the Welsh posts, as a Frenchman or two began to raise arms of triumph. But it had been a blustery day in Cardiff, and in those split seconds which are crucial, a gust of wind caught the ball. It tugged at it agonizingly, fatally, as it neared its target . . . and pulled it feet wide of the far post. He had the length, but not the glory. The final whistle sounded. Poor Lacaze: he crouched down, head buried in his hands, utterly disconsolate – another magnificent victim of the sporting melodrama which has fuelled imaginations and inspired young men and women through the decades.

England elected not to go for glory at Cardiff. It was their final chance, not of a place in history, but of making history. They had lost 10–9. Bill Beaumont saw it from the commentary box. 'England had it so easy for three years. But they have got into a rut and now have some fundamental changes to make. The captaincy was in a rut, the leadership was in a rut. You have to treat every international as though it is your last one. England got carried away with their own success. All this euphoria . . . the Five Nations standard has never been lower.'

The ending of England's dream of sporting immortality was, strangely, nowhere near as shattering as the experience of Murrayfield, 1990. After all, England had fallen so often on the big occasion. The first time it happened, it had stunned the English to a man. This time, expectations had not exactly been adjusted commensurate with that knowledge but there was, in the back of everyone's mind, the memory of Scotland. If it could happen then, it could happen again. Now, it did.

England had reason to rub their eyes, not to discard the tears but in disbelief. For Wales, 1993, read Australia, 1991. The only difference was the sea of celebration which broke over the National Stadium immediately the final whistle sounded. Any stranger would have concluded that the Welsh had just won the Triple Crown, the Five Nations Championship, the Grand Slam and the national lottery (had there been one). The nation was ecstatic; a victory over the English tasted sweeter than any other. To have done it now, thus denying England their chance of history, induced delight not seen at the ground for decades. Cardiff was an orgy of celebration all night long.

Through the long evening, Geoff Cooke, Will Carling and the rest of the English party bit their lips, smiled shallowly and shared the celebrations of their hosts. Smile through the pain – that is rugby's way. The dull ache in the pit of each man's stomach was a personal ailment to be hidden. Cooke seethed in private frustration at the influence which he believed had cost his team everlasting glory.

The wise men of the International Rugby Board's law-making committee had delved deep into their lucky-dip box some while earlier, and come up clutching a major law reform straight out of Mickey Mouse and Disney-land. It stated that a team on the attack would lose the put-in at a scrum if they failed to work the ball clear in loose play. This was a policy as fair and reasonable as the belief that Paris is the capital city of Cambodia. The idea had been to force teams to speed up and be more creative, to avoid the constant stoppages for set scrums. It would make sides show greater invention. If they could not protect the ball when in possession, then tough luck – they would have to give it to the other side, at the scrum.

No one in their right mind could accuse Will Carling's England side of being the Arsenal of the rugby world: boring and predictable. They had scored some wonderful tries and played some vivid attacking rugby. But now it was England who suffered the most. Others seized the opportunity to play a spoiling, muddling game which made life intolerable for any side wishing to attack. England's manager, Geoff Cooke, and their coach, Dick Best, complained long and loud about it. If you thought that condemned them as the arch-complainers, then you'd also have to indict Bob Dwyer, coach of world champions Australia. Dwyer also hated the new laws, and with reason: they helped moderate sides to create a game which was suddenly without any cohesion or pattern. The best teams were sucked into a morass of mediocrity in which creative, sustained, attacking rugby was virtually impossible.

The fudge the International Board came up with in March 1994 to deflect some of the intense criticism of this law spoke volumes for the sort of people they were. Rather than admit they had been wrong, they preferred a compromise which few applauded.

Cooke fumed at this absurd intrusion into a game which had seemed perfectly good enough before the meddling of the lawmen. After all, the 1991 World Cup had been a glittering illustration of all the finest elements of the sport, whether it was being played by Australia, Argentina, Ireland, Western Samoa, the French or the

English. No one ended that tournament saying the laws were all wrong and clamouring for change. Now, suddenly, we were being told that a radical re-think was required. Not in the view of the players or the coaches, mind you, just of the law-makers, who went ahead quite arbitrarily without apparently making any attempt to elicit the views of those at the sharp end – the people who actually played the game. 'All the changes have completely thrown our pattern of play out of the window,' said Cooke. His assessment was correct, too. England hadn't fired all season and the new laws were a major factor.

The midfield was now as congested as rush hour on Broadway, bodies cluttering up every inch of turf because it was no longer necessary for all the forwards to commit themselves to the hurly-burly up front. The onus was on the attacking side to release the ball: consequently, even the most bone-headed of forwards quickly ascertained that it was more profitable to stand off and await the transference of the ball down the opposition's back-line. Then three forwards could help a centre hammer into the fly-half or centre on the other team and tie in the ball until the referee's whistle sounded, giving the defending team possession at the resultant scrum. It was a philosophy thought up in the lunatic asylum.

Nevertheless, it was instrumental in denying England a third Grand Slam. Their minds became as muddled as the cluttered fields, for orthodox attacking play was suddenly reduced to a premium. It would be stretching the truth to say that quality attacking rugby was no longer possible, for the try that the recalled Stuart Barnes fashioned for Rory Underwood against Scotland demonstrated that exquisite talent could always prevail. But it has been made intensely more difficult. England, by dint of the fact that they possessed an ageing pack of forwards, lacked the capacity to adapt. This was not their fault.

Barnes made a difference, when he came in for Rob Andrew against Scotland, and the old enemy was beaten 26-12. However, there was one mitigating factor of some importance: Scotland were actually leading when they lost their influential fly-half Craig Chalmers with a broken arm. England then broke the shackles, Guscott sweeping gloriously upfield from Barnes's pass on a wide arc to put Rory Underwood over for the try of the season.

It had been just like the old times, but the moment was fleeting. Dublin, for the last match of the Championship, offered England at best a share of the title with the French. It was the weekend when the British Lions squad would be chosen, and the word was that when Will Carling got to Dublin he heard that he had no chance of winning the captaincy of the most famous British rugby touring team. Newspaper reports alleged that he promptly withdrew his name from consideration. Whether the story was true or apocryphal is not important. What is beyond dispute is that England never came to terms with the motivation required against an Irish side that was charged up with emotion from their previous unexpected victory over Wales in Cardiff. They had not been a million miles away from defeating the French at Lansdowne Road earlier in the Championship, and now they attacked the tired, dispirited English relentlessly. There was not a great will to resist in the English camp.

An unknown named Eric Elwood emerged from the ranks of Irish second division rugby to play that long dreamed of renaissance role all Irishmen sought. At the end of a long, frustrating season, England never escaped the Hibernians' wily hold. Ireland 17, England 3, it finished; there was more rubbing of eyes in sheer disbelief afterwards on both sides of the Irish Sea.

The match against Ireland was, in a sense, the end of an era for England. The fine side which had dominated European rugby was breaking up. Peter Winterbottom had long since planned his retirement, and Wade Dooley shared his timing. Both were subsequently selected for the British Lions tour of New Zealand, thereby delaying the end of their careers until July 1993. Jonathan Webb, forever juggling hospital duties and rugby training sessions, also decided to retire at the end of the season. By April, Jeff Probyn had reached thirty-seven and surely could no longer defy the ageing process. But the Wasps' tight head prop had much cause for dejection when the British Lions squad for New Zealand was announced. Selection is the ultimate accolade for a player, and transcends even the material reward some seek from their association with the game. To wear the Lions shirt elevates rugbymen into an exclusive, prized club. This is the gold top brigade: only the finest ever come this way.

Both Carling and Probyn had missed out in 1989 when the Lions went to Australia, the former through injury but the latter because of non-selection, which mystified observers. Now, however, Carling achieved the reward he merited; but for Probyn, by now the holder of as many caps as years, there was only another crushing disappointment when he was not selected. Personalities may have had as much to do with it as playing ability.

But even Probyn's absence paled into insignificance as an issue beside the selectors' decision to overlook Carling as captain. On the face of it this was astonishing.

At the beginning of the season, there seemed no debate to conduct regarding the captaincy; it had appeared a closed book. England, under Will Carling, had dominated European rugby since the start of 1989 and had been far and away the most successful side, even allowing for the fatal slips. Had they gone through the 1993 season to their intended destiny, it seems inconceivable that the Lions selectors would have been able to deny Carling the leadership. But failure in Wales was now used against him. The old flaws were re-examined; the boy was analysed and dissected. By an overwhelming majority, the Lions selectors decided that they wanted someone other than Carling to take the British Isles team to New Zealand.

This was no attempt to get the Englishman off the trip; he was immediately named in the party. But it spoke volumes about the way Carling was perceived by selectors outside England. It was understood at the time that the support for Carling as leader was confined to one representative, presumably the England and Lions manager Geoff Cooke. But there were no other Carling fanciers. Five other voices are said to have expressed firm views against the Englishman.

But if not Carling, who? Gavin Hastings had only the briefest of experience as an international captain, Ieuan Evans had been the leader of a struggling Welsh side which offered no sort of platform for him to demonstrate his leadership qualities, and Ireland's skipper, Michael Bradley, would not make the trip because he was not one of the two best scrum-halves. Other candidates hardly leapt to mind, but all the same, the British Lions selectors made it perfectly clear at an early stage that they did not want Will Carling as captain.

The decision could only have been founded on the

belief that Carling was not the man to weld together the Welsh, the Irish and the Scots with his England colleagues. The reason, almost certainly, was his remote, aloof image, the antithesis of the character required to unite differing factions from Britain and Ireland. Was Will Carling the best equipped to handle the difficult times which might develop on and off the field in New Zealand? Would he present the right image as captain of a British Isles touring team abroad? The resounding reply from those charged with selection was firmly and emphatically 'No'.

After the decision had been made to appoint Gavin Hastings as leader, the predictable comment from Carling to the effect that he preferred making the tour without the responsibility of captaincy was irrelevant. The mask was back in place, quickly erected to hide the inner blow to his pride. Of course Carling had wanted to be leader – had he not, he would have announced at the start of the Five Nations Championship back in January that he wished to tour with the Lions but not as captain, preferring a break from the pressure. His words after Hastings had been chosen came too late, and smacked of hurt pride.

Judged by results and experience, the decision was absurd. Carling had led England thirty-five times: Hastings had captained Scotland four times. Furthermore, the Scotsman's captaincy under the intense pressure of a hugely improved England performance at Twickenham in March had gone badly off the rails. Experience, success and overwhelmingly superior knowledge went out of the window in the captaincy debate. There must have been some extremely compelling reason for that; and the perception of Will Carling as the arrogant, stand-offish leader of a select England coterie was one of the very few plausible explanations. Perhaps, too, the formation of the Lions management team did not help. Geoff Cooke had won the position of manager, while England coach Dick Best was chosen as assistant to the Scottish coach Ian McGeechan. Had Carling toured as captain, three of the four key positions would have been held by Englishmen. Politically, this was probably seen as untenable, yet it would have been fully justified by results over previous seasons. Wales and Ireland had achieved virtually nothing, so Scotland had provided the only sustained challenge to England's ascendancy. Hastings's appointment balanced the influence, but there were dark scowls of disapproval from certain members of the England camp.

'The Celtic fringe got into Carling; it was disgraceful he didn't get the captaincy,' said one insider. There was, perhaps, more than a modicum of truth to that, but in the end, whatever history may suggest concerning the outcome to the tour, I believe the Lions selectors made the correct decision for the touring party and for Will Carling, too. His had been an onerous burden for too long: the experience of being sniped at incessantly can very rapidly chip off the gloss of satisfaction at being leader. For Carling to have stepped off the treadmill with England and instantly clambered back on board in the cause of the British Lions would have been a wearying experience.

As a club colleague at Harlequins said: 'He has never been just one of the boys, one of the anonymous group who can sit back and enjoy their time off and do things together. It is always different for the captain, and to make a major tour not as leader would be highly beneficial to him.' This is a view with which Geoff Cooke concurred.

The other reason for not choosing Carling was that Gavin Hastings was the better candidate. Not in experience of leadership, success or such criteria – plainly, he could not hold a candle to the Englishman in that respect. But Hastings had far more natural appeal as a figurehead for a British Isles squad. He was welcoming and genuine, warm, able to mix comfortably, and at ease whatever the company. He was also a player capable of getting his men behind him, a critical factor. He could handle the media, and greet all comers with a conviction Carling has never mastered. Such qualities from the captain are essential on a British Isles tour. 'The kind of man,' said one Scot, 'whom you would choose to go with you into the jungle.' Which is never a bad judgement of a fellow human being. Hastings always had the potential to let his hair down with his team, if the situation demanded that. He could be comfortable and convincing when exerting his authority, but also capable of integrating with his players. Such qualities were almost certainly decisive when the Lions selectors came to assessing the man they wanted to lead their squad.

So Will Carling missed out on the highest accolade available to a British rugby player. He had seemed the clear favourite for the job, at one time the only horse in the field, but the selectors had wanted a thoroughbred in every sense. Their decision to choose Gavin Hastings was by no means entirely credible, for the reason that full-back is just about the worst position on the field from which to direct a side. Because of that, they also pondered at some length the contribution Peter Winterbottom might make. New Zealanders would have nodded with firm approval had he been chosen. Ever since Wilson Whineray retired in 1965, every All Black touring party on a major overseas visit to the British Isles or France has been led by a back-row forward, with the exception of the 1983 tourists, who were captained by a wing, Stu Wilson. A wholly unsuccessful diversion that proved to be, too, according to a member of that party, the former All Black hooker Hika Reid.

Reid was a coach with the Courage League club London Irish until May 1994. But his knowledge of the game is sound, and he says emphatically: 'Winterbottom should have got the Lions job. He was widely respected, knew New Zealand well because he played there and also made the last Lions tour there in 1983. But above all that, he was in the ideal position to make decisions on the run. Critical, instant decisions have to be made during internationals and if your leader is out at full-back, he is in no position to act straight away. I agreed with the decision not to choose Carling, for that same reason. A back-row forward is far better placed to see the game at close hand.'

Wayne Shelford, a former captain of the All Blacks, also applauded the decision to overlook Carling but had a different view about Hastings's appointment: 'Gavin Hastings was without doubt the right choice. He had a good Championship, notwithstanding his kicking. He gives off the right signals and obviously knows how to delegate. Will has been shown to be fallible. He lost the game in Cardiff when he had forty minutes to turn it around and he didn't do it. A test captain has got to be able to think on his feet. Even if it means radically changing the game plan you've spent weeks planning and days rehearsing, it has got to be ditched in mid-stream. Will has not proved that he can do that. In part, that is because England themselves have not looked versatile enough in what they do, as was shown once again in Dublin.'

Before Carling flew out of London with the British Lions squad on 13 May, there was one final match for him to play at the end of the northern hemisphere season. Harlequins had reached another Pilkington Cup final – perilously again, it has to be conceded, by a single point victory in the semi-final over Wasps. So they crossed the A316 from their home base at the Stoop on 1 May to confront Leicester, convincing conquerors of Northampton in the other semi-final.

Harlequins arrived for their third successive final, a tribute to their competitive instincts but, said their critics, a shocking indictment of their lack of consistency in league rugby during the greater part of the season. This might have been an easy charge to lay, but it by no means told the proper story. With internationals such as Carling, Moore, Winterbottom, Leonard, Coker and Edwards in the club they had an intrinsic difficulty. None could pretend that a Harlequins team without them was anything like a first-strength side. But sometimes, in deep midwinter, a Harlequins team with them seemed nothing like a full-strength side, either, because of the influence of international rugby – on their minds and bodies.

Asking players to perform from January to March in the cauldron of the Five Nations Championship and then slip back into club rugby in the intervening weeks with no reduction in mental intensity or physical commitment was to expect the impossible. International rugby drains players in the mind and exhausts their bodies. How could anyone seriously criticize the likes of Will Carling if, seven days after the fearsome intensity of an England international in Paris, he found a

Harlequins League game at Bristol somewhat of a diminution in motivational terms? Players are not machines, they cannot be fine-tuned and just revved up to maximum performance by turning a key. In 1991, when England won their first Grand Slam in the match against France at Twickenham, Harlequins provided seven players for the England match squad, five in the side itself. Bath, by clear evidence the greatest club side in England, indeed in the northern hemisphere, these past ten years, had only two players in the team, with one more on the bench.

By 1993, and England's final home match of the Championship, the balance had been redressed. Four Harlequins, four Bath men in the England team, with two other Bath players on the bench. Bath, incidentally, had been eliminated from the 1993 Pilkington Cup by contriving to lose at Second Division club Waterloo. Then, needing to win their final League match at Saracens to become League champions, they stuttered and stumbled, trailing with eight minutes remaining against a team already relegated to Division 2. The weariness induced by a long, enervating season had caught up with Bath just as surely as it has influenced Harlequins' league performances for some years past. Bath escaped, to win the title, but the fatigue that had crept insidiously into their club had been the same virus afflicting Harlequins in league rugby for years.

Before the start there was a revealing moment of contrasts. The captain, Winterbottom, representing Harlequins for the last time before retirement, was busily engaged in counselling some of his younger troops prior to the kick-off. Carling, meanwhile, stood in silent isolation, staring at the turf in front of him. He was, quite obviously, deep in concentration for the impending contest; able, for once, to enjoy time for reflection, a luxury denied to the captain. Soon we saw the familiar sight of his sweat-glistening, jet-black hair at the heart of the action – reading the game, map-like, to cover the mistakes of others in defence, anticipating where possible so as to position himself in the most advantageous of positions for the attack. At half-time he was used extensively by Winterbottom to share the team talk, offering lengthy advice on first half trends which might suggest second half ploys.

Harlequins led 13–10 at half-time but this, alas, was the extent of their achievement on the day. Leicester, taking a stranglehold in the second half, dominated the game. Carling, without the influential Halliday alongside him, looked isolated, lost amid his side's young threequarters. He had few opportunities to break the shackles and contrived to find fewer still himself. It was another Cup final defeat for Harlequins, Leicester winning 23–16 to take the Cup to the Midlands for the first time since 1981, when they had beaten Gosforth.

The final revealed, once more, the insanity of the scrum feed change-over law. The sole attacking weapon in the game was the high up and under kick: little else was employed to break either defence. Throughout the season, it had been increasingly difficult to get through the congested middle of the field. The only answer was to kick, and hope to induce an error on the part of the defending team. It had ruined the sport as a spectacle for most of the season and was counter-productive to everything the game needed in terms of attractive, creative, open play. Rugby union had become a poor imitation of rugby league, with big forwards bashing their way down the middle. The ball was spread wide only at rare moments. Exciting, entertaining players of class and skill like Will Carling had found themselves all but shut out of the game in an attacking sense. Was this really what the lawmakers, honest but hopelessly flawed judges, had wanted when they began meddling?

14 Portrait of a Player

'I am afraid I play no outdoor games at all, except
dominoes . . . I have sometimes played dominoes outside French cafés.'

Oscar Wilde

By the time Will Carling set off for New Zealand with
the British Isles at the end of the 1992–3 British season,
he was twenty-seven years of age. He was also exhaus-
ted, in a physical and mental sense, if his play towards
the end of the season was any yardstick. Within his short
life-span he had experienced a great variety of sporting
and personal emotions, travelled the world, and generally lived the life of four less fortunate folk. He had
scaled the new heights of each rugby team he represented with an assurance, a talent, which marked him
out as special. For schoolboy, University and Divisional
Championship sides he had displayed all the rich
promise which had marked him out from his early years.
For England, he had performed commendably.

The question is: good or great? The rugby world is
utterly different from how it was twenty years ago.
Comparisons, always odious, were rendered quite ineffective by the changing of the game in so many ways.
The business of comparisons has always intrigued the
punter. How would Stanley Matthews have fared in
football today? Would even the late Bobby Moore have
been undermined by the exceptionally greater pace and

physical power of the modern game? The comparisons can also be made in rugby, but are for the rugby illiterate. They mean nothing and never can have a value: the game has changed so much, even in the last ten years.

What is undeniable is that the rugby world has seen some excellent illustrations of the centre threequarter species in recent years. There have been the powerhouse men, like the Frenchman Philippe Sella and the Australian Tim Horan, players whose strength has been at the core of their game. The contrast has been provided, vividly and exuberantly, by the Irishman Mike Gibson and France's Denis Charvet. These men of graceful, intuitive skills darted through gaps with quicksilver genius, sliding elusively and enigmatically into spaces none except them had seen. Gibson was a class apart – from all others, probably; and Charvet possessed a rare attacking genius.

Sella and Horan were different. Rugged, hardened competitors, they resembled the grand 1930s steam engines, workhorses with thighs pumping at pace like pistons attached to flywheels on those magnificent engines. Carling is a player in the same mould, his upper body strength being of paramount importance in the modern-day game. But not in Sella's class, says the Australian player David Campese.

'Will is a very good player but not a great player. To me, when you have a backline the inside centre gives the outside centre room to run. But Carling is not a ball player; he takes the ball on and sets the forwards up. I don't think you would rate him as one of the best around. Certainly he is nowhere near as good as Sella has been. There is no flair in Will's game, he just does the basic things right, which is what the English want. He sometimes tries to run on the outside break. But you know what he is going to do all the time. Great players can do different things and show different skills. But to be fair, England have a style of play and he fits in perfectly. He sets the ball up for the forwards.'

Campese's fellow Australian Tim Horan agrees that the role of Carling allied to Guscott in the England centre requires some reconsideration. The Queenslander, who has made a dramatic impact on the amateur code and is coveted by every rugby league club in Australia, says: 'Both Will and Jerry have to back their own ability a lot more. They get starved of the ball but they have to look for it more. Will Carling could run with the ball on the counter-attack far more. In my view, the two together have not shown how good they are.'

The law change, which gave the scrum feed to a side able to contain opponents taking the ball into loose forward play and failing to work it back, made Carling's role even more critical. To be caught and then lack sufficient upper body power to release it meant that possession was lost. To facilitate this requirement of power, Carling works slavishly in pursuit of peak fitness, attaining levels quite beyond the scope of most people. He looks after his body with the care and attention a pianist gives his hands.

Few people have the physical strength which Carling has always enjoyed. He can be held by an opposing centre, then caught from behind by a covering back-row flank forward from the opposition, and perhaps also wrapped up by the No. 8 moving across, but his ability to stand amid not merely the tackle but the challenge of two or three opponents is legendary and a fundamental element of his game. Countless times, while suffering the intense blows which have become a feature of modern-day international rugby, Carling has demonstrated the ability to remain on his feet. He is quickly supported by colleagues, who prise the ball loose ensuring continuity in the movement. The opposition may enjoy numerical superiority in the clinch yet be denied by Carling's iron grip upon the ball. Then help arrives to release it.

Power at short range is fundamental to his running. At speed he is considerably pacy, but it is the combination of speed and power which makes him so difficult to stop in full flight. Only the most committed of tackles succeeds. Seeing any player running flat out is an increasingly rare sight in the modern game, thanks to the constant tampering with the laws. But when Carling does achieve it, the spectacle is inspiring. Power is an inherent part of his make-up. He has worked on it constantly, understanding its relevance in the game. Of course, the frame to exploit was already there. But strength alone is by no means the sole solution for every scenario; even the night-club bouncer occasionally needs a lighter touch.

Carling has had a great deal to offer. The delicate, short pass to release a colleague through the gap his presence has created a little further out; the awareness, the ability to put a short, stabbing little kick over the head of or through a back-line laying up flat in defence to stifle attacking intent; the shrewdly placed chip through, perhaps of no more than ten or fifteen yards, that can rupture any defensive pattern if it carries sufficiently delicate weight and is perfectly placed. These are skills that Carling has constantly demonstrated.

His outside swerve has been noted approvingly by the former Welsh rugby union player Jonathan Davies: 'Maybe Will is not the most skilful with flashes of brilliance. But he is very strong, deceptively quick and has a very good swerve. He does the latter well. He is a 100 per cent player; he chases everything. Everyone talks about Guscott but I think Carling is underrated. When Wales played England in 1988, Carling and John Devereux [now, like Davies, with Widnes rugby league club] had a good battle. Those two are very, very similar.'

Carling also possesses a kick like a mule's. This attribute is essential to the inside centre threequarter in the modern game. Pressure can be so intense upon the outside half from the opposition's on-rushing open side flank forward that the player best positioned to make the long, raking downfield clearance kick from his own 22, or even the one slanting into touch inside the opposition's 22 to establish a potent attacking position, is frequently the inside centre. The outside centre is too far down the line; too much risk is attached to moving the ball so wide before clearing it to safety. The inside man, as one removed from the pressurized fly-half, is the ideal player to fulfil this role, and Carling performed it to perfection in the 1992 Pilkington Cup final between Harlequins and Bath. The length of his kicks, their power and accuracy, forced Bath into retreat, but this should not be dismissed as simply a powerful man hoofing the ball as far as he possibly can.

It is an impressive skill. Paul Dodge showed it throughout his club career for Leicester, for England and in two Test matches for the 1980 British Lions in South Africa. It is a key element in any side's potential. In 1971 the New Zealand full-back Fergie McCormick, an international since 1965, was utterly and ruthlessly destroyed by the British Lions outside half, Barry John, with a display of controlled precision kicking which was as intricate and graceful as a spider's web, and about as deadly, too, to the unsuspecting. John rolled touch kicks tantalizingly beyond the covering McCormick; he created anguish in his foe by placing the ball just those few yards from his reach. The ground he gained was invaluable, but his execution of McCormick (for the All Black never again played international rugby) was both lethal and elegant. Truly, the bashful assassin.

Peter Dixon, Carling's coach at Durham, says: 'Will is like Paul Dodge in many ways. But he is quicker off the mark than Dodge was. Dodge, however, showed the ball more. That is why Jeremy Guscott is, in my view, the permanent centre in the England side. He shows the ball and his eyes are wandering. Will Carling looks ahead and says to himself, "I am going to boot the ball." There are times when he has already decided what he is going to do, when the chance isn't really on as the ball arrives.'

There is much evidence that Carling would 'show' the ball altogether more often, as a schoolboy player. But this is not surprising. As a schools player, he was a boy apart, bigger, stronger and quicker than almost all rivals. He enjoyed running the ball constantly to utilize such qualities to their utmost. On the international stage, when set alongside only the finest players in each country, the ability to stand apart is considerably reduced. The opportunity to run free with the ball is necessarily lessened by the fiercer commitment and far higher class of opponents.

Peter Dixon identifies another weakness in Carling's game, the tendency to become blinkered regarding the position of others around him when in possession. He explains: 'Will tends to make breaks and then he looks straight down the field. He is not especially aware of what is available and he tends to step inside too much.

This was demonstrated in the England–Ireland match of the 1992 Five Nations Championship. Will made the break and had he just swung out, he would have picked up Guscott alongside him. But he didn't, he stepped inside and when the tackle hit him he had to throw the ball along the ground. It could have meant the try, which was certainly on, being lost. But Guscott took it and put Webb over through the broken defence.

'We have often seen him bowled over by the cover defence. He has gone straight down the park and been turned one way, inside, by the defence. I can think of other games when he has been hit again from the right. Because he stepped in and went too far instead of linking with his wing and outside backs. I think in that sense, he has still got that problem that he had here in Durham. Because he has not got the vision of a player like Guscott. He doesn't link with both sides of the field.'

Dixon regards Carling's role as that of the New Zealand second five eight. 'Either kicking from inside centre or bashing in over the advantage [or gain] line, particularly off balls from short line-outs. It is quite a different role to Guscott's. You don't need to do much if you get the ball into Guscott's hands. He is such a superbly balanced runner. His quality in showing the ball, holding it up front with a variety of options open to him, is extremely high. Simon Halliday was also very good at this, perhaps better than Carling.' Hence, perhaps, the worry Carling communicated to Dixon, after he had left Durham and was in the England side, that the selectors might prefer a Guscott–Halliday centre axis in the England team.

The notoriously flawed idea of comparing players from different generations is condemned by Dixon. Certainly, he finds it hard to do. 'I don't think it was the same position, centre, in those days as it is today. Will is a very fine player and longevity may say he is a great. You think of a player like Barry John in the latter category, and Jeremy Guscott would be up there, for he has produced some superb touches of rugby and is an absolute delight to watch. If Carling cured one or two things I have said, he would be right there on the top pedestal of all-time greats.'

Has Carling made the most of his talent? Dixon ponders the question carefully. 'In his first two years he played some super stuff in running the ball with England. But it is very hard being captain, particularly of so many older players. Actually to get a grip of a side like that and then perform yourself to the utmost is tremendously difficult. I would say Will Carling's game could have been in danger of that and it hasn't. But I still think he can play better, and it may come when England realize up front because the laws have changed they are not going to be able to play an emphatic forward game as in previous years. They will have to move it around, and then we will see some vintage Carling.'

Wayne Shelford, the New Zealander, is another who finds too many faults in Carling's game to consider him suitable for membership of a club containing only world 'greats'. He said of the England captain before the British Isles departed for New Zealand: 'Maybe now that the pressure is off Will, we may see what he's made of as a player. Certainly he's not in my top bracket of world centres. He's too much of what I call a "tucker" – that is, his first instinct is to tuck the ball under one arm and head towards the tackler. Even if he is crash-balling, a good centre never tucks the ball at the outset. It signposts intentions and leaves no scope for the hand dummy. Will has got to be more creative and must work harder. He needs to support on the outside more, and be ready to take the inside or outside pass. I think he's maybe got the disease of many inside centres here and wants to score himself too much. They can't. They are there to link, to create and to support. Perhaps Will has been hampered by his own status as captain. He needs coaching, he needs advice, just like any other player.'

This tendency to tuck the ball under an arm and set off into the war zone is closely related to Dixon's view that Carling does not show the ball. It is a question of, as Shelford intimates, keeping your options open, keeping the opponent guessing as to your true intentions. It suggests an element of predictability creeping into Carling's game.

In the 1992 English Cup final he showed he could play the kicking role as well as most. For he can plant the kick ahead, or downfield to diffuse pressure, with control and precision. Paradoxically, it is a task England have only occasionally asked him to perform. It was the strongest feature of Rob Andrew's game during the years from 1985 to 1993 when he was accumulating fifty-two caps. Perhaps England simply did not require the contribution of their captain in that particular area.

That may be one plank in Dudley Wood's contention that we have not yet seen the best of the England captain. 'His is an outstanding talent and his ability for direct, straight running in the centre is tremendous. We have not seen the best of him because we have not been able to play the type of game that would show him at his best. He possesses great strength but he looks after himself. He doesn't play every game, takes a little holiday during the season which I respect and admire him for. You can burn yourself out in this game.'

Wood, an Oxford University blue in 1952 and 1953,

is of course of the old school. He knew a quality centre or two in his time. Bleddyn Williams, of Cardiff, Wales and the British Lions, for example: now there was a player. As my own grandfather once reminded the assembled throng during an Oxford University v. Major R. V. Stanley's match at Iffley Road at the start of the 1950s, Williams was different. A genius with the side-step and swerve, Williams took on the student defence and destroyed it with a dazzling step inside and run to the posts for an individual try. Rising instantly to his feet, Grandfather exclaimed: 'There's class for you.' He was right, too.

Wood agrees. 'Bleddyn Williams and Mike Gibson are two of the greatest centres I have ever seen. They were different. Bleddyn had an electric side-step which he used to gain pace. You don't see anything like that now. But you realize how quick Will Carling is when he has half a gap.' The pressures which Wood has observed piled on to Carling's shoulders convince him that the days of the international playing into his thirties are numbered. The life-span of the top players is bound to decrease in playing terms, he says. 'People like Jeff Probyn, who has still been playing international rugby at thirty-seven will be rare. For a lot of players it will be a shorter career at the top. That is sad, but it reflects the outside pressures to which they are subjected.'

But until the time comes for Carling to stop – and that might be after the 1995 World Cup, when he will be almost thirty – his insatiable appetite for achievement will remain. A close colleague at Harlequins says: 'He has an incredible drive to succeed. His rugby has been highly successful and his business is flourishing. Motivation is a major part of his life. That explains his successes and his weaknesses. For example, Will Carling despises a player who steps back and says, "I am doing all right." He just cannot come to terms with such a view. As a player, I do not believe we will ever see the best of him until he is not captain. Nor can he be expected to play in every game; not even a figurehead should do that. This year, however, his commitment to Harlequins has been tremendous, for he has played a lot of matches. That is no mean achievement when you remember that most international players cannot even bend down for a few days after an international match.'

The constant desire for further achievement is a powerful factor in Carling's motivation. As his club confidant says: 'If he had won three Grand Slams, he would have wanted four. There is no limit to his desire to do well.'

Though by any standards Carling is an outstanding player, some elements of his game remain below the level of the others. His kicking can lack speed. A tendency to take two steps before releasing the ball from the boot has cost him several charge-downs during his career. It happened in his first school match at Sedbergh; it has been apparent on the international field with England. That fatal delay, perhaps of no more than two seconds, can be decisive; the slight span of time, the hesitation, can be enough. An opponent is by then close enough to block the kick.

Assurance in possession of the ball and natural timing are the keys to this. The natural performer can act and think in tandem, releasing the ball towards the foot for a kick almost the instant the hand has touched it. In international rugby we are talking about split seconds. It's the same in cricket, against the fast men of the world's bowling scene. To face Curtley Ambrose on a pacy wicket requires instant judgement of length and line. Hesitation becomes the tool with which inscriptions are carved on the sportsman's gravestone.

Another comparative imperfection in Carling's play is his passing from left to right. The other way is fine, crisp, sharp and well directed, but the reverse route is less convincing. There is a dilution of the snap to the delivery of the ball: it can be slightly less than the flat, fast distribution in the other direction. This is an aspect which requires constant topping up as a skill. One leading coach conceded: 'You could only give him seven out of ten on this discipline and frankly that is not high enough for a world-class centre.'

Nor is Martin Offiah, long since established as an outstanding rugby player in the professional code, convinced that Carling measures up. Not for rugby league anyway. 'People are always asking me about what kind of players would make it in rugby league. Someone said that Will Carling would be a better choice than Jeremy Guscott but I said no. Jonathan Davies and Jeremy Guscott are players who have got more to offer rugby league because they've got something which league may not have. A player like Will Carling in rugby league would not make such an impression because, although he is a strong player, there are a lot of players like that. You can't bring something into rugby league which they have already got, which is straight running.

'I think Will is a very good player but I also believe if I was looking to make an investment in a rugby union player, I would probably go for someone who has speed and skill . . . Therefore, I would pick Guscott. Someone like Dewi Morris, who is a bit more tricky, would do very well in league, and Gary Armstrong of Scotland, too, because they have got the toughness and they're slippery runners. If Will came to play this game he'd probably get cleaned out. He's the England captain and people would be looking for him, he couldn't suddenly change his game. Take the try he scored against Wales in 1990 when he was bumping people off. There's no way he would be able to do that in rugby league.'

The league player writing off the union 'softie' is nothing new. Geoff Cooke offers a more complete view of his England captain. 'He can improve as a player. He has constantly got to work on his skills so at the real height of pressure, the crucial moments when he gives a pass, they are spot on. He has to work still on his awareness and on decision-making as a midfield player. He will take on a player that doesn't need to be taken on when the ball should have been spread wide. He has to keep at it. But I believe him to be very near his potential: he just needs to improve little areas of his game.'

Cooke's realistic assessment is tempered by his insistence that the British have a problem in handling their sports stars. 'Once you have made it in this country, people are out to knock you down. British sport is riddled with examples of that. People love to criticize other people – it is part of our national characteristic. We find it very difficult to praise others. We get lured into stereotyped images about people. We choose to believe what it suits us to believe, and we are predisposed to making judgements. We make assumptions about people who may be very nice; judgements which are superficial. This is something Will Carling has got to learn to live with.'

Unfair press reports, like lousy weather, can be banished from the mind. But Cooke believes that one thing the modern-day players will never succeed in escaping is the pressure. 'The players, especially those who are successful, will be on their knees. We will find it increasingly difficult to meet the demands of international rugby and be successful at the highest level plus meet all the demands in club rugby as well. Already this season, there is no slack at all.'

Cooke continues to paint a dire picture for the England captain and his colleagues. 'Every Saturday this year is filled with meaningful rugby. There is no relaxation. To Harlequins' credit, they accept at the moment that top players cannot play in every match. That is why they often struggle in league rugby. We have some major conflicts ahead. The top players should be playing twenty-four or twenty-five games maximum per season. It cannot be more because the demand on their bodies is so intense. They are taking a pounding and there is a mental fatigue, too. Plus any preparation they have got to do.

'As England selectors we try to be reasonable about it but the situation concerns me. If we want to beat the best in the world we have to be well prepared. So if the situation isn't addressed within five years we will have a problem. It will either kill representative rugby or we will have the problems of the international team getting players released from their clubs. Because as clubs grow in stature through tougher leagues they will have contracts with their players. Players already have benefits to go to clubs; soon, clubs will want something in return. In the future, players won't be free to decide whether to play every club match. Then clubs will say, "You can't go to an international squad next week because we have an important league match coming up." Already, New Zealand are talking about compensating clubs and provinces for taking players away for international duty. All these conflicts will emerge.'

In many ways Will Carling has been a trendsetter, a

marker for others to follow, the first of his kind. English rugby has never placed so many burdens of expectancy on its leading players, for a game which was once played for fun and pleasure now takes on the air, in the minds of some at least, of a nationalistic war each winter. This is plainly daft and highly dangerous but it will be hard to stop. Competition is the essence of our modern lives; sport, as a variation on the theme, is as susceptible to this direction as anything else.

Pressures are beyond the scope of players to change, but aspects of their game can always be altered – for the better. Both Ted Wood and Bill Beaumont insist that component parts of Will Carling's game can certainly be improved. Wood calls him the best centre he has ever seen but says: 'There is so much more we haven't seen. He is playing at the top of international rugby, is so strong, stands on his feet in the tackle and goes for the high ball. But I think he has got more subtlety to offer, aspects like side steps and dummies. I feel sure that extra subtlety is there but I wonder whether there is the space to show it in today's international rugby.'

Beaumont is unequivocal in his praise. 'A great player. Without doubt. But his one major fault is his slight lack of knowing when to offload the ball. He has been able to get away with hanging on to it too long because of who they have been playing. He has had so much ball. As I said earlier, he has been most fortunate to be there at this time. His first movement now when he gets the ball is to run straight. Will knows that is very predictable. It is quite obvious, too, that he will kick the ball on his right foot with a diagonal kick. I think defensively he is tremendous in the tackle. And in attack, he chases and catches the ball so well. He has scored several tries from it. He is a tremendously strong player.'

The try Carling snatched from above, rather than under, Welsh noses in the first minute of the 1992 Five Nations Championship Grand Slam match against Wales emphasized his determination in pursuit of the high kick ahead. His timing, too. Arriving too early to reach the ball makes the player as irrelevant as if he were too late – he lacks impetus and cannot do much more than simply wave his arms at the ball as it is coming down. But the player who times his run to such an effect that he meets it in mid-air as it is dropping has a comprehensive advantage over his opponents. The momentum of his run can assist his leap into the air, and if he can catch the ball cleanly, then any kick which drops near an opponent's goal line may very well create a score.

In the 1993 Pilkington Cup final, this quality was emphasized by Carling in the creation of Harlequins' opening try. Challinor's high kick soared to the Leicester posts, where a trembling Liley waited. Carling, timing his run in support of the kick so well, seemed almost to hang in the air after his leap. Liley, greatly troubled by the intimidating physical presence of the airborne England captain, could not cope and, from the release of the loose ball, Harlequins scored. This ability to jump, as though spring-heeled, is priceless. Carling has shown it countless times.

The defence? Ah well, there's a sight – one of the grandest in all international rugby: the dark eyes search, darting suspiciously to spy their prey, and the seriousness of it all is emphasized by the creased forehead, tramlines of concern spread across it like ripples from a pond disturbed by a stone. The tackling technique has been finely honed, from an excellent starting point. As Peter Dixon remembered all those years earlier at

Durham, Carling's method of putting his opponent on the floor was crushingly effective. No going for the shins and clinging, pathetically, around the man as he lost balance in slow motion, like some giant log being felled. He takes man and ball for the most part, which is the vital method in present-day rugby when support for the ball carrier has become an art. To prevent the ball's release is crucial. With that in mind, Carling's ability to obliterate both man and ball is a fundamental part of his team's potency.

There is an explosion of power upon contact in the tackle, for the primary intention in the technically refined modern game is either to bury both man and ball, thereby forcing the referee to stop the game and award the scrum feed in your favour, or to turn your victim in the tackle or upon impact with the ground, so as to enable your own players to rip away the loose ball from the opponent's possession.

There is no intrinsic defensive weakness in Carling's game. Rather, this ingredient has probably been the finest part of his play, in a technical sense. Revealingly, Bill Beaumont adds: 'Will Carling is an outstanding player. And speaking personally, I would far rather be remembered as a great player than a great captain.'

But few chronicles of Will Carling's life can be complete without some mystery, some additional complication. It seems somehow inevitable: this the player who is as brave as any, more committed than most, has been strangely plagued by injuries, especially during training. Former England international full-back Dusty Hare says that Carling is like another player he has known in this respect. 'I see this in a very similar way with a young man at Nottingham. I have never before seen players with their ability get what I call side-tracked from injuries. Yet they are always feeling them.'

Hare believes that Carling has sustained injury unnecessarily because of a flawed technique. Shortly before the 1991 World Cup, Hare wrote that Carling exacerbated the physical side of the game by failing to release the ball at the most propitious moment for his team. 'Perhaps at times Will goes a fraction too far with the ball. Sometimes when he does that he gets his body in the wrong position and sustains slight injuries,' he said at the time. Hare went on: 'I rated Will Carling very highly from early on in his career. When I saw him play in a match at Leicester, it may have been for the Barbarians, I was very impressed. But as time progresses, I only wish that we'd had a better backs coach for the England side or that England had played a more expansive game so that Will could become a better player. I think we see Will playing in fits and starts. I just think there is a lot more to come from Will. He has the capacity to go another notch.'

That was two years ago. How does Hare view the England captain now? 'He has learned a little bit since then; he is not as bad as he was in getting what I call isolated. But the new laws have helped that. Now players know that if they go too far with the ball, they will lose it at the scrummage. Before that, there was many a time Carling would go too far, the ball would be killed but his side would receive the put-in. I still think there is more to come from Will. I don't think he uses his ability as much as he should do in attack. He is a good strong runner but because he has been Will Carling and has been marked closely, he has been a little bit careful lately because people have hit him. He has been clobbered in internationals because of who he is and he is now getting rid of the ball earlier. He uses the easy option by kicking or passing it.' The relatively ordinary quality of Carling's play throughout most of the 1992–3 season and with the Lions in New Zealand emphasized this point.

Hare also concurs with the decision to overlook Carling as captain for the British Lions. 'There was absolutely no way he would have gelled the four countries together.'

By common consent, Carling's vast potential still remains to be exploited to the full. But whether that will now be possible within the confines of the crushing expectations of both the social world and the physical nature of the modern game seems open to doubt. Any ordinary player should be nearing his peak at twenty-seven and able to sustain that exalted level of performance for the next three years. But then Will Carling is no ordinary player, and he has no ordinary lifestyle. Attempting to make a man of the boy overnight by burdening him with the captaincy so young has induced a weariness of off-the-field responsibilities which may impair any more progress upon it. This is a tragedy, for it has denied Carling the space, time and anonymity with which he could have polished further his magnificent natural skills.

15 A Captain Considered

'At twenty years of age, the will reigns; at thirty, the wit; and at forty, the judgement.'

Benjamin Franklin

England lost a genius of a rugby player the day they made Will Carling captain. There is compelling evidence that subjecting one of the finest young talents ever discovered to the excruciating pressures of leadership impeded his natural progress in the game. He had the potential to become perhaps the player of his age. Captaincy dulled that promise: it was a burden imposed, although gratefully accepted.

What was regarded at the time as a gamble and later accepted as a bold, enterprising step has come subsequently to be seen as a mistake. One can trace the validity of that belief by assessing Carling as a player and understanding, in the light of study and judgement, that he has not acquired the sheen of quality that ought to have elevated so outstanding a talent from being one of the best to *the* best.

Indisputably, the cares of captaincy have struck at the heart of what should have been an inevitable progression towards the acquisition of an ultimate talent. Leadership is a lonely, often a desolate chore. It can be a painful, humiliating experience, not entirely overlooked even in the moments of achievement and success. 'If things are not going well it is a bloody hard job,' says Bill Beaumont. 'It can be lonely. I still think you have got to be part of the lads. I don't think you can get away with not doing that. I think if you are part of it, they respect you more if you do bollock them on the training field.'

Will Carling may have seemed the perfect choice as captain. After all, he could play magnificently and was assured of a distinguished future career. But he was deeply sensitive, insecure, sometimes touchy. The images, impressions, suspicions and assumptions which have always occupied Carling's mind have never been appropriate to the role of leadership. Nor is he a man of great charisma. He offers the world a cold, detached impression, frequently appearing bored and ill at ease in the company of strangers, an aspect almost certainly a result of his cloistered childhood and school days.

But leadership, when the peripheral activities have been laid aside, is intrinsically about inspiring others – not just those around you, but almost everyone you meet. Nigel Melville, another ex-England captain, identifies precisely this trend in the current time: 'We expect so much of an England rugby captain. He is expected (a) to have a good job and do it well; (b) to train like a professional sportsman and perform on the field every time he goes out, like a professional; (c) he must act on the field, and be sharp, well-heeled and polite off it; (d) he is expected to do it all for nothing, whether it is promoting the senior game, helping youth rugby or whatever; (e) he is expected never to turn down invitations; (f) he is expected to speak at dinners and not just that, but be funny; (g) to impress his peers as a regular guy.

'The minute one of those things is out of balance you

have a label and once you have got it, it is hard to change. I think underneath, Will Carling is a very quiet guy. Probably very shy, too.' Furthermore, becoming leader so young induced an anxiety which he has never completely overcome. As Melville says: 'He was only out of school three or four years and he was captain of England. Probably he treated those around him as he had those at school. That is bound to be seen as arrogant.'

There is some evidence to suggest that sympathy ought to be a prime consideration for the often beleaguered Will Carling in his role as England captain. But, as has been demonstrated consistently throughout his career, there is always another side to ponder: the diplomatic process has never been part of Carling's make-up. From his school days, a picture emerges of the boy who drew comfort from a close group of friends. Others were treated with disdain or suspicion. This was hardly likely to qualify the young man for leadership of his country's rugby team, a task which at times requires the patience of Florence Nightingale, the diplomacy of a British Ambassador in Serbia and the judgement of Solomon.

Off the field, Carling often seems uncomfortable with the attentions of the media and the public. While one can sympathize with this, sporting leaders throughout the world have nowadays become public figures. Throughout his many years in international rugby, for example, the former French rugby captain Serge Blanco offered his home telephone number to anyone in the media who seriously needed it. 'As a French rugby player, I am public property,' he once explained. Equally fairly, within months of retiring from the game, Blanco had changed his number in order to achieve seclusion, reasoning that his private life was no longer of concern to others. It would be wrong to suggest that no one can contact Will Carling at home. But contacting him there and extracting conversation in the way one has done for many years at Chez Blanco has been another matter entirely.

Blaming Carling for this might seem wrong – surely those who appointed him captain ought to accept the responsibility? Clearly they made an error of judgement, but it is worth recalling that Carling was not their first choice anyway, but third, behind Nigel Melville and Rob Andrew. Melville's analysis of the media is startlingly different from Carling's. The now retired Yorkshireman, who helps coach Otley, says: 'The media have a job to do. I felt I was the one who was privileged they wanted to talk to me. I always used the media for my own gain in rugby.'

Melville is anxious to explain his position precisely. 'The England captain is expected to work and act like a professional. That is resented a little in your family life. If you are the England footballer Alan Shearer on £9,000 a week or something, you should talk to people. But if you are earning nothing and people ring you up at ten at night and ask you questions, and your wife hasn't seen you all week, it could appear that the media are being intrusive. But it is the game that is putting people in that position. It is a successful sport. I believe the game will become professional at international and possibly League 1 level.'

The inference from Melville is twofold: the explosion in the game should mean professionalism for its top performers, but until that occurs, the captain still has a duty to perform the functions expected of the England leader. Carling, alas, has rarely come to terms with his obligations in this respect. However, the Rugby Football

Union chose Carling to be president of the Young England Rugby Club, ahead of other figures who might have seemed more appealing to youngsters, like Gareth Chilcott and Mickey Skinner. They waited and watched how Carling handled the job, and have been hugely impressed. Dudley Wood says: 'He has been absolutely meticulous in turning up for everything. It is a tremendous coup getting him to do it but he has really enjoyed it. He talks to the children, answers questions and does it well. Will wouldn't agree with my views on certain aspects of the game. But you can see sportsmen who are a great credit to their game, such as Gary Lineker. Will Carling is certainly in that category. I have never found him in the least arrogant in my dealings with him. He has always been very helpful. He is thoughtful, he thinks a lot about the game and leadership, and how best to handle the other players. This has been a learning process.'

The process has, undeniably, improved Carling, but only to a certain extent. He remains largely uncomfortable in unfamiliar company, unable to lead the throng as one might expect from a natural motivator and assured communicator in the style of Lineker. Carling gives the impression that he is a victim of the circumstances which impel today's sporting captains to be a mixture of supreme player, consummate speaker and brilliant humorist – and a paragon of confidence, too.

As Ed Campbell, second master at Sedbergh School, put it: 'Will Carling has been under pressure no other captain has ever known with England. You are judging this chap against a background of an entirely new set of rules. Any rugby player that grows up under this has a host of problems. Will is not always popular because he has to raise defences, understandably. It is difficult for a youngster to come to terms with that.' Especially the introverted, occasionally melancholy youngster. More particularly, the youngster denied a grooming for the awesome responsibilities, through the natural progression handed down over the years. Fran Clough, a player who knew him with the North Divisional side, says tellingly: 'Insecurity is what motivates a lot of the things he gets involved with.'

Few know or understand Will Carling better than Rob Andrew, the man nearest to him in the England side, geographically speaking, and a close confidant of the captain. Andrew points to the pressures inherent in a game which has become so much more high-profile in just a few years. 'We all enjoy the coach trip to Twickenham on the big day, the drive through the crowded car park. You enjoy running out with thousands watching you. But you can't have your cake and eat it all. Certainly not when you have that sort of profile. You can't go into your private life and pretend the world outside doesn't exist. That is just a function of what the game is about now and what we have created by our achievements. Every single person wants some peace and quiet, sometimes you want some privacy. Before, we had peace and quiet and a lot of very average Saturday afternoons playing for England. But now, I wonder where the cutoff comes; how you stop this drift to professionalism. Profiles will only get bigger and there is no way future England captains will be able to avoid this. The pressures on the captain are always going to be there, the clock will not be turned backwards now.'

The constant attention, the feeling that you are a target for every face, crowds in. 'You get to the stage where you can't go out, you don't want to go out because of it. You almost groom yourself to have to handle this public profile. That is a fact of life everybody has to cope with. We have got the best and worst of all worlds.'

But Will Carling and Rob Andrew differ greatly. Andrew is altogether more of a secure, assured character, matured by marriage. He may not have emerged from his youth with the reputation enjoyed by the England captain, but he would, I believe, have taken on board the myriad demands of the national captaincy with a great deal more equanimity than Carling. The selectors presumably felt the same way.

If Carling was to prove a failure when judged by the most exacting criteria of captaincy, then one thing should be made perfectly clear. It was not his fault. He was ill-equipped for the job from the start: youthful, immature, poorly qualified, with no experience of leadership apart from at schoolboy level. To draw assumptions from that segment of anyone's life can be hugely misleading. The inspiration of boys is not necessarily a leader of men. So it proved.

Carling, as captain, has been rooted in his own image; often unsure of both himself and his team's best route forward. He is obedient and stereotyped, ordered: not prone to largesse or excesses in any field. It is inevitable that a team led by such a man will be vulnerable to a lack of balance. Will Carling and his side have rarely gambled. Only occasionally did England take any opponent by the throat, and there was a reluctance to (as the Irishman Mick Doyle used to say) give it an opportune lash. Under the captaincy of the conservative, sober Will Carling, this was not a serious option, and when it *was* employed, it was often at quite the wrong moment.

Everything had to be planned; but captaining an international sports team demands greater flexibility than this. Meticulous planning has its role, indeed its importance; but the great moments in sport arise, almost without exception, from the off-the-cuff approach, the bold and perhaps last throw of the gambler. Those who reach out for glory might just touch it; those, alas, who meekly accept their fate consign themselves to anonymity.

Carling brought to the captaincy the qualities which had been present throughout his young life: an ability to play rugby exceedingly well, and a never-yielding enthusiasm. But an insecure personality does not change plans in mid-stream due to his own doubts. Such a person is comforted, made secure in his mind only by the status quo.

Amid the far greater intensity and pressures of leadership of a senior England team, however, these traits came more strongly into play. There was far more pressure, much greater scrutiny – and Carling no longer looked the supreme leader. Captaining a school side is one thing, because the best player is assumed to be the most suited to lead. At this junior level, the intricacies, the psychologies of leadership are not dissected. At the top of the tree they are, and very carefully.

Those susceptible to insecurity tend to cling to companions they trust deeply. Their nature makes them reluctant to strike out alone down the unknown road of real captaincy, to the isolated arena of leadership. Carling might protest to the contrary – indeed, he has done so. But the reality was that he always remained close to his chums. This is always the reaction of those who are unsure, uncertain.

Under the grievous burden of leadership, Carling's own game marked time. I do not think it a complete coincidence that the performance I, and many others, believe to have been his finest ever came in the 1992 Pilkington Cup final against Bath, when he was plain and simple W. D. C. Carling, just another player and not the captain. Here he was presented with the opportunity to concentrate completely on his own game, disregarding tactical plans or words of motivation for those around him. He looked what we have always believed him to be, the supreme player. It was a revealing glimpse into the world of excellence that Carling would almost certainly have attained time and again, had captaincy not intruded.

Will Carling always took the leadership of his country seriously. He is not a flippant person. Besides, the intense focus now placed upon international rugby and its main players requires a formidable attention to detail and concentration. It is quite different from the occasion not so long ago when an England rugby captain, rather in the style of the Aborigines, decided to go walkabout. This was a perfectly reasonable occupation except for one factor – he was due to give the team talk at 11.30 on the morning of the match. At 11.25 there was some private discussion as to where he was. At 11.35 a certain degree of anxiety had surfaced concerning his lackadaisical approach. At 11.45 it was decided the meeting must start without him, and at 12.30 it finished with him nowhere in sight. At 12.50 the players filed out of the hotel on to the team bus, the chairman of selectors having decided whom to name in his place to lead England that afternoon.

At which point . . . the captain strolled into the far end of the hotel car park, to be confronted by a red-faced chairman of selectors. 'Oh, I'm awfully sorry, I got involved in a terrific book at the local library, it really was fascinating . . .'

Rob Andrew watched England's fledgling captain take his first steps. 'Initially when he was made captain, he sat back: at the age of twenty-two, he couldn't come in and demand this and that and say, "We are going to do it this way – I have captained Sedbergh so this is the way I will captain England." You cannot do that. He talked to a lot of senior players and got the feeling for what they thought was wrong. He listened. He is actually very shy and he had to get used to the limelight. Suddenly, in a very short space of time. From playing the game just for fun you become a personality just because you happened to be good at what you were doing. That is not easy to handle.

'He was surprised to get his first cap and was surprised to be given the captaincy. He gathered as much information as possible about what people wanted. He gradually built up information about people, too: he did a lot of talking to those away from the game. He really made an effort to talk to people in the team and get their opinions and advice. Now, of course, he has been through it all. He has developed from the youngest player in the side and the least experienced to the bloke now whom others rely on. His views are now stronger, he has got more conviction in what he thinks. But he hasn't detached himself from what others are thinking. He is constantly looking for things to move on to. All the way through there has been this basic desire to succeed. He had that when he first played for the North.'

But, says Andrew significantly, Geoff Cooke was the brains behind the England renaissance. 'He is still very much the man in charge.' Are they compatible? 'They have hit it off from Day 1,' says Andrew. 'I don't know they are that similar, although both are thoughtful and fairly quiet in their own way. Both have a deep down enormous desire to succeed, without shouting from the rooftops about it.'

No one in rugby, as Andrew emphasizes, was prepared for the fall-out from such an explosion of interest in their sport. 'Rugby union players are now better known than some professional sportsmen, whereas a few years ago professional players were on a different plane. What Will has done is handle it extremely well. Yes, he has had his ups and downs, but no one in rugby was prepared for this. If you are a professional footballer you can argue that you went into the sport knowing all this. As a rugby player, you never imagined it. All of a sudden this World Cup thing has exploded and the pressures have been comparable to many other professional sports. The pressure has been amazing. Will Carling is now heavily public property, he cannot put a foot out of place. Everything he does is closely monitored. He didn't set out to create this. It has just been created.'

But others might have handled better this blanket of attention which descended upon the game. Carling has never come properly to terms with it, though he has done his best; because it is not in his nature to become so open a figure.

Carling's captaincy has been marked by misjudgements. They began early, with consequences for Rob Andrew, among others. 'We were going to make him captain of the North Divisional side,' remembers Dave Robinson. 'But he couldn't get there for training the night we were to announce the choice and so we gave the captaincy to someone else' – Rob Andrew.

But if the mistakes have suggested a lack of judgement in the tightest situations, and from Edinburgh 1990, the World Cup Final 1991 and Cardiff 1993 we can glean much evidence to prosecute such a case, then it is indisputable that the role of England rugby captain has changed out of all recognition. Mike Weston was the last captain of England before coaches, that strange and hitherto unknown species, appeared on the scene. 'It was 1968, and I can remember having to organize everything. The captain had to make sure there were balls available for the training session, arrange the signals the team would use during a game, prepare and deliver the preparatory team talk and then the dressing-room chat. Then do the after-match interview with David Coleman.'

But Weston believes that all that pales into insignificance beside the demands made on an England rugby captain today by the media. 'For Will Carling the media attention is incredible. But he has caused his own pressure by his success. You can tell he is sensitive and shy. He is clearly embarrassed by it all.'

It is on the field that Peter Dixon judges him as a leader. Dixon's view is that Carling has not had to do a tremendous amount of motivational work regarding his own players, because most of them have been sufficiently experienced to know precisely their own task and the job expected of them. 'There has been so much experience he has had quite an easy ride in that respect. England should have won the Grand Slam the year before they did, and the year before that, too [1989 and 1990]. Especially the time they went to Wales and the forwards kept battering away at a Welsh plan specifically to counter that. A more mature captain would have changed the game. Even though it was wet and the ball was slippery, they could have won the game further out. Perhaps the same sort of thing happened in the Grand Slam match in Scotland. The Scots are always difficult but the England captain should have changed the tactics.'

Most revealingly of all, and here he touches on a subject of critical importance in the story of Will Carling, Peter Dixon says: 'Anyone going for a Grand Slam who has had it torn away from him . . . it must have a dramatic impact.' Edinburgh, 1990, was a turning point for Will Carling. It inhibited his captaincy even further, making him more cautious than before. The insecurity again came to influence his career, for the pain caused by the Scots remained with him for the better part of two years. Even amid the Grand Slam successes of 1991 and 1992, Carling remembered the agony of Edinburgh. Particularly when it returned to haunt him in Cardiff, 1993.

Peter Dixon shares Bill Beaumont's view on the 1992 Grand Slam. 'All the other countries were in utter chaos. It was easy to win a Grand Slam that year.' Beaumont is equally unequivocal regarding Carling's part in the failure against Wales in 1993. 'He should have told Jonathan Webb to kick the goal in the last minute. I would have told him to kick the bloody thing. Nor is that being wise after the event. In 1980 against Wales, when we were going for the Grand Slam, we had a penalty in injury time far out on the right touchline. I didn't need to tell Dusty Hare he had to kick it. He did – we won 9–8 and went on to beat Scotland for the Grand Slam.

'Will hasn't had to stamp his authority as captain because England have never been under pressure. Except at critical moments. For example, they made mistakes captaincy- and coaching-wise in the 1991 World Cup Final. They played into Australia's hands. What had been successful before, we should have stuck with.

Then, during the game, it was possible to change that approach. There were quite a few games I played in when you thought, "Right, I have to change this." You have to rely on players to help change the pattern as well. Others should have said that to Will during that Final. But at the end of the day someone has to make a decision. But only two blokes could decide to change the tactics. Perhaps there was a need for someone in the forwards to help.'

Eddie Butler, rugby correspondent for the *Observer*, says the 1991 World Cup final was an aberration from England's point of view. 'An aberration from start to finish. But then England have got away with a lot of misjudgements. Against Wales, in 1993, that was the first time Carling had actually played badly himself. I just think he allowed Gibbs and Hall to get to him physically. For the first time people read him. He is a good player but a strong forward player. An opponent like Gibbs will stand toe to toe with him and say "Let's bash it out". Maybe that affected his leadership that day.'

As a player, most of his opponents considered him an outstanding performer. Former Welsh captain Paul Thorburn says: 'As a centre he is a very skilful, all-round player. Perhaps his captaincy has taken the headlines rather than his ability to play. But you never know about captains. What would Will have been like behind a losing pack? He has been fortunate: he arrived on the England scene when they started to get it together. Perhaps the public think he is arrogant but if there is any bitterness it is probably only jealousy. We would all like to have been captain of a Grand Slam side.'

Jonathan Davies adds: 'In his position people are jealous – it's as simple as that. He has had a lot of pressure on him but I think he has been a tremendous boost for English rugby. I was a bit sceptical when they said he is captain until the next World Cup [in 1991]. They put a lot of pressure on young shoulders with that decision. Being captain of England is totally different to being captain of any other home nation. If they lose they have people rubbishing him, if they win everybody adores him and the other three nations are jealous.'

The intense study of Carling as a captain invoked this thought from a Harlequins confidant. 'Every time the boy shows a slight sign of weakness, the media go for the jugular. We tend to focus on Carling but why? Are we being hyper-critical and looking, or is it he is successful and doesn't need the press, so that when the chance arises they put the knife in? Perhaps people are hyper-critical because he is built up to be this great leader. A lot of people are incredibly jealous.' This is undoubtedly true. Nevertheless, the evidence is overwhelmingly clear that Carling as a captain falls some way short of greatness.

16 Personal Profile

'Let us, then, be up and doing,
  With a heart for any fate;
Still achieving, still pursuing,
  Learn to labour and to wait.'
  Henry Longfellow

To understand the driving force behind Will Carling is not easy. He is a complex young man, whose personality, as we have seen, offers a clutch of contradictions. It is one of our human paradoxes that those of us who are unable to love or truly like other people are those who seek the incentive the most.

Phenomenal success in his chosen sport helped Will Carling, separated for long periods from his parents at an early age, to find approval and favour among his closest childhood and young adulthood friends. He continues to cling to that group, enjoying the familiarity they provide. But the challenges and demands of the outside world often find him unprepared.

There is a parallel here with the case of Prince Charles, of whom a psychiatrist wrote recently: 'He finds great difficulty in giving others something which he never had: a sense of worth acquired from ... freely available parents.' As with Charles, too, Carling's privileged position in adult life has led him to become a rather solitary, self-absorbed individual who approaches friendship with caution and experiences difficulties in integrating with his peers.

He is cautious about ventures that would place him beyond the security of his own small, tightly knit group. This closed set has been a constantly recurring feature of his life: at school, university and now with his club. Breaking into that circle can prove difficult. A colleague says: 'Will would not know how to handle situations without his trusted friends around him. He has travelled the world, yet he is not especially worldly.'

The importance of this group was emphasized by Carling himself when he announced plans for his marriage to Julia Smith, a twenty-eight-year-old public relations girl and former girlfriend of rock stars Eric Clapton and Jeff Beck. Carling told the *Mail on Sunday*: 'I have some very, very close friends and Julia gets on very well with them. Her being there has not made any difference.' It was as though she had to be approved, accepted by his trusted pals, before he could embrace the possibility of marriage.

Another example. A close colleague at Harlequins says: 'New situations Will struggles with. If you asked him to go into our committee room after a match and just chat with a few people for twenty minutes or so, he wouldn't have a clue how to conduct himself. That is why he keeps to his own group of friends. He is regarded as somewhat aloof, so the younger guys won't approach him. And it is not his manner to go up to them and say "Hi, I'm Will Carling" to a nineteen-year-old or third team player.' Thus the impression, accurate or erroneous, persists through Carling's inability to project a more positive self-image.

By general consensus, the happiest times of Will Carling's life were played out in his schooling environment. The schoolboy who had such fun in the company of a select few friends has found the outside world a harsh place, quick to judge and to condemn him for any failings. This is a factor Carling struggles to accept.

Bill Beaumont believes that Carling distrusts outsiders. 'I think he finds it hard to make close friends. Perhaps there is a slight mistrust. I think he is a lonely lad. England's success at the World Cup brought Will Carling into the living room of everyone in the country. He is obviously very much in the public eye.' But even Geoff Cooke, ex-manager of the England squad and a man very close to Carling, says of him: 'Occasionally, he has been overtly sensitive to criticism and reluctant to accept any view other than his own. He is strong-willed, strong-minded. He does not suffer fools gladly and is very intolerant of other people's weaknesses and failings. He sets himself very high personal standards and is so committed and dedicated to being the best that anybody who doesn't appear to have that same commitment and same sense of purpose, he gets very irritated with. He finds that difficult. It has not led to serious friction, but it has led to tensions. He is particularly intolerant of players who really don't understand the demands of being an international player. In Argentina, for example, he made his feelings very obvious to the players in that category.'

The constant need to succeed, the driving force behind Carling, is at work here. Sensitivity to criticism is derived in part from the perpetual adulation of his school days. He always succeeded, he was always being lavished with praise. Such praise fuelled still further the inner desire to go on achieving. When, suddenly, he stepped into another world where commentators and onlookers were by no means as laudatory, he was ill-equipped to deal with criticism of his ability as a player and, perhaps more importantly, his conduct as a man.

Some people have been astonished to be confronted by Carling or his representatives, complaining at critical comments written or spoken about the England captain. It has been as though any criticism is a direct assault, which must result in the breaking of relationships. He often seems unable to accept another viewpoint, an opinion different from his own, and simply shrug it off.

Clem Thomas was one of those startled to be approached by a representative of Carling. 'John Holmes, his agent, came up to me, introduced himself, and said "Will tells me you've never written anything positive about him at all." I told him I'd never written anything bad, either. Will Carling was lucky because I'd never really gone for him. He'd certainly have known had I done that.'

The emotional side of Carling was presented dramatically to another *Observer* journalist, Eddie Butler, after the dinner following the Barbarians match against Australia in 1992. Butler, who captained Wales and also represented Cambridge University, Pontypool and the British Lions, was nonplussed to be sought out by Carling after he had written a story saying that there had been no adventure in the England camp and that the most advantageous thing he (Carling) had done in the last four years had been to take himself into the City and hawk himself as Captain of England plc. Granted, it was not the sort of remark likely to earn Butler a Governorship of Sedbergh School, but it was a bright enough throwaway line that few would have taken terribly seriously. But Will Carling did.

'He was almost out of control,' said Butler. 'He was stamping his feet and his eyes were filled with tears.

He was way over the top. He said I had let him down completely, he said he had been stabbed in the back by so many people. It was a display of immaturity for someone who claims to be able to keep his emotions in check. There is obviously something quite effervescent beneath the surface. It is something insecure.

'There are doubts over his ability to cope with the whole thing. I am not sure England have coped with the pressures on the field when they have come. When they are in control they are very powerful, but in the instances when the opposition have proved themselves very resilient, England just ran out of ideas long before the end. The captain must carry some of the blame.'

Butler says that tensions exist within the England camp. 'Will has his own little gang of Andrew, Rory Underwood, etc. They are quite a chummy little clique. But I think a snooze factor takes over among the forwards when Carling starts talking.'

As a character, Carling 'certainly lacks that cuddlyness', in Butler's words. Certainly, compared to many of his peers, it is difficult to get close enough to him to create an enduring friendship . . . That suggests that he is either quick to pass judgement or cannot bring himself to make a measured assessment of an individual for fear of being wrong. For the sake of his own security and peace of mind, he is prepared to remain a man alone.

The misjudgements are a recurring theme. Promoting himself so boldly was clearly likely to rebound on him, at cost to his own privacy. Some people have thicker skins than rhinoceroses. They can be dreadfully intrusive once a celebrity has been sighted. Carling has found it hard to come to terms with those who walk up to his dinner table at a restaurant, request autographs while he is in the middle of conversation or dinner and then start pulling up a chair, quite uninvited, to discuss a recent match. But some can take this treatment. In New Zealand, the former All Black Bryan Williams regularly attracts a queue for his autograph at his restaurant dining table. This, despite the fact that he retired from the game long ago. Yet the charm, the courtesy with which Williams handles such situations are an object lesson to all. Each request for an autograph is met with the pleasant response: 'Would you like it signed to anyone in particular?' His duty done, and the last in the queue satisfied, he returns to his private conversation. But then Williams understands this is an accepted part of the game, even in retirement. He enjoyed great times in the game; his view is that any small thing he can do to give something back is just his pleasure.

Commendably, Carling is known throughout the game as the player who always signs autographs for children. Given the number of requests he must receive, that is no mean feat. And, as with many top sportsmen, his high profile can have unwelcome consequences. His Harlequins colleagues remember him sitting in the corner of a Richmond pub late one evening, after one of the 'Quins Pilkington Cup finals. To their dismay, a sober Carling had been buttonholed in a corner by some crass bore with too much drink inside him, and was being poked in the chest by the fool to emphasize some point he insisted the 'Quins man must know. 'That sort of thing makes you become a recluse,' said a fellow player.

You can confidently put people into certain categories. But then suddenly Will Carling comes along and proves there are dangers in such generalizations. 'There are traces of insecurity, yet I have seen traces of incredible warmth,' says a friend. 'I have seen him be really kind to people, but also cold to others. Personally, I like him: he sets standards to everybody. He needs friends.'

Another friend describes him thus: 'He is a very sensitive kid. Kid is the operative word although he is very far from the all-American-type-boy image. His parents still have an enormous effect on him. He goes home to see them for lunch almost every Sunday. He is devoted to his mother.

'Everywhere I go, people say, "What is Will Carling really like?" They say to me, "He appears to be a money-grabbing bastard." But he is not like that, even though he does want to be the best in the world in all he does. He has a single-minded pursuit of that and anything that gets in the way gets it with both barrels.'

Which maybe links rather well with Dudley Wood's summary of him. 'I would never underestimate him. He is a slightly enigmatic character, not easy to read.' A gentle understatement, by the respected secretary of the RFU!

The story of his career reveals his failure to come to terms with the high public profile he misguidedly pursued in his early days of celebrity. The chaos in Cardiff, in 1991, when England's first win in Wales for twenty-eight years was overshadowed by a petulant act; the naïve, off-hand remarks he made late in 1990 at a conference, pouring scorn on Paul Gascoigne and his game; after-dinner speeches which shocked even rugby club men; the regrettable attempt to get an England coach pushed out; the mystifying silence at his own book launch; the extraordinary scene he created with the journalist Eddie Butler after an official dinner: all these things are born of insecurity and unease with his role as national rugby captain. Indeed, it is hard not to feel sympathy for someone saddled with so immense a responsibility when their nature is simply not conducive to such a role. The wrong decisions, the rank misjudgements, the misguided remarks, the petulant outbursts, the gaffes: these are plainly symptoms of a character under considerable strain; of a loner, a man who finds it hard to handle people, thrust into an alien environment that he is far from ideally equipped to handle. No one in their right mind rejects the captaincy of the England rugby team, but it could be argued that had Carling done so he would be fêted as the finest rugby player in the world today.

The problem, states Nigel Melville, concerns the general perception of him. As a player, a captain and a person. 'I believe to be a top sportsman you need a certain arrogance, self-belief . . . call it what you will. How that is perceived by other people is Will's problem. People are jealous of his age and his success.' But Melville detects a change since Carling came under the influence of John Holmes, one of the shrewder agents available to leading sports stars in this country. 'I think since Will went to John Holmes he has mellowed. Because people don't book the straight arrogant guy. I think it is Holmes' tuition which is at play, for he has begun to model Carling on Gary Lineker.

'There is a broader market for him if he is seen as a basic decent guy. You can work off that other image because people forget the early days. I have no doubt he has changed. I think he changed after the first Grand Slam. He has grown up a little since then.

'He had put himself a bit in the firing line with this corporate motivational speaking. That from a twenty-three-year-old was a little strange. What experience had he got? That probably came across as a certain amount of arrogance. It was seen as jumping on the band wagon, taking the money.

'His problem is that people do not like those who are larger than the game. It is like David Campese. People think he is arrogant. It is this resentment of players making money out of an amateur sport. But many other players are greedier than Will Carling. People just think these guys are laughing in their faces. But their arrogance is misunderstood.'

Is it myth, therefore, that dogs Will Carling? The myth of the arrogant, aloof money grabber who is determined to exploit his position for the maximum gain? Unluckily for him, myths tend to perpetuate themselves. This is the difficulty confronting Carling.

Arrogant, aloof? It's more complex than this. He is often misunderstood, for which he himself is partly to blame. His misjudgements off the field have not helped him gain universal acceptance. He suffers from acute shyness, a trait which has led others similarly to be accused of arrogance and aloofness. Carling finds it virtually impossible to dispel this notion because his own behaviour is rooted in his deep insecurity. That quality of remoteness, which in turn is regarded as a form of arrogance, is essentially a lack of the self-confidence, the assured mien which is expected, even demanded, of someone in Carling's position.

An accumulator of vast sums? Well, he sees only justice in his view that those who contribute so much to an amateur sport ought to be allowed to reap any financial dividends in their spare time. I agree with him, though it is easy to understand the sniping from those who take the view that the England captain driving around in a sponsored Mercedes worth £80,000 or more hardly provides a role model in a sport that still likes to call itself amateur. Carling is not, after all, advocating revolution, or calling for the RFU committee to come out into the streets to be shot!

If businessmen wish to pay thousands of pounds to hear the England rugby captain speak, then good luck to the England rugby captain. We live, it is worth recalling, in a free society; if you wish to go and pay such sums, it is your own decision. If Will Carling has the attendant masses of rugby groupies in the palm of his hand, then that is their choice. He is taking an honest shilling, whatever his critics may intimate. Yet through such activities, he perhaps personifies professionalism in the game and offers his critics, always quick to seize gleefully on his misjudgements, an armoury full of weapons to fire at him.

Will Carling's difficulty in adapting to new circumstances, confirmed by a close colleague back at Harlequins, was undoubtedly a factor in his disappointing tour with the British Lions in New Zealand. Certainly, injuries intruded at crucial moments, but by his very nature Carling was likely to find the situation hard.

For five years England had regarded him as an automatic selection, initially as a player and then as captain. Bereft of the captaincy, the insecurities of Will Carling were exposed, with dramatic consequences. Others in his position, Scott Gibbs of Wales and Scott Hastings of Scotland, mounted a strong challenge for the centre berth alongside Jeremy Guscott. Hastings' tour was wrecked by injury but Gibbs sustained his challenge, forcing Carling into the anonymous backwaters of the midweek team.

No one had a hope of even daring to challenge Carling's international position during all those years with England. Now, suddenly, Gibbs was to do so, and

Carling failed to match the challenge. His form was on the whole at best modest. The Welshman's achievement in winning the Test place for the decisive second and third internationals against New Zealand was a crushing blow to Will Carling's self-esteem, particularly as the Lions had turned to Englishmen to rescue their tour after the loss of the first international.

It was a bitter irony, with harsh side effects that saw Carling, the England captain, left out of the Lions' first choice side as eleven Englishmen went out to face New Zealand in the Wellington Test – and emerge victors by 20-7. But Carling himself conceded he had found it hard away from the familiar environs of the English dressing room, where he had been surrounded by colleagues he had known for years and from whom there had been no threat to him. Now, in an alien country and among many alien companions, Carling failed the ultimate challenge.

Very, very few achieve the pinnacle of sporting excellence and personal maturity simultaneously. The expectation of both has been an enormous burden for Will Carling. Few people are so consistently in the spotlight as he; his high profile puts him firmly in the category of the professional sportsman. This grand contradiction within the game itself is possibly at the root of so many of his difficulties. But how he now copes with this position will determine the making of the man.

17 *A Fortuitous Twist*

If the law changes in rugby union had conspired to undermine English aspirations of a third successive Grand Slam in the Five Nations Championship of 1993, then plainly they now worked to the benefit of the England captain.

Will Carling had returned from his humbling experiences on the 1993 British Lions tour of New Zealand a very different player. Gone was the searing burst of attacking speed, the quality with which he had destroyed defences in all grades of rugby for many years. Such a quality had been gradually eroded by the frequent heavy and intimidating hits, the crunching tackles which had taken their toll. Judged by world standards, Carling was no longer the same potent attacking force as a centre threequarter.

Yet by a grand irony, the game had been so altered by the controversial law changes that in many positions a different breed of player was now required. At open-side flank forward, for example, the traditional terrier of a player, hunting the loose ball like a Jack Russell, was rendered obsolete. Teams like England, France and New Zealand wanted big, strong, pounding men able to play anywhere in the back row. Benazzi did it for France, Clarke for England. Both were really No. 8s or blind-side flankers but hardly role models for the open-side berth. Now, however, the game had been so dramatically changed by the lawmakers' meddling that the whole structure was different.

In the midfield, defences reigned. The field was cluttered by stray forwards from both packs, no longer finding it necessary to bind into the scrum, ruck or maul but able to float out wide and help congeal the middle part of the field. This changed the whole nature of the kind of midfield player required. The opportunities for fast, silky handling threequarters who could dart here, there and everywhere, transferring the ball in the blink of an eye and slipping through gaps into open country, were frankly non-existent.

To put it bluntly, the game of rugby union, one which was once the epitome of craft and skilful play, had entered the world of biff-bang more familiar in rugby league. Tackling and blocking up the game in a static midfield required strong, squat players able to go on tackling throughout the match. Such centres had to demonstrate bravery and stamina in defensive duties, for these often now constituted as much as 80–85 per cent of the individual's involvement in a match. As the England centre Phil de Glanville said: 'The opportunities for finding space and running into it are now very few and far between.'

Thus it was that Carling's loss of pace and the diminution of his attacking skills did not greatly matter in the context of the new game. His defence had always been excellent and it now became simply world class, on a par with any player in the game in his position.

The second irony of the situation was that on the morning of England's first international in Pretoria on their tour of South Africa in June 1994, *The Times*' chief sports writer, David Miller, penned a major article proclaiming that England could no longer launch their backline as any kind of meaningful threat to the opposition because of one man, the fly half Rob Andrew. It was time, said Miller, for Andrew to go because he lacked the pace required at this level and the best had been seen of him. It is highly likely that Andrew, a cool, calculating individual, saw, or at the very least heard, about that article before he went on to the field at Loftus Versfeld for that first Test. But whatever the motivation, Miller's embarrassment must have been hard to bear as the England fly half rattled up a personal tally of 27 points in England's astonishing, magnificent victory by 32 points to 15. The biggest joke, of course, was that Miller had got the wrong man. He should have had Will Carling.

The common factor in all England's difficulties throughout the 1993/94 season was their inability to create and score tries. Statistics are the tool of disingenuous politicians, and their employment can be deemed scurrilous. What cannot be falsified is the evidence of the human eye. Anyone with even one good eye could discern the problem within the English three-quarter line. In the absence of the seriously injured Guscott, whose replacement, de Glanville, was new to international rugby and could hardly be expected to dictate a playing pattern, England had no one to create in midfield. For Carling, very much the senior man, had long since lost the art of creativity. Not, it should be said, the capability and indeed the right to play international rugby, because his defence was so good. And the way the game had moved in the direction of defence, Carling's credentials for a place were better than any other's. His tackling had always been technically sound and strong; now it became solidly consistent and reliable. Only very very rarely did anyone elude his grasp.

De Glanville, too, was a tough, firm tackler and the

pair formed a barrier which became all but impenetrable under normal circumstances. Alas, de Glanville was the only one likely to add creativity to the package and as a consequence England struggled all season to score tries. They banged over four penalties and a dropped goal to beat New Zealand, and tripped up Scotland at the death in Edinburgh through five penalty goals by Callard, who kicked four more in the single point defeat by Ireland at Twickenham. Off to Paris, a different setting, a changed environment but the same outcome – five penalties and a dropped goal, this time by Andrew, securing an 18–14 victory which was forged up front by the English pack. Penalty kicks everywhere, not a try in sight.

Amid the euphoria of England's outstanding first Test demolition of South Africa in Pretoria, there was, however, a similar story to be told. Andrew kicked almost everything offered and scored a try himself from his own high kick to the South African line. Only Ben Clarke's try from a break by Tony Underwood could be said to have been creative. And then in the second Test of the tour, England were again sterile, Andrew's three penalty goals their only offering in a 27–9 defeat. Seven internationals in the course of the season with some damning figures to present: of 116 points scored by England, 96 came from kicks – 101 if you consider that Andrew's high kick to the South African line, where he only had to catch the ball and fall down to score, was virtually created from another kick. 101 points from kicks out of 116 points scored suggests some grave weaknesses somewhere within the England side. Handing Carling all the blame for this sorry state of affairs would clearly be ridiculous. England's forwards must take some of the condemnation for failing to produce sufficiently fast ball to offer the threequarter line some space and time in which to operate. The half-backs, Morris and Andrew, were brave, doughty fighters whenever they went on to the field but hardly likely to be confused with greyhounds in terms of speed. Yet they too fitted the requirement for a modern game plunged into mediocrity by ill-judged law changes which had wrecked the game aesthetically. Solid players who could tackle all day and kick the leather off the ball when no other option was possible (and it usually wasn't) were now required by international teams everywhere. Thus, players lacking sufficient speed such as Carling, Andrew and Morris could mask their deficiencies with other qualities which the game now demanded. Go back to the 1991 World Cup and the laws then operating and you would find all three wanting in creativity. But the changes in the laws had worked in their favour, undoubtedly prolonging their international careers.

Carling, certainly, had lost the ability to carve out scoring opportunities either for himself or his colleagues. The long-term absence of Guscott meant the selectors avoided having to confront a decision which might have given them sleepless nights had, for example, the Bath inspiration returned in mid-season. Given that England had played New Zealand, Scotland and Ireland without sniffing a try, the pressure might have become intense to remove Carling and pair Guscott and de Glanville. As it was, fate was decided by Guscott's extended absence from the game.

England therefore played a game of safety first all season. It was justified under the law changes and amid adversity but no one would have known better than their new manager Jack Rowell, who had replaced Geoff Cooke at the end of the Five Nations season, that such tactics would never be good enough to win a World Cup. Rowell said as much, too, when his side got to South Africa for their historic tour. But Rowell, like Cooke in the winter season, had to get by without arguably the best attacking centre in world rugby, Jeremy Guscott. To have considered omitting Carling with Guscott settled and in form in the side might have been permissible. To think about leaving him out with only the young (albeit highly promising) de Glanville alongside, who had won only nine caps even after the South African tour, would have been folly. So the issue never arose. But in normal circumstances it could and indeed should have done.

England recognized the problem themselves. They had been so desperate to rush the Harlequins player David Pears back into the side at the earliest opportunity, that they paid scant attention to his disturbing injury record. Pears played against France but never reappeared for the rest of the season and lasted just one match on the South African tour. On the face of it, to put so much faith in a player dogged by injuries over the last eighteen months was quite unjustified. The reason for that desire to see Pears inserted at full-back was that England knew he was one of the few players around who could help cover the attacking deficiencies at centre, by getting into the backline at speed off both orthodox first phase and also broken play possession. His incursions into the line gave England their only variation from de Glanville's search for gaps, for the captain was rarely seen in any attacking vein. As the *Daily Mail*'s Peter Jackson reported at the end of the South African tour: 'Carling was without peer as a defensive centre but the breaks were few and far between.'

In one revealing moment during the second Test match at Cape Town, Carling confirmed suspicions that his burning pace had gone, and with it much of the confidence to take on opponents, attributes that had been the hallmark of his early career. England, under the cosh for long periods, retrieved a ball and suddenly came out of deep defence in a propitious attacking position. South Africa were stretched, and when Carling received possession, there was a glorious opportunity at last for the England captain to counter-attack in the grand style. But over the years Carling's ambition and attacking intent have been dulled by the conditioning of England's cautious play and his own loss of confidence in his pace. Instead of finding another gear to take on and pass two less than speedy opponents, he opted for the safe kick downfield and the moment was lost. It was a revealing commentary on his own reduced horizons and spoke volumes for England's inability to mastermind raids from defence – often, in these days of cluttered and rigidly formed defences, the best situation for the release of backs.

By now, too, Carling's widespread experience, not just of captaincy but of leading this particular England squad, was undoubtedly a strong factor in his retention. He had during the course of the season created a new world record for captaining his country, having led them forty-two times when he appeared in the second Test against South Africa at Newlands. To have overthrown so long-standing a leader barely twelve months before the 1995 World Cup in South Africa would have required a watertight case for the prosecution. Such a move would never have been considered in the era of Geoff Cooke, who had appointed him in the first place and always stood by Carling. If there was a suggestion that Cooke's replacement, Jack Rowell, might not be so lenient and understanding a manager, then those who made it should have understood that Rowell could hardly walk into the job clutching a Kalashnikov. For a start, he knew he had been by no means an overwhelmingly popular candidate for the job in every committee member's mind and secondly, he was aware of the great difference to be negotiated between achieving success at club level and on the international stage. Rowell had been the mastermind behind Bath's towering successes at club level but translating that into the international game was never going to be a simple matter. Rowell, as a businessman of much experience and wisdom with the Dalgety Food Company, understood that better than anyone.

To have toppled Carling with his first movement would have been risky in the extreme. Nor, as we have seen, would it have been justified. But what Rowell did do was make it perfectly plain that the squad was not one of his choosing. He had inherited it and as such could claim only a partial association with it. The words went unspoken but the suspicion lingered; had Rowell taken charge of England two or more years before the '95 World Cup, it is doubtful whether Carling would have survived the change of personnel at boardroom level.

But if there had been any whispers of 'dropping the captain', Carling decisively allayed them on the day England beat the All Blacks. It was in every sense a historic day and a performance to match; an England side depleted by the absence of Bayfield, Guscott and Morris forced to hand new caps to players in critical positions, like Bracken and Callard. Carling's job was twofold – to integrate the new men in the team's plans, familiarizing them with the ways of the squad and helping them adapt to their considerable task against renowned opponents. Secondly, he had to produce a performance which not only showed the way but inspired everyone both in his team and in the crowd. Twickenham was crammed full of 68,000 supporters, the new East Stand having received its final permit only hours before the big day.

He did it, to the jubilation of a nation. No tries, admittedly, but a performance by every member of the England team which was soaked in blood, sweat and tears of eventual joy. Carling, magnificent in defence and inspirational as a leader, could be said to have come of age as a captain that day. It was, he intoned, 'our greatest win, an incredible effort'. He called it the most significant of the forty-three internationals he had played for his country, and he was probably right. England that day exorcized a ghost, they deflated a legend. To suggest otherwise would be both churlish and factually incorrect, for not only was it a great victory but also a magnificent demonstration of courage, commitment and total concentration. In all respects, Carling led his men better than ever before. And yet the old insecurities were never far below the surface. 'Triumph of the worried Will' headlined a *Guardian* report, explaining how Carling had put to flight, for the moment anyway, the doubters and critics.

Then, within days, he had put into words the thoughts of so many English followers sickened by the brutality handed out by New Zealand players such as Jamie Joseph, who recklessly trod on the ankle of Bracken in a brazen but craven attempt to force the youngster out of the Test match. Earlier in the tour, de Glanville had required fifteen stitches in an ugly head wound after being stamped in a ruck. Carling said in the *Mail on Sunday*: 'New Zealand will be remembered mostly as a dirty side. That is sad for them but I think they deserve it. Some of their play has been beyond the conventions we obey and I feel more sad about the damage they have done to rugby's image. This tour was a great showcase for the game but how many mothers will now be saying "I don't want my son to play rugby". The All Blacks arrived with a specialist public relations man to improve their image but they have failed. The image that sticks is of a team prepared to win at any cost.'

All of which needed saying, but it took guts for Carling to say it. He was perfectly correct to do so. The All Blacks' cynicism was a disgrace to the good name of the game and it needed someone with the good name of the England captain to speak out. Once the partying had ceased, England had a lengthy lay-off before the Five Nations Championship season began for them, for they sat out the first round of games on 15 January, making their debut at Murrayfield against the Scots. Alas, the momentum established against New Zealand had gone AWOL in Edinburgh, with a scrappy disjointed match apparently going to Scotland when Townsend dropped a last-minute goal for a 14–12 lead. Then came the hand of God, Act 2, as Andrew, allegedly, shovelled the ball back from a ruck and the referee was somehow convinced it was a Scottish mit in disguise. Up stepped Callard, outwardly the calmest man on the ground, to pot the goal with the calm aplomb Doug Sanders could have used on that famous 18th green in a British Open golf championship all those years before. The final shot was high quality; what had gone before rather less impressive. Still, England had got away with a lucky win and with Ireland next up at

Twickenham, the All Black scalp proudly displayed from the flagpole, it would be normal service resumed. Or would it?

'NO EXCUSE: I lost control as England crashed', screamed the *Mail on Sunday* headline above Carling's exclusive column. In it, Carling admitted that at times in England's 13–12 defeat he was not in control. He had tried to change things but players acted as they saw fit. Fair enough. But then it was back to the old cop-out – 'great sides don't just have one leader'. Which I think we have heard before from the England rugby captain in times of adversity. The point is, great sides *do* just have one leader. But then, Carling had apparently always preferred captaincy by majority, a view which many others find baffling.

The defeat of Ireland was costly for England. It denied them the Grand Slam and the Triple Crown. Only the Championship trophy, newly minted, remained available, but the astonishing defeat of France in Cardiff on the same day that England had fallen to Ireland devalued the France–England match in Paris two weeks later. No matter, England still won it, with another performance of valour amid adversity, Andrew finding the richest seam of goalkicking form even he could have imagined. His five penalty goals and a dropped goal soared high over the crossbar as England, although again tryless while France scored the only touchdown of the match, got home 18–14. Winning in Paris has become elementary for England but a seemingly unattainable feat for Scotland (who last won there in 1969), Ireland (last win there 1972) and Wales (last win 1975). England, by startling contrast, had now won seven consecutive matches against France including four straight wins at the Parc des Princes. 'We know how to beat France in

Paris', was Geoff Cooke's understatement, but doing so ought not to be underestimated. It requires strong commitment, resolve and meticulous planning. England performed on all three fronts, again, on 5 March 1994.

Expecting too many lavish attacking movements and Barbarians-style rugby in the white-hot cauldron of a France–England game in Paris would be absurd. So any thoughts of dismay with Carling's side at failing once more to score tries was tempered by the location and nature of the courageous performance. At Twickenham, in the Championship decider against Wales, England needed to deliver in the matter of tries – and they did. To a point.

Rory Underwood and Rodber got one each in England's 15–18 win. So what was this headline, on the following Monday morning in the *Daily Telegraph* relating: 'Subdued Wales let off the hook by "soft" England'? Churlish, vindictive, perhaps? No, factually accurate. For when Wales were at the point of extinction, England holding a 15–3 lead with over half an hour of the match still to come, there should have been a steady, inevitable progression to the clear sixteen-point winning margin England required to take the Championship trophy on points. Wales had been set up for the kill by an outstanding England forward effort but, as so often before, the job remained only half done. They had their opponents on the rack but did not finish them off, the crucial lack of killer instinct once more apparent. Again, it raised question marks over certain performers and Carling could hardly escape censure. England had lacked the finishing power to put Wales to the sword and a match which had been overwhelmingly one-sided on the pitch looked closely contested on the scoreboard, a grand indictment of English failings. It had long been thus.

So what of the future, what remains for Will Carling and Will Carling's England side? The 1995 World Cup looms, iceberg-like, upon the horizon. It will be, surely, one of the final acts of Carling's career, for it seems doubtful whether he would continue beyond that stage. To have led England an astonishing fifty times or more, a landmark he will pass at the World Cup if he retains his position and the captaincy, would be in anyone's language an extraordinary achievement. Those closest to him in English international circles, Rob Andrew, Brian Moore and Rory Underwood, may similarly choose to bow out on the grandest stage, and Carling would almost inevitably join them if they went.

His life is now ever more hectic. Combining and balancing the demands of a busy job, an overwhelmingly enervating sporting hobby and a new wife, the former Julia Smith whom he married in much style one week after returning from the England tour of South Africa in June 1994, would tax a man with ten days available in a week. Rugby barely tolerates other activities in its practitioners' lives – which is, of course, the nub of so much debate over the future course of the game. Whatever it may claim, it is certainly not an amateur sport for players constantly put upon by its requirements.

So what can Carling anticipate as he embarks upon his final phase in the international game? Clearly, England need to rediscover the art of creating and scoring tries around the field. That is the first priority and attention will understandably be focused upon an area which has not performed as expected in recent times. The return of Jeremy Guscott, if and when it happens, will give England a new dimension but it is essential that Carling, too, contributes and in ways other than just defence. Whether he still has it in him to do so, the 1995 World Cup will finally decide.

Bibliography

The Book of English International Rugby, 1871–1982, ed. John Griffiths, Collins Willow, 1982.

David Campese with Peter Bills, *On a Wing and a Prayer*, Macdonald/Queen Anne Press, 1991.

Will Carling, *Captain's Diary 1989–1991*, Chatto & Windus, 1991.

Mick Doyle, *Doyler*, Gill and Macmillan, 1992.

The Heinz Official Book of the Rugby World Cup 1991, ed. Ian Robertson, Stanley Paul, 1991.

Barry Newcombe, *Carling's England: The Making of the World Cup Team*, Harvill Press, 1991.

Rothmans Rugby Union Yearbook, editions 1980–81 to 1992–3.

The Rugby Union Who's Who 1992–93, ed. Alex Spink, Collins Willow.

David Sole with Derek Douglas, *Heart and Sole*, Mainstream Publishing, 1992.

Philip Warner, *The Harlequins*, Breedon Books, 1991.

Various editions of *Rugby World and Post* and *Rugby News* magazines.

Various issues of *The Times, Daily Telegraph, Observer, Daily Mail, Daily Express, Sunday Telegraph, Sunday Times* and *Mail on Sunday*.

Will Carling's Record for England as Player and Captain

AS PLAYER

January 1988	v. France	(A)	Lost	9–10
February 1988	v. Wales	(H)	Lost	3–11
March 1988	v. Scotland	(A)	Won	9–6
March 1988	v. Ireland	(H)	Won	35–3
April 1988	v. Ireland	(A)	Won	21–10
June 1988	v. Australia	(A)	Lost	8–28
June 1988	v. Fiji	(A)	Won	25–12

AS CAPTAIN

November 1988	v. Australia	(H)	Won	28–19
February 1989	v. Scotland	(H)	Drew	12–12
February 1989	v. Ireland	(A)	Won	16–3
March 1989	v. France	(H)	Won	11–0
March 1989	v. Wales	(A)	Lost	9–12
November 1989	v. Fiji	(H)	Won	58–23
January 1990	v. Ireland	(H)	Won	23–0
February 1990	v. France	(A)	Won	26–7
February 1990	v. Wales	(H)	Won	34–6
March 1990	v. Scotland	(A)	Lost	7–13
July 1990	v. Argentina	(A)	Won	25–12
August 1990	v. Argentina	(A)	Lost	13–15

November 1990	v. Argentina	(H)	Won	51–0
January 1991	v. Wales	(A)	Won	25–6
February 1991	v. Scotland	(H)	Won	21–12
March 1991	v. Ireland	(A)	Won	16–7
March 1991	v. France	(H)	Won	21–19
July 1991	v. Fiji	(A)	Won	28–12
July 1991	v. Australia	(A)	Lost	15–40
*October 1991	v. New Zealand	(H)	Lost	12–18
*October 1991	v. Italy	(H)	Won	36–6
*October 1991	v. USA	(H)	Won	37–9
*October 1991	v. France	(A)	Won	19–10
*October 1991	v. Scotland	(A)	Won	9–6
*November 1991	v. Australia	(H)	Lost	6–12
January 1992	v. Scotland	(A)	Won	25–7
February 1992	v. Ireland	(H)	Won	38–9
February 1992	v. France	(A)	Won	31–13
March 1992	v. Wales	(H)	Won	24–0
October 1992	v. Canada	(H)	Won	26–13
November 1992	v. South Africa	(H)	Won	33–16
January 1993	v. France	(H)	Won	16–15
February 1993	v. Wales	(A)	Lost	9–10
March 1993	v. Scotland	(H)	Won	26–12
March 1993	v. Ireland	(A)	Lost	3–17
November 1993	v. New Zealand	(H)	Won	15–9
February 1994	v. Scotland	(A)	Won	15–14
February 1994	v. Ireland	(H)	Lost	12–13
March 1994	v. France	(A)	Won	18–14
March 1994	v. Wales	(H)	Won	15–8
June 1994	v. South Africa	(A)	Won	32–15
June 1994	v. South Africa	(A)	Lost	9–27

* World Cup

Index